Charles William George St. John

Short Sketches of the wild Sports & natural History of the Highlands

Charles William George St. John

Short Sketches of the wild Sports & natural History of the Highlands

ISBN/EAN: 9783337157739

Printed in Europe, USA, Canada, Australia, Japan

Cover: Foto ©ninafisch / pixelio.de

More available books at **www.hansebooks.com**

The Wild Sports & Natural History

OF

THE HIGHLANDS

CHARLES ST. JOHN

SHORT SKETCHES

OF THE

Wild Sports & Natural History

OF

THE HIGHLANDS

By CHARLES ST. JOHN

A NEW EDITION, WITH THE AUTHOR'S NOTES, AND
A MEMOIR BY THE REV. M. G. WATKINS

LONDON
JOHN MURRAY, ALBEMARLE STREET
1893

PREFACE

THE appearance of another, the ninth, edition of St. John's *Highland Sports* renders a few words of introduction necessary for readers separated by nearly half a century from the time when the book was first published. It delighted a past generation, and has probably done more than any book since written to foster a love of out-door sport among the wilder birds and animals of the British Isles. But the author possesses a stronger claim to the gratitude of naturalists and sportsmen. He upholds the highest traditions of true sport: on the one hand setting the example of refraining from all that savours of taking an ungenerous advantage over these wild creatures; on the other, trying to inculcate humanity towards them, believing that a fondness for observing their habits confers a higher pleasure than the mere shooting of a great quantity of game.

Mr. St. John was specially qualified to write on the birds and beasts of Scotland. A happy concurrence of circumstances connected with his residence in the district of Moray gave him unrivalled opportunities of observing its quadrupeds, while he has paid even greater attention to the birds of the country. He says (Preface to *Natural History and Sport in Moray*, p. ix.): "I have taken the nests of all the birds which breed in Scotland, without, I believe, an exception. I have also watched the habits of feeding, etc., of all, from the golden eagle to the golden-crested wren, from the wild swan to the teal, and have had opportunities of so doing which perhaps no other person has had."

Independently of the charm of St. John's writing, what at present renders his *Wild Sports* especially valuable is that Scotland and the Scotch fauna have considerably changed during the last half-century. The variety and abundance of wild life here described can never again be seen. Fortunately a true picture of that departed past is preserved in St. John's vivid narratives. Population has increased; and railways, driven far into what in his days were wastes of trackless bog and heather, now admit countless sportsmen and tourists to the most retired districts. An increasing taste for shooting and fishing, and the charm of a freer life during the beautiful northern summer than can be found in great cities, have planted castles and shooting lodges all over Scotland. Sport of any kind can now only be obtained at a considerable cost. For economical reasons, all lovers of Scotland must rejoice at this tendency of the age; but it has pressed with great severity upon all wild life. Indeed, where they have not been specially protected, several kinds of birds and beasts, such as the osprey, the kite, and the marten, have either died out or are rapidly approaching extinction. Were it not for legal restrictions and private watchfulness others would be seriously endangered, or linger on remaining scantily represented.

Thus many animals and birds which were sufficiently common in St. John's time are now rare and seldom seen. It has been thought advisable, therefore, in this edition to add a few notes in order to illustrate the instincts or traits of these creatures, their prevalence or scarcity. Some more general remarks have also been appended here and there to clear up any obscurity or bring out associations which might otherwise have been forgotten. There has been no tampering with the original text.

The additional notes of the author, marked C. St. J., are printed word for word from an interleaved copy of Jenyns's *Manual of British Vertebrate Animals*. They are interesting as showing the exactitude and brevity of St. John's notes. At times they also throw further light upon the text. For permission to use them the editor is indebted to the kindness of the writer's son, Admiral H. C. St. John.

M. G. W.

KENTCHURCH RECTORY, *July* 1892.

LIFE OF C. ST. JOHN

MANY men well known in the literary world possess no history, because their life has been spent with their books. Mr. St. John's days were passed on the moorland or by the river, devoted to sports and natural history, consequently there is little to tell of his life except the distinctive facts which mark off one human being from another. His love of animated nature, his perseverance and keenness in capturing the rarer birds and beasts, are only matched by the acuteness with which he caught their habits and instincts and transferred them into these pages. In them and in his other two books may be read his real life-work.

Charles William George St. John was son of General the Honourable F. St. John, himself the son of Frederick, second Viscount Bolingbroke. He was born at Chailey, Sussex, 3rd December 1809, and sent in due time to Midhurst School, under Dr. Bayley. Here it is upon record that under the careful tuition of an old pensioner, who acted as drill-sergeant to the school, the characteristic bent of his mind showed itself, and he became a proficient in spinning for pike and setting night-lines for eels in the river Arun. During his stay of about four years his box was usually filled with some kind of pets; dormice, guinea-pigs, or stag-beetles. He was appointed to a clerkship in the Treasury in 1828, but only remained for some two years at his desk, the confinement and regular hours being little suited to his tastes. At this time of his life St. John was fond of society, and was enabled to enjoy it to his heart's content through the kindness of his aunt, Lady Sefton. He had a slight impediment in his speech, but it almost disappeared when he was among friends, and then his conversation was easy and flowing. When in London he was wont to drive or ride out of town to shoot blackcock and return the same day. The distance was eighty miles, and he used four horses in getting over the ground, each horse doing twenty miles.

A new phase of life opened upon him after leaving the Treasury, owing to the kindness of his cousin, Lord Bolingbroke, who lent him Roschall, a shooting-box on the Oykell in Sutherland. The retirement, the shooting, the wild stretches of moorland around him, exactly suited his genius. Many of his observations on animal life, and much of his experience as a deer-stalker, were here acquired. On an expedition from Roschall he met Miss Ann Gibson, the daughter of a rich banker in Newcastle, and married her in November 1834. She possessed some fortune, in which he had been somewhat deficient, and much sympathy with his tastes and habits. Henceforth he devoted himself to the life of a sportsman and naturalist, living in succession at several houses in the Highlands in Ross-shire, Inverness, Nairn, and Moray. The need of schools for his growing family brought him nearer to towns. But he found the "laigh" of Moray best suited to his tastes—"a fertile and well-cultivated country, with dry soil and bright and bracing climate, with wide views of sea and mountain, within easy distance of mountain sports, in the midst of the game and wild animals of a low country, and with the coast indented by bays of the sea and studded with frequent fresh-water lakes, the haunt of all the common wild-fowl, and of many of the rarer sorts." Amid such scenes St. John lived for ten years, the best part of his working life, before his fatal illness.

It was in Moray that St. John became acquainted with Mr. C. Innes, Sheriff of Moray, in the autumn of 1844, while the latter was shooting partridges. He had shot one and lost it among some potatoes; but St. John offered to let his own rather ungainly-looking dog find it if the Sheriff would permit him. This the dog speedily did, and an acquaintance thus commenced of much pleasure to both, and the source of a new and unexpected interest in St. John's life. He was then living at Invererne, below Forres; and Mr. Innes, captivated by his stories of sport and adventure, induced him to write out a few reminiscences for an article he was himself preparing for the *Quarterly Review*. The editor (Lockhart) was delighted with them, especially with the story of "the Muckle Hart of Benmore." St. John now began to see how he could utilise the varied information he had gathered, and one winter diligently put together the charming pages of *The Wild Sports of the Highlands*. The Sheriff had the satisfaction of arranging for the sale and publication of this in 1845; and then for the first time naturalists and sportsmen obtained accurate information of the wild life of Northern Scotland; while the simple charm of St. John's narratives, and the boundless enthusiasm for sport which these chapters evoked, speedily made his name famous, and have given the utmost pleasure ever since to all lovers of rural life. Thenceforth St. John kept more regular journals, and acquired a scientific interest in his sport. The sand-hills of Culbin, the Black Forest stretching away beyond Brodie and Dalvey, the sand-spits on the coast where the seals might be seen basking in the sun, the Findhorn with its ever-varying prospects and the "sea-pyes" haunting its gravel banks, these and other contiguous fields of research furnished him with inexhaustible objects to observe and comment upon.

In 1848 and 1849 St. John was obliged for the sake of his family to reside much in Edinburgh; but he loved to make excursions on the one side to Newcastle, where dwelt Mr. Hancock, whose tastes were similar to his own, and on the other to Sutherland. This county had always possessed many attractions for him in its fishing and deer-stalking, and led to his publishing two volumes upon its sport.

Of all the houses St. John had inhabited, perhaps the College, Elgin, is the most identified with his pursuits and literary work. Here he came in the autumn of 1849. It was in the neighbourhood of many friends,—Sir A. G. Cumming of Altyre, Major Gordon Cumming, and others,—while there were good schools close at hand for his boys. The house itself, with its old trees and rambling garden and the ivy covering the walls, was exactly suited to the studies in natural history of himself and his family. Here he could shoot and fish in much happiness; and here, owing to his habits of vigour, active exercise, and temperance, he spent several happy years. It is worth while extracting a pleasant picture of his home-life at Elgin from the pages of Mr. Innes:

The boys were the constant companions of his sport when school permitted, and sometimes the schoolmaster was forgotten when the car came to the door to take papa and Rennie (Donald) to the loch. Then, on the return, there were the contents of the game-bag to examine,—rare specimens to note, and sometimes to preserve and stuff after Mr. Hancock's directions, who was a great friend and ally of old and young. In the evening the drawing-room was a pretty sight. Some rare bird, or, if no rarity offered, a good handsome old blackcock, was displayed *en pose* for the artists, and father and children made studies in water-colours of a head, a claw, or a tail of the fine bird. Without pretending to much skill in art, St. John drew easily and coloured dexterously what was placed before him, and he made all his children able to do the same.—P. xxviii.

But the end of this happy, industrious life was approaching. The pen which had delighted so many lovers of nature by its graphic accounts of sport and natural history was soon to drop useless from the hand. St. John had been a sufferer for a long time from severe headaches. After a violent attack in the beginning of December 1853 he seemed better, and was on his way to shoot at Pluscardine, when on 6th December he was struck down by paralysis of the whole left side. Quite powerless, yet perfectly conscious, he was carefully tended and taken home by Major Campbell. For many weeks he was tenderly nursed by him and by his own devoted family. He never recovered the use of his limbs, but was enabled to go south for change of scene and air. Brighton, however, and Southampton did not appear to do him much good. He still cherished the hope of ending his days in the Highlands; but death released him on 12th July 1856 at Woolston, and he was buried hard by in Southampton Cemetery. At his feet inside the coffin was placed the skull of a favourite retriever, the successor of "Grip." During the two years of his illness his patience and resignation were wonderful after the active life that he had almost always led out of doors among his favourite sports and in the observation of nature. It might have been expected that he would have pined for freedom and exercise, but no sign of such a feeling ever showed itself. He left three sons and one daughter, who are still living.

Charles St. John is famous as a sportsman, a naturalist, and a writer. As a sportsman, his fire and eagerness were extreme; and he was especially fond of seeing his dogs work as he shot, never taking life merely for the wantonness of killing. But fishing and shooting were always subordinate to his ardour for observing the habits of the wild creatures which he possessed so many opportunities of noting. He insisted on seeing with his own eyes, and never cared to take facts on hearsay. Enthusiastic, cautious, and diligent, he was the model of a zoologist; country pursuits and love of the country almost amounting with him to a passion. St. John's style is plain and straightforward, frequently rising to a poetical appreciation of scenery, and redolent of heather scents and the freshness of the mountain breeze. Imagination is strictly subordinated to sober details of what he actually saw, and heard, and did. There is no attempt to rise to gorgeous or even fine writing, and this is the reason why his books still prove so fascinating. Without either eccentricities of thought or of language, they tell their own tale, and appeal strongly to all who sympathise with nature and sport. Therefore they never become antiquated, or disgust readers with the affectations and sporting jargon of a bygone day. When Walton and White of Selborne are forgotten, then, and then only, will the world tire of St. John. Few authors in his own peculiar range of sport and natural history combined can vie with him; few indeed have surpassed him. It is believed that many lovers of nature who have grown up since the early editions of the *Highland Sports* were published will be as delighted to make St. John's acquaintance as were their fathers, to whom his experiences of the sport to be obtained in Scotland came like a revelation.

St. John's insight into animal life was as keen as that of Jefferies, but wider, more particular and exact. Nature was as dear to him as to Thoreau; but St. John's love of sport drew him nearer to the birds and beasts of his native land. Perhaps the late Mr. J. Colquhoun most resembled him in united enthusiasm for sport and nature and skill in writing on these subjects; but St. John far excels him in the accuracy of his knowledge and the extent of his observations on animals, their habits and traits. An untimely death removed one who would probably have largely increased sportsmen's sympathy and acquaintance with their quarry, and might have considerably widened the domain of the sciences which preside over the birds and animals of his adopted country. Besides the *Highland Sports*, St. John has left two excellent books, one on *The Natural History of Moray*, the other on *Deer-stalking in Sutherland*.

This memoir has been put together from the Life of St. John written by the late Mr. C. Innes and prefixed to the former of these two books, and from notes supplied by the eldest son of the author, Admiral H. C. St. John. To his kindness also this edition is indebted for the portrait of the author, the first which has hitherto been made public.

CONTENTS

INTRODUCTION 1

CHAPTER I

Highland Lakes—Steam-boats—Small Lochs—Wild Cats—Ravens—Dragging the Lake—The Char—Fishing at Night—Pike—Trolling large Trout on Loch Ness—Flies, Otters, etc.—Fishing with the Otter—Spawning Trout . 8

CHAPTER II

Roe: Mischief done by—Fawns—Tame Roe—Boy killed by Roe—Hunting Roe: Artifices of—Shooting Roe—Unlucky shot—Change of colour—Swimming—Cunning Roe 19

CHAPTER III

Grouse's Nest—Partridge Nest—Grouse-shooting—Marten Cat—Witch: Death of—Stags—Snaring Grouse—Black Game: Battles of—Hybrid Bird—Ptarmigan-shooting—Mist on the Mountain—Stag—Unsuccessful Stalking—Death of Eagle 27

CHAPTER IV

The Wild Cat: Strength of; Rencontre with—Trapping tame Cats: Destructiveness of—Poisoning vermin—Trapping vermin 43

CHAPTER V

Poaching in the Highlands—Donald—Poachers and Keepers—Bivouac in Snow—Connivance of Shepherds—Deer killed—Catching a Keeper—Poaching in the Forests—Shooting Deer by Moonlight—Ancient Poachers . . 50

CHAPTER VI

Salmon-fishing—Salmon ascending Fords—Fishers—Cruives—Right of Fishing—Anecdote—Salmon-leaps—History of the Salmon—Spearing Salmon—River Poaching—Angling—Fly-making—Eels—Lampreys . . 62

CHAPTER VII

Short-eared Owl: Habits of—Long-eared Owl—Tame Owl—White Owl—Utility of Owls—Mice—Rats: Destructiveness of—Water Rats: Food of—Killing Rats—Ratcatchers 72

CHAPTER VIII

Crossbills: Habits of; Nest—Snowy Owl—Great-eared Owl—Hoopoe—Shrike—Tawny and Snow Bunting—Lizards—Singular Pets—Toads: Utility of; Combats of—Adders—Dog and Snakes—Large Snake—Blind-Worm . 80

CHAPTER IX

On the Peculiarities and Instinct of different Animals—Eggs of Birds—Nests—The Fox—Red-Deer Hind 87

CHAPTER X

The Eagle: Habits; Greediness; Anecdotes of; Killing Eagles; Trapping; Food of—The Peregrine Falcon: Manner of Hunting—Tame Falcon: Anecdotes of—Guinea-Hen and Ducks—The Osprey—The Kite: Trapping—The Buzzard: Nests and Habits of 93

CHAPTER XI

The Hen-Harrier: Destructiveness to Game; Female of; Trapping—The Sparrowhawk: Courage of; Ferocity; Nest—The Kestrel: Utility of—The Merlin: Boldness—The Hobby—Increase of Small Birds . . 103

CHAPTER XII

The Otter: Habits—Catching of—Shooting—Attachment to each other—Anecdotes—Fish killed by 110

CHAPTER XIII

Weasels—Ferrets: Fierceness of—Anecdotes—Food of Weasels—Manner of Hunting for Prey—The Stoat: Change of Colour; Odour of; Food of: Their catching Fish—Polecat—The Marten Cat: Habits; Trapping: Eating Fruit; Activity of; Different Species . 116

CHAPTER XIV

Anecdotes and Instinct of Dogs—Anecdotes of Retriever—Shepherds' Dogs—Sagacity—Dogs and Monkey—Bulldog—Anecdotes of Shooting a Stag—Treatment of Dogs 124

CHAPTER XV

Increase of Wood-Pigeons and other Birds—Service to the Farmer of these Birds—Tame Wood-Pigeons: Food of—The Turtle-Dove—Blue Rock-Pigeons: Caves where they breed—Shooting at the Rocks near Cromarty . 135

CHAPTER XVI

Wild Ducks: Edible kinds of—Breeding-places of Mallards—Change of Plumage—Shooting—Feeding-places—Half-bred Wild Ducks—*Anas glacialis*—*Anas clangula*: Habits of—Teeth of Goosander—Cormorants—Anecdotes . 144

CHAPTER XVII

Birds that come in Spring—The Pewit: Pugnacity; Nests of; Cunning—Ring-Dotterel—Redshank—Oyster-Catcher: Food; Swimming of; Nest—Curlew—Redstart—Swallows, etc. . . 154

CHAPTER XVIII

Sheldrake: Nest; Food—Teal: Breeding-places; Anecdotes—Landrail: Arrival of—Cuckoo—Nightjar: Habits of—Quail—Grebe: Arrival: Account of Nest and Young—Bald Coot—Water-Hen—Water-Rail . . 162

CHAPTER XIX

Wild Geese: Arrival of; Different kinds of; Anecdotes of—Shooting Wild Geese—Feeding-places—Wariness—Habits—Breeding-places—Black-headed Gull—Birds that breed on the River-banks . . . 172

CHAPTER XX

The Sandhills of Morayshire: Description of; Origin of—Foxes: Destructiveness and Cunning of; Anecdote of—Roe-hunting in the Sandhills—Anecdotes . 183

CHAPTER XXI

Death of my first Stag . 192

CHAPTER XXII

The Findhorn River—Excursion to Source—Deer-stalking—Shepherds—Hind and Calf—Heavy Rain—Floods—Walk to Lodge—Fine Morning—Highland Sheep—Banks of River—Cottages . . . 200

CHAPTER XXIII

Findhorn River—Bridge of Dulsie—Beauty of Scenery—Falls of River—Old Salmon-fisher—Anglers—Heronry—Distant View—Sudden Rise of River—Mouth of River 211

CHAPTER XXIV

Migration of Birds in October—Wild Swans: Pursuit of; Manner of getting a Shot; Two Killed—Habits of Wild Swan 218

CHAPTER XXV

The Water-Ouzel: Nest; Singular Habits; Food; Song of—Kingfisher: Rare Visits of; Manner of Fishing—Terns: Quickness in Fishing; Nests of . 225

CHAPTER XXVI

The Muckle Hart of Benmore . 232

CHAPTER XXVII

Different kinds of Gulls: Large Collections of—Breeding-places—Islands on a Loch—Eggs of Gulls—Young Birds—Food and Voracity of Large Gulls: Salmon-fry killed by—Boatswain-Gull—Manner of procuring Food . 244

CHAPTER XXVIII

Woodcock's Nest: Early Breeding of; Habits of, in Spring; First Arrival of; Anecdotes of; Manner of carrying their Young—Habits of Snipe—Number of Jacksnipes—Solitary Snipe 251

CHAPTER XXIX

Seals—Destruction to Fish and Nets—Shooting Seals in River and Sea—Habits of Seals—Anecdotes—Seal and Dog—Seal and Keeper—Catching Seals—Anecdotes 256

CHAPTER XXX

Fox-hunting in the Highlands . 265

CHAPTER XXXI

The Badger: Antiquity of; Cleanliness; Abode of; Food; Family of—Trapping Badgers—Anecdotes—Escape of Badger—Anecdotes—Strength of—Cruelty to 270

CHAPTER XXXII

Autumn Day on the Mountain—Stags and Hinds—A Bivouac—Death of the Stag 278

CHAPTER XXXIII

Peculiarities and Instinct of different Animals—Feeding Habits—The Beaks of Birds—Wings of Owl—Instinct in finding Food—Ravens—Knowledge of Change of Weather—Fish 289

CHAPTER XXXIV

Coursing Deer . 295

CHAPTER XXXV

Tameness of Birds when Sitting . . 311

CHAPTER XXXVI

Variety of Game . . 315

LIST OF ILLUSTRATIONS

BY HARRISON WEIR, CHARLES WHYMPER, A. C. CORBOULD,
A. H. COLLINS, A. T. ELWES, AND A. H. HALLAM MURRAY
ENGRAVED ON WOOD BY J. W. WHYMPER

PORTRAIT OF THE AUTHOR	*Frontispiece*
ROUGH WEATHER	*Title-Page*
	PAGE
DONALD INSTRUCTING HIS YOUNG MASTER	1
FISHING BY MOONLIGHT	8
PLOVERS	18
ROEBUCK	19
ROE SWIMMING LOCH	26
SHOOTING A WITCH	27
MOUNTAIN SCENERY	39
PTARMIGAN	42
WILD CAT	43
THE RIGHT SORT OF GAMEKEEPER	49
AFFRAY WITH POACHERS	50
BIVOUAC ON THE HILLS UNDER THE HEATHER	61
SPEARING SALMON OR BURNING THE WATER	62
RAPIDS ON THE FINDHORN	71
THE LONG-EARED OWL	72
RATS CARRYING OFF EGG	79
THE SNOWY OWL	80
YELLOW-HAMMER'S NEST	87
WHITETHROAT'S NEST	92
THE EAGLE AND MOUNTAIN HARE	93

	PAGE
My Pugnacious Peregrine	102
The Sparrowhawk	103
Kestrels	109
The Otter in his Haunts	110
The Otter's Attack	115
The Weasel's Victim	116
Deer and Hounds	123
A Hunting Bulldog	124
My Pets	134
Wood-Pigeons	135
Across Cromarty Bay	143
Wild Duck	144
The Sympathetic Mate	153
Oyster-Catchers at Home	154
Logie House	161
Water-Hen	162
Loch Indorbii	171
Shooting Wild Geese	172
Site of Heronry on the Findhorn	182
Sandhills of Moray	183
A Cautious Peep	191
Death of my First Stag	192
Findhorn Bay	199
The Findhorn River	200
The Valley of the Findhorn	203
Crossing the Burn	205
Valley of the Findhorn	210
Dulsie Bridge	211
The Hills of Sutherland from the Moors above the Findhorn	215
Relugas House	217
The Sentinel	218
Swans in the Bay	224
The Water-Ouzel	225
Terns on Salmon Stakes	229
The Moray Firth from Dava	231

LIST OF ILLUSTRATIONS

	PAGE
"I dashed my Plaid over his Head"	232
Bringing Home the "Muckle Hart"	243
"The whole Community attacked Him"	244
Gulls coming Inland	247
The Findhorn from Altyre Woods, looking north	250
Woodcocks Tilting	251
Donald and the Seal	256
Looking up the Findhorn Valley from Dulsie Bridge	264
Fox-hunting in the Highlands	265
Highland Mowing	269
Badger and Wasps' Nest	270
Group of Highland Dogs. From Sir E. Landseer, R.A.	277
"The next Moment He was Passing Full Broadside to Me"	278
"On the Height of the Hill He Halted"	283
Bridge after Flood	288
The Raven	289
Highland Barometers	294
The Stag at Bay	295
Malcolm holding the Dogs	310
Young Ducks catching Moths	311
Curlew and Golden Plover	315
Dead Stag	319

THE WILD SPORTS & NATURAL HISTORY
OF
THE HIGHLANDS

DONALD INSTRUCTING HIS YOUNG MASTER

INTRODUCTION

I HAVE lived for several years in the northern counties of Scotland, and during the last four or five in the province of Moray, a part of the country peculiarly adapted for collecting facts in Natural History, and for becoming intimate with the habits of many of our British wild birds and quadrupeds. Having been in the habit of keeping an irregular kind of journal, and of making notes of any incidents which have fallen under my observation connected with the zoology of the country, I have now endeavoured, by dint of cutting and pruning those rough sketches, to put them into a shape calculated to amuse, and perhaps, in some slight degree, to instruct some of my fellow-lovers of Nature. From my earliest childhood I have been more addicted to the investigation of the habits and manners of every kind of living animal than to any more useful avocation, and have in consequence made myself tolerably well acquainted with the domestic economy of most of our British *feræ naturæ*, from the field-mouse and wheatear, which I stalked and trapped in the plains and downs of Wiltshire during my boyhood, to the red deer and eagle, whose territory I have invaded in later years on the mountains of Scotland. My present abode in Morayshire is surrounded by as great a variety of beautiful scenery as can be found in any district in Britain; and no part of the country can produce a greater variety of objects of interest either to the naturalist or to the lover of the picturesque. The rapid and glorious Findhorn,[1] the very perfection of a Highland river, here passes through one of the most fertile plains in Scotland, or indeed in the world; and though a few miles higher up it rages through the wildest and most rugged rocks, and through the romantic and shaded glens of the forests of Darnaway and Altyre, the stream, as if exhausted, empties itself peaceably and quietly into the Bay of Findhorn, a salt-water loch of some four or five miles in length, entirely shut out by different points of land from the storms which are so frequent in the Moray Firth, of which it forms a kind of creek. At low-water this bay becomes an extent of wet sand, with the river Findhorn and one or two smaller streams winding through it, till they meet in the deeper part of the basin near the town of Findhorn, where there is always a considerable depth of water, and a harbour for shipping.

From its sheltered situation and the quantity of food left on the sands at low-water, the Bay of Findhorn is always a great resort of wild-fowl of all kinds, from the swan to the teal, and also of innumerable waders of every species; while occasionally a seal ventures into the mouth of the river in

---

[1] Every one interested in the Findhorn should read Sir T. D. Lauder's admirable book, *The Moray Floods in 1829*. The character of the river, and the calamities which in that year followed the sudden floods to which it is liable, are particularly pointed out in it.

pursuit of salmon. The bay is separated from the main water of the Firth by that most extraordinary and peculiar range of country called the Sandhills of Moray,[1] a long, low range of hills formed of the purest sand, with scarcely any herbage, excepting here and there patches of bent or broom, which are inhabited by hares, rabbits, and foxes. At the extreme point of this range is a farm of forty or fifty acres of arable land, where the tenant endeavours to grow a scanty crop of grain and turnips, in spite of the rabbits and the drifting sands. From the inland side of the bay stretch the fertile plains of Moray, extending from the Findhorn to near Elgin in a continuous flat of the richest soil, and comprising districts of the very best partridge-shooting that can be found in Scotland, while the streams and swamps that intersect it afford a constant supply of wild-fowl. As we advance inland we are sheltered by the wide-extending woods of Altyre, abounding with roe and game, and beyond these woods again is a very extensive range of a most excellent grouse-shooting country, reaching for many miles over a succession of moderately sized hills which reach as far as the Spey.

On the west of the Findhorn is a country beautifully dotted with woods, principally of oak and birch, and intersected by a dark, winding burn, full of fine trout, and the constant haunt of the otter. Between this part of the country and the sea-coast is a continuation of the Sandhills, interspersed with lakes, swamps, and tracts of fir-wood and heather. On the whole I do not know so varied or interesting a district in Great Britain, or one so well adapted to the amusement and instruction of a naturalist or sportsman. In the space of a morning's walk you may be either in the most fertile or in the most barren spot of the country. In my own garden every kind of wall-fruit ripens to perfection, and yet at the distance of only two hours' walk you may either be in the midst of heather and grouse, or in the sandy deserts beyond the bay, where one wonders how even the rabbits can find their living.

---

[1] One district alone, Culbin, which belonged to the Kinnairds, and consisted of more than 3600 acres of the finest land, was entirely destroyed in the autumn of 1694 or spring of 1695. A great drifting of the sands then took place, which nearly overwhelmed the whole estate in a very sudden manner (see Chapter XX.) Some say that Culbin consisted of 9000 acres. These hillocks, like the French "dunes," are blown into different sized masses and alter in height from time to time.

The varieties of the soil and its productions, both animate and inanimate, will, however, be best shown in the extracts from my note-books, with which these pages are filled. My memorandums, having for the most part been written down at the moment, and describing anecdotes and incidents that fell under my actual observation, will at all events contain correct descriptions of the nature and habits of the animals and birds of the country; though, not being originally intended for publication, they are not arranged in any regular order. Here and there I have quoted some anecdote of animals, which I have heard from others: these I can only offer as I received them, but I can safely assert that I have quoted the words of those persons only upon whose veracity and powers of observation I could depend. My subject, as connected both to natural history and sporting, has led me back to my former wanderings in the more northern and wilder parts of the country, where I had great opportunities of becoming acquainted with the habits of the wilder and rarer birds and beasts, who are natives of those districts; and the pursuit of whom always had greater charms for me than the more commonplace occupations of grouse or partridge shooting.

I hope that my readers will be indulgent enough to make allowances for the unfinished style of these sketches, and the copious use of the first person singular, which I have found it impossible to avoid whilst describing the adventures which I have met with in this wild country, either when toiling up the rocky heights of our most lofty mountains, or cruising in a boat along the shores, where rocks and caves give a chance of finding sea-fowl and otters; at one time wandering over the desert sand-hills of Moray, where, on windy days, the light particles of drifting sand, driven like snow along the surface of the ground, are perpetually changing the outline and appearance of the district; at another, among the swamps, in pursuit of wild ducks, or attacking fish in the rivers, or the grouse on the heather.

For a naturalist, whether he be a scientific dissector and preserver of birds, or simply a lover and observer of the habits and customs of the different *feræ naturæ*, large and small, this district is a very desirable location, as there are very few birds or quadrupeds to be found in any part of Great Britain, who do not visit us during the course of the year, or, at any rate, are to be met with within a few hours' drive. The bays and rivers attract all the migratory water-fowl, while the hills, woods, and corn-lands afford shelter and food to all the native wild birds and beasts. The vicinity too of the coast to the wild western countries of Europe is the cause of our being often visited by birds which are not strictly natives, nor regular visitors, but are driven by continued east winds from the fastnesses of the Swedish and Norwegian forests and mountains.

To the collector of stuffed birds this county affords a greater variety of specimens than any other district in the kingdom, whilst the excellence of the climate and the variety of scenery make it inferior to none as a residence for the unoccupied person or the sportsman.

Having thus described that spot of the globe which at present is my resting-place, I may as well add a few lines to enable my reader to become acquainted with myself, and that part of my belongings which will come into question in my descriptions of sporting, etc. To begin with myself, I am one of the unproductive class of the genus Homo, who, having passed a few years amidst the active turmoil of cities, and in places where people do most delight to congregate, have at last settled down to live a busy kind of idle life. Communing much with the wild birds and beasts of our country, a hardy constitution and much leisure have enabled me to visit them in their own haunts, and to follow my sporting propensities without fear of the penalties which are apt to follow a careless exposure of oneself to cold and heat, at all hours of night and day. Though by habit and repute a being strongly endowed with the organ of destructiveness, I take equal delight in collecting round me all living animals, and watching their habits and instincts; my abode is, in short, a miniature menagerie. My dogs learn to respect the persons of domesticated wild animals of all kinds, and my pointers live in amity with tame partridges and pheasants; my retrievers lounge about amidst my wild-fowl, and my terriers and beagles strike up friendship with the animals of different kinds whose capture they have assisted in, and with whose relatives they are ready to wage war to the death. A common and well-kept truce exists with one and all. My boys, who are of the most bird-nesting age (eight and nine years old), instead of disturbing the numberless birds who breed in the garden and shrubberies, in full confidence of protection and immunity from all danger of gun or snare, strike up an acquaintance with every family of chaffinches or blackbirds who breed in the place, visiting every nest, and watching over the eggs and young with a most parental care.

My principal aide-de-camp in my sporting excursions is an old man, who, although passing for somewhat of a simpleton, has more acuteness and method in his vagaries than most of his neighbours. For many years he seems to have lived on his gun, but with an utter contempt of, and animosity against, all those who employ the more ignoble means of snaring and trapping game; and this makes him fulfil his duty as keeper better than many persons trained regularly to that employment.

He is rather a peculiar person in his way, and has a natural tendency to the pursuit of the rarer and wilder animals, such as otters, seals, wild-fowl, etc.—which accords well with my own tastes in the sporting line—many a day, and many a night too, at all seasons, has he passed lying in wait for some seal or otter, regardless of wet or cold.

His neighbours, though all allowing that he was a most inveterate poacher, always gave him credit for a great deal of simple honesty in other things. So one day, having caught him in a ditch waiting for wild ducks, on my shooting-grounds, instead of prosecuting, I took him into my service, where he has now remained for some years; and though he sometimes shows an inclination to return to his former way of life, he lives tolerably steady, taking great delight at all idle times, in teaching my children to shoot, fish, or trap vermin—a kind of learning which the boys, young as they are, have become great proficients in, preferring Simon Donald to their Latin master; and though they attend regularly and diligently to the latter, they make equally good use of the lessons of the former, and can dress a fly and catch a dish of trout for dinner, gallop on their Shetland ponies across the wildest country, or hit a mark with a rifle as well as most boys of double their age. And, after all, this kind of education does boys more good than harm (as long as they do not neglect their books at the same time, which I do not allow mine to do), as they acquire hardihood of constitution, free use of their limbs, and confidence in their own powers. But I have said enough of me and mine, and must refer those who may have any curiosity on the subject to the following sketches, as illustrating my doings and observations in my temporary home.

It may be proper to mention that Chapters XXVI. and XXX. have already appeared in print; some learned critic having deemed it expedient to publish them in the 153rd Number of the *Quarterly Review*.

FISHING BY MOONLIGHT

CHAPTER I

Highland Lakes—Steam-boats—Small Lochs—Wild Cats—Ravens Dragging the Lake—The Crea—Fishing at Night—Pike—Trolling large Trout on Loch Ness—Flies, Otters, etc.—Fishing with the Otter—Spawning Trout.

THE beauties of Loch Lomond, Loch Awe, and several other of the Highland lakes, are almost as well known to the English as Regent Street or Hyde Park. Lovely and magnificent as all these visited lakes are, and worthy of the praise of the poet and the pencil of the painter, there are unnumbered other Highland lochs whose less hackneyed beauties have far greater charms for me. Visit Loch Lomond, or many others, and you find yourself surrounded by spruce cockneys, in tight-waisted shooting-jackets, plaid waistcoats, and (so called) Glengarry bonnets, all of whom fancy themselves facsimiles of Roderick Dhu, or James Fitz-James; and quote Sir Walter to young ladies in tartan scarfs, redolent, nevertheless, of the land of Cockayne. Steam-boats and coaches are admirable things, but they spoil one's train of ideas, and terminate one's reverie when enjoying the grandeur and sublimity of one of these spots of beauty. Though a steam-boat, at a certain number of miles' distance, with its stream of smoke winding over the rocky shore of a large lake, and adding a new feature to the scene, may occasionally come in with good effect;—when it approaches and comes spluttering and groaning near you, with its smoke drifting right into your face, and driving you from some favourite point or bay, you are apt to turn your back on lake, boat, and scenery, with a feeling of annoyance and disgust. I well remember being one bright summer's day on the shore of Loch Ness, and enjoying the surpassing loveliness of the scene. The perfectly calm loch was like a mirror, reflecting the steep red crags of the opposite shore; and the weeping-birch trees, feathering down to the very edge of the water, and hanging over its surface, as if to gaze at their own fair forms in its glassy depths, were as distinctly seen in the lake as on the shore; while here and there a trout rising at a fly dimpled the smooth water, and in my idle mood I watched the circles as they gradually widened and disappeared. The white gulls floated noiselessly by, as if afraid to disturb the stillness of the scene, instead of saluting their common enemy with loud cries. I had been for some time stretched on the ground enjoying the quiet beauty of the picture, till I had at last fallen into a half-sleeping, half-waking kind of dreaminess, when I was suddenly aroused by a Glasgow steamer passing within a hundred yards of me, full of holiday people, with fiddles and parasols conspicuous on the deck, while a stream of black sooty smoke showered its favours over me, and filled my mouth as I opened it to vent my ill-temper in an anathema against steam-boats, country-dance tunes, and cockneys.

There have come in my way, during my rambles through the Highlands, many a fair and beauteous loch, placed like a bright jewel in the midst of the rugged mountains, far out of reach of steam and coach, accessible only to the walking traveller, or at most to a Highland pony, where the only living creature to be seen is the silent otter playing its fantastic gambols in the quiet of the evening, or the stag as he comes to drink at the water's edge or to crop the succulent grass which grows in the shallows. There are so many small lochs which are known but to few individuals, but which are equally beautiful with those whose renown and larger size have made them the resort of numberless visitors, that it is difficult to single out any one as pre-eminent. In Inverness-shire there are many lovely lakes, and many an hour and day have I passed in fishing on some of these. There was one beautiful lake to which I used sometimes to take net and boat, as well as rod. It was a piece of water about four miles long, and one or two broad; at one end were two sandy bays, forming regular semicircles, with their beaches covered to a width of a few feet with small pebbles. Between these two bays was a bold promontory running into the lake, and covered with fine old pine trees. Along one side was a stretch of perhaps three miles of grey precipitous rocks nearly covered with birch and hazel, which hung over the water, casting a dark shade on it. The other end of the lake was contracted between the rocks till it was lost to the view, while on the remaining side was flat moorland. The whole country round and within view of the lake was picturesque and bold. In the rocks near the water were a colony of wild cats, whose cries during the night deterred the shepherd from passing that way; while on the highest part of the grey precipice was a raven's nest, the owners of which always kept up a concert with their voices of ill-omen whenever they saw a human being near their dominions—there they would sit on a withered branch of a tree or a pointed rock, croaking, and playing their quaint antics for hours together. Their nest was so protected by a shelf of rock which projected below it, that I never could get a rifle-ball into it, often as I have tried, though I must have frequently half-filled it with the splinters of the rock.

In dragging this lake we were obliged to restrict ourselves to the two sandy bays, as the rest of the bottom was covered with old tree-roots and broken sticks, which tore our nets, and prevented our using them.

In the quiet summer evenings it was interesting to see my crew of five Highlanders, as, singing a Gaelic song, they rowed the boat in a large semicircle round one of the bays, letting out the net as they went, one end of the rope being held by a man on the shore at the point from which they started. When they got to the other side of the bay, they landed, with the exception of one man, who remained in the boat to right the net if it got fixed in roots or stones. The rest hauled in the net gradually, bringing the two ends together. As it came in, a fine trout or pike now and then would be seen making a dart round the enclosed space within the net, or dashing at the net itself, dragging for a moment half the corks under water. The head man of the crew, a little peppery Highlander, invariably got into a state of the most savage excitement, which increased as the net approached the shore; and if any stoppage occurred from its being caught by a root or stick, he actually danced with excitement, hallooing and swearing in Gaelic at the net, the men, and the fish. When all went on smoothly and well, he acted the part of fugleman with no little dignity, perched in the bow of the boat, and keeping the men in proper place and time as they dragged in the net. We generally caught a great number of trout and pike, some of very large size. By the time we had killed all the fish, and arranged them in rows to admire their beauty and size, the little captain (as the other men called him) subsided into a good-humoured calm; and having offered a pinch of snuff to the gamekeeper, whom he generally fixed upon in particular to shout at, in consequence of a kind of rivalry between them, and also in consequence of his measuring some head and shoulders higher than himself, he made a brief apology for what he had said, winding it up by saying, "And after all, that's no so bad, your Honour," as he pointed to some giant trout; he then would light a pipe, and having taken a few whiffs, deliberately shove it alight into his waistcoat pocket, and extracting a netting-needle and string, set to work, mending any hole that had been made in the net. This done, and a dram of whisky having been passed round, the net was arranged on the stern of the boat, and they rowed round the wooded promontory to the other creek, keeping time to their oars with some wild Gaelic song, with a chorus in which they all joined, and the sound of which, as it came over the water of the lake, and died gradually away as they rounded the headland, had a most peculiarly romantic effect.

Sometimes we did not commence our fishing till sunset, choosing nights when the full moon gave us sufficient light for the purpose. Our object in selecting this time was to catch the larger pike, who during the day remained in the deep water, coming in at night to the shore, and to the mouths of the burns which run into the lake, where they found small trout and other food brought down by the streams. During the nighttime, also, towards the beginning of autumn, we used to catch quantities of char, which fish then, and then only, approached near enough to the shore to be caught in the nets. In the clear frosty air of a September night the peculiar moaning cry of the wild cats as they answered to each other along the opposite shore, and the hootings of the owls in the pine-wood, sounded like the voices of unearthly beings, and I do not think that any one of my crew would have passed an hour alone by that loch side for all the fish in it. Indeed, the hill-side which sloped down to the lake had the name of being haunted, and the waters of the lake itself had their ghostly inhabitant in the shape of what the Highlanders called the water-bull. There was also a story of some strange mermaid-like monster being sometimes seen, having the appearance of a monstrous fish with long hair. It was a scene worthy of a painter, as the men with eager gestures scrambled up, the fish glancing like silver in the moonbeams ; and then, as they rowed round, sometimes lost in the shade of the pine-trees, which completely darkened the surface of the water immediately below the rocks on which they grew, or came again into full view as they left the shadow of the woods, the water sparkling and glancing from their oars. Frequently they stopped their wild chant, as the strange cries of the different nocturnal animals echoed loudly from the rocks, and we could hear the men say a few words of Gaelic to each other in a low voice, and then recommence their song.

We always caught the largest fish at night-time, both trout and pike, the latter frequently above twenty pounds' weight, with the teeth and jaws of a young shark. Sometimes the net brought in a great number of char, which appear to go in large shoals ; but these latter only in the autumn.

In these lochs I killed great numbers of pike and the larger trout by means of floating lines, which we put in at the windward side of the lake, to be carried down by the wind. On favourable days, in March or October, when there was a brisk wind, the lines went but half-way across the loch before every hook had a fish on it, and then commenced a rare chase. When we neared a float with a large pike hooked to it, as the water was very clear, the fish took the alarm and swam off at a great pace, often giving us some trouble before we could catch him. I have seen an empty corked-up bottle, with line attached, used as a float for this kind of fishing, instead of the corks. Pike are very capricious in taking the bait, and some days not one would move, although the wind and weather all seemed favourable; while on other days every float had a fish to it. Again, the fish would be quiet for some time, and then suddenly a simultaneous impulse seemed to seize them, and they would seize the baits as quickly as we could wish, for the space of an hour or so.

The trout seldom take a dead bait during the daytime, but we often caught them on hooks left in the water all night. In all the Highland lakes on which I have fished in this way, large eels would sometimes take the hook, and often break my lines. It is frequently said that putting pike into a lake would destroy the trout-fishing; but I have invariably found that in all lakes of a considerable size, where the pike were plenty, the trout have improved very much in size and quality, and not diminished even in numbers to any great extent. In fact, the thing to be complained of in most Highland lakes is, that the trout are too numerous, and consequently of a small size and inferior quality. The only way to kill the larger trout is by trolling. In Loch Awe and several other lakes I have seen this kind of fishing succeed well. If the sportsman is skilful, he is sure of taking finer trout in this way than he would ever do when fly-fishing. In trolling there are two or three rules which should be carefully observed:—Choose the roughest wind that your boat can live in; fish with a good-sized bait, not much less than a herring, and do not commence your trolling until after two o'clock in the afternoon, by which time the large fish seem to have digested their last night's supper and to be again on the move. You may pass over the heads of hundreds of large trout when they are lying at rest and not hungry, and you will not catch one; but as soon as they begin to feed, a fish, although he may have half-a-dozen small trout in his stomach, will still run at your bait. The weight of sinkers on your line, and the depth at which you fish, must of course depend on the depth of water in the lake. A patient fisherman should find out how deep every reach and bay of the lake is before he begins to troll. The labour of a day spent in taking soundings is well repaid. The strength and activity of the large loch trout is immense, and he will run out your whole reel-line if allowed to do so. Sometimes he will go down perpendicularly to the bottom, where he remains sulky or attempts to rub off the hooks: get him out of this situation, and away he goes, almost towing your boat after him. Then is the time for your boatman to make play to keep up with the fish and save your line; for a twenty-pound Salmo ferox[1] is no ignoble foe to contend with when you have him at the end of a common fishing-line: he appears to have the strength of a whale as he rushes away.

I was crossing Loch Ness alone one evening with my rod at the stern of the boat, with my trolling-tackle on it trailing behind. Suddenly it was seized by a large trout, and before I could do anything but take hold of my rod he had run out eighty yards of line, and bent my stiff trolling-rod like a willow, carrying half the rod under water. The loch was too deep for me, and he snapped the line in an instant, the rod and the twenty yards of line which remained jerking back into the air, and sending the water in a shower of spray around. Comparing the strength of this fish with that of others which I have killed when trolling, he must have been a perfect water-monster. Indeed I have little doubt that the immense depths of Loch Ness contain trout as large, if not larger, than are to be found in any other loch in Scotland.

For fly-fishing in lakes, it is difficult to give any rule as to the colour and size of your fly. The best thing you can do is to find out some person whose experience you can depend on, and who has been in the habit of fishing in the particular water where you want to try your own skill, for most lakes have a favourite fly. I have always, when at a loss, had recourse to a red, white, or black palmer. There are very few trout who can withstand these flies when well made. The size of the palmer should depend on the roughness or smoothness of the water. On a dark windy day I have frequently found a white palmer succeed when nothing else would tempt the fish to rise;

---

[1] Mr. Colquhoun contributed a very interesting chapter on this fish to the *Field* paper (13th November 1880), from which a few sentences are extracted. The largest feroxes taken in Scotland, not even excepting Loch Awe, have been taken out of Loch Rannoch, but of late years the constant trailing of spoons and other gaudy baits over them has made the very large fish of all our trolling lochs so shy that few will run at any trolling bait. The largest Mr. Colquhoun has ever known to be taken in Loch Awe by rod was twenty-one pounds. At Loch Rannoch, in twenty-eight years, three of twenty-three, twenty-two, and twenty pounds' weight have been taken. Feroxes are sometimes hooked with a trout-fly when from three to six pounds, but he has never known a large one so taken, though he once saw a ferox of seventeen pounds taken at the head of Loch Awe with a large spring salmon-fly. Many so-called large feroxes are often found to be kelt salmon.

while on a bright calm day a small black palmer should be tried. There are endless favourite loch-flies, and it is seldom that a person cannot be found to give you the requisite information as to which to use: however, I never feel much at a loss as long as I have some palmers in my fly-book.

In putting night-lines into a large lake, the best places are those where any burn or ditch runs into it, or along some shallow sandy or gravelly bay, for in these places the fish feed during the night-time. Worms, frogs, and small trout are the best bait for night-lines. In trolling, the small silvery fish supposed to be the young of the salmon, or the small kind of herring called garvies, are the best bait. Preserved in spirits of wine, they keep for a long time, and become so tough, that they do not tear or break off your hook. If you take a fancy to fish with a fly during the night in a lake, a large black fly is the best, but unless it is drawn very slowly through the water, the fish, though they rise, will miss it.

A small fly which I have found to be always a favourite with trout, is one made as follows:—Body yellow floss silk, with landrail wing, and a turn or two of red heckle near the head. In most waters this fly succeeds. In some of the small black-looking lakes, far up in the solitudes of the mountains, where no person is ever seen, unless a shepherd may chance now and then to stray in their direction, or the deer-stalker stops to examine the soft ground near the water edge for the tracks of deer—in these lonely pools the trout seem often as unconscious of danger as birds are said to be on a newly discovered island; and they will rise greedily at the rudest imitation of a fly fastened to a common piece of twine, five or six trout rising at once, and striving who should be caught first. The fish in some of these lakes which are situated at a great height, are excessively numerous, but generally black and small. I have seen little black pools of this kind actually crowded with small trout.

The otter takes to the waters far up in the hills during the summer time, where she may rear her young in the midst of abundance and in solitary security. Making her lair on some small island or point of land covered with coarse grass or rushes, she lives in plenty and peace, till her young having grown strong, and the frosts of winter having commenced, the family remove, like their betters, to the seaside, passing over hill and valley in a straight line, to some remembered rocks and caves, where the dam has wintered before.

Round the small hill-lake, too, are seen the tracks of the fox and wild cat. Their nightly maraudings seem to lead them always in the direction of water. During the heats of August, when at a loss for grouse, I have always found it a good plan to hunt round any lake that may be at hand—as the old birds lead their young daily to the water's edge to drink, and to pick up the small angular stones, numbers of which are invariably found in the stomach of the grouse, being probably necessary to grind down their dry and hard food. The hen-harrier and falcon, too, seem to hunt in these places, knowing that if grouse fail them, they are sure to find either a duck or snipe, or perhaps a large flock of plovers huddled together on the pebbles which edge the water. In fact, the mountain lake seems to be always a kind of rendezvous for all wild animals; and I doubt if any grouse-shooter or deer-stalker ever passes near their clear waters without going out of his way to look along the margin, or to refresh himself by gazing over the cool surface.

When you are shooting, too, there is the inducement of hoping to find a brood of ducks or teal, which few hill-lakes are without. I have sometimes found great numbers of these birds, collected in some quiet pool on the hills, in August or September, before they have descended to feed on the corn in the low country.

Many a Highland lake has a legend attached to it, and however improbable the tale may seem to the incredulous Sassenach, the Highlander believes firmly in the truth of it.

Some person, endowed doubtless with a prominent organ of destructiveness, has within the last few years invented an implement for fishing the lakes, called the *otter*; and though it is rather a poaching sort of affair, still I consider it quite a fair way of catching trout in some of the mountain lochs, where a rod could be used to no good effect, and where it would be impossible to launch a boat. Its principle of motion is exactly similar to that of a boy's kite. Acted upon by the resistance of the water, the otter, which consists of a small thin board, about fourteen inches by eight, and leaded on one edge so as to swim nearly upright, carries out a long line, which is attached to it by four short strings, and is wound on a large reel. To this line are fastened a dozen flies on short lines, which, being carried along by the board, rake the surface of the water; and in windy weather I have caught numbers of trout in this way, where the rod would have been of no use whatever.

Many a grilse, and salmon too, have I killed in Loch Ness with the otter. There are, however, some great drawbacks to the merits of this implement. The fish are very apt to escape after being struck by the hooks, and, being thus wounded and frightened, become shy, and unwilling to rise again. Also, if a large fish is hooked very near the board, there is a great risk that he will break your fly off, and go away with it sticking in his mouth. For these reasons, the otter, though of great use in certain localities, should never be used in waters where the rod can be brought into play. Though exciting enough in an unknown and remote lake, where you seldom fish, the actual sport which it affords falls far short of rod fishing.

I have tried it for pike, but did not find it answer, as the fish were constantly struck without being hooked—in consequence of their requiring some time to gorge their prey. The angling in some of the best trout lochs is completely spoilt by the introduction of these instruments of destruction. Every shepherd's boy or idle fellow can make one, and carry it about with him; and in lakes where this kind of fishing is prohibited, he has nothing to do, if he sees a keeper or watcher in the distance, but to wrap up the whole thing in his plaid, and walk away with it. There are but few Highland lochs in which a net can be drawn with good effect, owing to the unevenness of the bottom, and the risk of getting your tackle entangled and broken by roots and remains of trees, which always abound in these waters—the remnants of forests of an age gone by. Their great depth too is another obstacle to net fishing, excepting here and there, where a sandy bay or tolerably smooth bottom can be found. To these places the trout always resort in the evenings, in order to feed on the insects and smaller fish that frequent the small stones.

In lochs containing pike, a hang-net, as it is called, placed across deep angles of the water or along the edge of weeds, is sure to catch them; this fish always struggling and endeavouring to press forward as soon as he feels the net, whereas the trout in these clear waters always escape the danger by turning back as soon as they touch the meshes.

The Highland shepherds kill numbers of the spawning trout in the autumn, in every little stream and rill, however small, which feeds the lake. At this time of the year the trout are seized with an irresistible inclination for ascending any running stream that they can find ; and I have seen large trout of several pounds' weight taken out of holes in very small runs of water, to get into which they must have made their way for considerable distances up a channel where the water could not nearly cover them. Still, as long as a trout can keep his head against the stream, so long will he endeavour to work his way up. Numbers of fish, and always the largest, fall a prey not only to men, but to every prowling fox or wild cat who passes their way during the autumn, and all vermin instinctively hunt along the edge of water during the night-time. A trout in shallow water is easily caught by any of these animals. Even the buzzard and the raven succeed in capturing them when they are left in small rills, as is frequently the case, having been tempted to ascend them by some shower, which swells the water for a short time and then leaves it as low as ever.

PLOVERS

ROEBUCK

CHAPTER II

Roe: Mischief done by—Fawns—Tame Roe—Boy killed by Roe—Hunting Roe: Artifices of—Shooting Roe—Unlucky shot—Change of colour—Swimming—Cunning Roe.

As the spring advances, and the larch and other deciduous trees again put out their foliage, I see the tracks of roe[1] and the animals themselves in new and unaccustomed places. They now betake themselves very much to the smaller and younger plantations, where they can find plenty of one of their most favourite articles of food—the shoots of the young trees. Much as I like to see these animals (and certainly the roebuck is the most perfectly formed of all deer), I must confess that they commit

[1] Roe have the first year one antler, second year two antlers, third year three antlers. This is always the case unless some accident happens to them. Sometimes they have four antlers, but seldom. The growth of the horns of all deer is irregular, depending much on the feeding which they get.—C. St. J.

great havoc in plantations of hard wood. As fast as the young oak trees put out new shoots the roe nibble them off, keeping the trees from growing above three or four feet in height by constantly biting off the leading shoot. Besides this, they peel the young larch with both their teeth and horns, stripping them of their bark in the neatest manner imaginable. One can scarcely wonder at the anathemas uttered against them by proprietors of young plantations. Always graceful, a roebuck is peculiarly so when stripping some young tree of its leaves, nibbling them off one by one in the most delicate and dainty manner. I have watched a roe strip the leaves off a long bramble shoot, beginning at one end and nibbling off every leaf. My rifle was aimed at his heart and my finger was on the trigger, but I made some excuse or other to myself for not killing him, and left him undisturbed—his beauty saved him. The leaves and flowers of the wild rose-bush are another favourite food of the roe. Just before they produce their calves the does wander about a great deal, and seem to avoid the society of the buck, though they remain together during the whole autumn and winter. The young roe is soon able to escape from most of its enemies. For a day or two it is quite helpless, and frequently falls a prey to the fox, who at that time of the year is more ravenous than at any other, as it then has to find food to satisfy the carnivorous appetites of its own cubs. A young roe, when caught unhurt, is not difficult to rear, though their great tenderness and delicacy of limb makes it not easy to handle them without injuring them. They soon become perfectly tame and attach themselves to their master. When in captivity they will eat almost anything that is offered to them, and from this cause are frequently destroyed, picking up and swallowing some indigestible substance about the house. A tame buck, however, becomes a dangerous pet; for after attaining to his full strength he is very apt to make use of it in attacking people whose appearance he does not like. They particularly single out women and children as their victims, and inflict severe and dangerous wounds with their sharp-pointed horns, and notwithstanding their small size, their strength and activity make them a very unpleasant adversary. One day, at a kind of public garden near Brighton, I saw a beautiful but very small roebuck in an enclosure fastened with a chain, which seemed strong enough and heavy enough to hold and weigh down an elephant. Pitying the poor animal, an exile from his native land, I asked what reason they could have for ill-using him by putting such a weight of iron about his neck. The keeper of the place, however, told me that small as the roebuck was, the chain was quite necessary, as he had attacked and killed a boy of twelve years old a few days before, stabbing the poor fellow in fifty places with his sharp-pointed horns. Of course I had no more to urge in his behalf. In its native wilds no animal is more timid, and eager to avoid all risk of danger. The roe has peculiarly acute organs of sight, smelling, and hearing, and makes good use of all three in avoiding its enemies.

In shooting roe, it depends so much on the cover, and other local causes, whether dogs or beaters should be used, that no rule can be laid down as to which is best. Nothing is more exciting than running roe with beagles, where the ground is suitable, and the covers so situated that the dogs and their game are frequently in sight. The hounds for roe-shooting should be small and slow. Dwarf harriers are the best, or good-sized rabbit-beagles, where the ground is not too rough. The roe when hunted by small dogs of this kind does not make away, but runs generally in a circle, and is seldom above a couple of hundred yards ahead of the beagles, stopping every now and then to listen, and allowing them to come very near, before he goes off again, in this way giving the sportsman a good chance of knowing where the deer is during most of the run. Many people use fox-hounds for roe-shooting, but generally these dogs run too fast, and press the roebuck so much that he will not stand it, but leaves the cover, and goes straightway out of reach of the sportsman, who is left to cool himself without any hope of a shot. Besides this, you entirely banish roe from the cover if you hunt them frequently with fast hounds, as no animal more delights in quiet and solitude, or will less put up with too much driving. In most woods beaters are better for shooting roe with than dogs, though the combined cunning and timidity of the animal frequently make it double back through the midst of the rank of beaters; particularly if it has any suspicion of a concealed enemy in consequence of having scented or heard the shooters at their posts, for it prefers facing the shouts and noise of the beaters to passing within reach of a hidden danger, the extent and nature of which it has not ascertained. By taking advantage of the animal's timidity and shyness in this respect, I have frequently got shots at roe in large woods by placing people in situations where the animal could smell them but not see them, thus driving it back to my place of concealment. Though they generally prefer the warmest and driest part of the woods to lie in, I have sometimes when looking for ducks started roe in the marshy grounds, where they lie close in the tufts of long heather and rushes. Being much tormented with ticks and wood-flies, they frequently in the hot weather betake themselves not only to these marshy places, but even to the fields of high corn, where they sit in a form like a hare. Being good swimmers, they cross rivers without hesitation in their way to and from their favourite feeding-places; indeed, I have often known roe pass across the river daily, living on one side, and going to feed every evening on the other. Even when wounded, I have seen a roebuck beat three powerful and active dogs in the water, keeping ahead of them, and requiring another shot before he was secured. Though very much attached to each other, and living mostly in pairs,[1] I have known a doe take up her abode for several years in a solitary strip of wood. Every season she crossed a large extent of hill to find a mate, and returned after two or three weeks' absence. When her young ones, which she produced every year, were come to their full size, they always went away, leaving their mother in solitary possession of her wood.

The roe almost always keep to woodland, but I have known a stray roebuck take to lying out on the hill at some distance from the covers. I had frequently started this buck out of glens and hollows several miles from the woods. One day, as I was stalking some hinds in a broken part of the hill, and had got within two hundred yards of one of them, a fine fat barren hind, the roebuck started out of a hollow between me and the red deer, and galloping straight towards them, gave the alarm, and they all made off. The buck, however, got confused by the noise and galloping of the larger animals, and, turning back, passed me within fifty yards. So to punish him for spoiling

---

[1] They do not unite in herds, but live in separate families. —Scrope, *Deer Stalking*, p. 183.

my sport I took a deliberate aim as he went quickly but steadily on, and killed him dead. I happened to be alone that day, so I shouldered my buck and walked home with him, a three hours' distance of rough ground, and I was tired enough of his weight before I reached the house. In shooting roe, shot is at all times far preferable to ball. The latter, though well aimed, frequently passes clean through the animal, apparently without injuring him, and the poor creature goes away to die in some hidden corner; whereas a charge of shot gives him such a shock that he drops much more readily to it than to a rifle-ball, unless indeed the ball happens to strike the heart or spine. Having killed roe constantly with both rifle and gun, small shot and large, I am inclined to think that the most effective charge is an Eley's cartridge with No. 2 shot in it. I have, when woodcock-shooting, frequently killed roe with No. 6 shot, as when they are going across and are shot well forward, they are as easy to kill as a hare, though they will carry off a great deal of shot if hit too far behind. No one should ever shoot roe without some well-trained dog, to follow them when wounded; as no animal is more often lost when mortally wounded.

Where numerous, roe are very mischievous to both corn and turnips, eating and destroying great quantities, and as they feed generally in the dark, lying still all day, their devastations are difficult to guard against. Their acute sense of smelling enables them to detect the approach of any danger, when they bound off to their coverts, ready to return as soon as it is past. In April they go great distances to feed on the clover-fields, where the young plants are then just springing up. In autumn, the ripening oats are their favourite food, and in winter, the turnips, wherever these crops are at hand, or within reach from the woods. A curious and melancholy accident happened in a parish situated in one of the eastern counties of Scotland a few years ago. Perhaps the most extraordinary part of the story is that it is perfectly true. Some idle fellows of the village near the place where the catastrophe happened having heard that the roe and deer from the neighbouring woods were in the habit of feeding in some fields of high corn, two of them repaired to the place in the dusk of the evening with a loaded gun, to wait for the arrival of the deer at their nightly feeding-ground. They had waited some time, and the evening shades were making all objects more and more indistinct every moment, when they heard a rustling in the standing corn, at a short distance from them, and looking in the direction they saw some large animal moving. Having no doubt that it was a deer that they saw, the man who had the gun took his aim, his finger was on the trigger, and his eye along the barrel; he waited, however, to get a clearer view of the animal, which had ceased moving. At this instant, his companion, who was close to him, saw, to his astonishment, the flash of a gun from the spot where the supposed deer was, and almost before he heard the report his companion fell back dead upon him, and with the same ball he himself received a mortal wound. The horror and astonishment of the author of this unlucky deed can scarcely be imagined when, on running up, he found, instead of a deer, one man lying dead and another senseless and mortally wounded. Luckily, as it happened, the wounded man lived long enough to declare before witnesses that his death was occasioned solely by accident, and that his companion, at the moment of his being killed, was aiming at the man who killed them. The latter did not long survive the affair. Struck with grief and sorrow at the mistake he had committed, his mind and health gave way, and he died soon afterwards.

The difference in the colour and kind of hair that a roe's skin is covered with, at different seasons of the year, is astonishingly great. From May to October they are covered with bright red-brown hair, and but little of it. In winter their coat is a fine dark mouse-colour, very long and close, but the hair is brittle, and breaks easily in the hand like dried grass. When run with greyhounds, the roebuck at first leaves the dogs far behind, but if pressed and unable to make his usual cover, he appears to become confused and exhausted, his bounds become shorter, and he seems to give up the race. In wood, when driven, they invariably keep as much as they can to the closest portions of the cover, and in going from one part to another follow the line where the trees stand nearest to each other, avoiding the more open parts as long as possible. For some unknown reason, as they do it without any apparent cause, such as being hard hunted, or driven by want of food, the roe sometimes take it into their heads to swim across wide pieces of water, and even arms of the sea. I have known roe caught by boatmen in the Cromarty Firth, swimming strongly across the entrance of the bay, and making good way against the current of the tide, which runs there with great rapidity. Higher up the same firth, too, roe have been caught when in the act of crossing. When driven by hounds, I have seen one swim Loch Ness. They are possessed of great cunning in doubling and turning to elude these persevering enemies. I used to shoot roe to fox-hounds, and one day was much amused by watching an old roebuck, who had been run for some time by three of my dogs. I was lying concealed on a height above him, and saw the poor animal go upon a small mound covered with young fir-trees. He stood there till the hounds were close on him, though not in view; then taking a great leap at right angles to the course in which he had before been running, he lay flat down with his head on the ground, completely throwing out the hounds, who had to cast about in order to find his track again; when one bitch appeared to be coming straight upon the buck, he rose quietly up, and crept in a stooping position round the mound, getting behind the dogs. In this way, on a very small space of ground, he managed for a quarter of an hour to keep out of view of, though close to, three capital hounds, well accustomed to roe-hunting. Sometimes he squatted flat on the ground, and at others leaped off at an angle, till having rested himself, and the hounds having made a wide cast, fancying that he had left the place, the buck took an opportunity to slip off unobserved, and crossing an opening in the wood, came straight up the hill to me, when I shot him.

The greatest drawback to preserving roe to any great extent is, that they are so shy and nocturnal in their habits that they seldom show themselves in the daytime. I sometimes see a roe passing like a shadow through the trees, or standing gazing at me from a distance in some sequestered glade; but, generally speaking, they are no ornament about a place, their presence being only known by the mischief they do to the young plantations and to the crops. A keeper in Kincardineshire this year told me, that he had often early in the morning counted above twenty roe in a single turnip-field. As for the sport afforded by shooting them, I never killed one without regretting it, and wishing that I could bring the poor animal to life again. I do not think that roe are sufficiently appreciated as venison, yet they are excellent eating when killed in proper season, between October and February, and of a proper age. In summer the meat is not worth cooking, being dry, and sometimes rank.

ROE SWIMMING LOCH

SHOOTING A WITCH

CHAPTER III

Grouse's Nest—Partridge Nest—Grouse-shooting—Marten Cat—Witch, Death of—Stags—Snaring Grouse—Black Game: Battles of—Hybrid Bird—Ptarmigan-shooting—Mist on the Mountain—Stag—Unsuccessful Stalking—Death of Eagle.

I FOUND the nest of a grouse with eight eggs, or rather egg-shells, within two hundred yards of a small farm-house on a part of my shooting-ground, where there is a mere strip of heather surrounded by cultivated fields, and on a spot particularly infested by colley-dogs, as well as by herd-boys, *et id genus omne*. But the poor bird, although so surrounded by enemies, had managed to hatch and lead away her brood in safety. I saw them frequently afterwards, and they all came to maturity. How many survived the shooting-season I do not know, but the covey numbered eight birds far on in October.

If the parent bird had selected her nesting-place for beauty of prospect, she could not have pitched upon a lovelier spot. The nest was on a little mound where I always stop, when walking in that direction, to admire the extensive and varied view—the Bay of Findhorn and the sand-hills, the Moray Firth, with the entrance to the Cromarty Bay, and the bold rocky headlands backed by the mountains of Ross-shire. Sutherland, Caithness, Inverness, and Ross-shire are all seen from this spot; whilst the rich plains of Moray, dotted with timber, and intersected by the winding stream of the Findhorn, with the woods of Altyre, Darnaway, and Brodie, form a nearer picture.

It is a curious fact, but one which I have often observed, that dogs frequently pass close to the nest of grouse, partridge, or other game, without scenting the hen bird as she sits on her eggs. I knew this year of a partridge's[1] nest which was placed close to a narrow footpath near my house; and although not only my people, but all my dogs, were constantly passing within a foot and a half of the bird, they never found her out, and she hatched her brood in safety.

Grouse generally make their nest in a high tuft of heather. The eggs are peculiarly beautiful and game-like, of a rich brown colour, spotted closely with black. Although in some peculiarly early seasons, the young birds are full grown by the 12th of August, in general five birds out of six which are killed on that day are only half come to their strength and beauty. The 20th of the month would be a much better day on which to commence their legal persecution. In October there is not a more beautiful bird in our island; and in January a cock grouse is one of the most superb fellows in the world, as he struts about fearlessly with his mate, his bright red comb erected above his eyes, and his rich dark-brown plumage shining in the sun. Unluckily, they are more easily killed at this time of the year than at any other; and I have been assured that a ready market is found for them not only in

---

[1] When she has small young ones, the partridge becomes very bold sometimes, and I have seen one attack and strike a dog which was passing with me close to the wood. The partridge conceals her nest and eggs, and even the entrance to it through the long grass with the greatest care. It is, however, often placed close to a road or path, on which occasion dogs, etc., seem to pass close to the old bird while sitting, without finding her scent. At the same time I have known an old partridge caught on her eggs by my retriever and brought to me. I released the bird, and the next day she was again on her eggs, which were all hatched in due time.—C. St. J.

January, but to the end of February, though in fine seasons they begin to nest very early in March. Hardy must the grouse be, and prolific beyond calculation, to supply the numbers that are yearly killed, legally and illegally.[1] Vermin, however, are their worst enemies; and where the ground is kept clear of all their winged and four-footed destroyers, no shooting seems to reduce their numbers.

I cannot say that my taste leads me to rejoice in the slaughter of a large bag of grouse in one day. I have no ambition to see my name in the county newspapers as having bagged my seventy brace of grouse, in a certain number of hours, on such and such a hill. I have much more satisfaction in killing a moderate quantity of birds, in a wild and varied range of hill, with my single brace of dogs, and wandering in any direction that fancy leads me, than in having my day's beat laid out for me, with relays of dogs and keepers, and all the means of killing the grouse on easy walking ground, where they are so numerous that one has only to load and fire. In the latter case, I generally find myself straying off in pursuit of some teal or snipe, to the neglect of the grouse, and the disgust of the keeper, who may think his dignity compromised by attending a sportsman who returns with less than fifty brace. Nothing is so easy to shoot as a grouse, when they are tolerably tame; and with a little choice of his shots, a very moderate

---

[1] Since the days of Mr. St. John the scourge known as the grouse disease has become only too familiar in Scotland. Its first recorded appearance was in 1838. It was again prevalent in 1856, and in 1868 a disastrous outbreak visited the greater part of the Scottish moors. Subsequently, in 1872-73, in 1880, and in 1889, it has been experienced with more or less severity. Various causes, more or less conjectural, have been assigned for this mortality. Although this is not the place to enter into a disquisition on the subject, we may enumerate some causes as follows: overstocking of moors, the artificial destruction of vermin, frosted heather, the large consumption of corn in some places by the birds, the existence of a parasitic worm in the intestines, etc.

To each of these theories a very probable, if not absolutely conclusive, refutation has been supplied. The widely-extended prevalence of the disease, when it does break out, is not compatible with the existence of any cause which is more or less local. We must be content to assume that the hitherto undiscovered cause is akin to those which produce widespread epidemics among mankind, though in all probability some of the foregoing conditions may tend to increase the virulence of the disease at certain times and in certain districts.

For an exhaustive treatment of the subject we would refer the reader to Dr. T. Spencer Cobbold's *The Grouse Disease*, and T. Speedy's *Sport in the Highlands and Lowlands*.

Dr. E. Klein (*Etiology and Pathology of Grouse Disease*: Macmillan, 1892) is the last inquirer into the malady. He deems it "an acute, infectious pneumonia," and has detected and cultivated the microbe characteristic of the disease. He can suggest no remedy, however, except the old-fashioned receipt to destroy all suspicious-looking birds.

marksman ought to kill nearly every bird that he shoots at early in the season, when the birds sit close, fly slowly, and are easily found. At the end of the season, when the coveys are scattered far and wide, and the grouse rise and fly wildly, it requires quick shooting and good walking to make up a handsome bag; but how much better worth killing are the birds at this time of year than in August. If my reader will wade through some leaves of an old note-book, I will describe the kind of shooting that, in my opinion, renders the sporting in the Highlands far preferable to any other that Great Britain can afford.[1]

October 20th.—Determined to shoot across to Malcolm's shealing, at the head of the river, twelve miles distant; to sleep there; and kill some ptarmigan the next day.

For the first mile of our walk we passed through the old fir woods, where the sun seldom penetrates. In the different grassy glades we saw several roe, but none within shot. A fir-cone falling to the ground made me look up, and I saw a marten cat running like a squirrel from branch to branch. The moment the little animal saw that my eye was on him he stopped short, and curling himself up in the fork of a branch, peered down on me. Pretty as he was, I fired at him. He sprang from his hiding-place, and fell half-way down, but catching at a branch, clung to it for a minute, holding on with his fore-paws. I was just going to fire at him again, when he lost his hold, and came down on my dogs' heads, who soon despatched him, wounded as he was. One of the dogs had learned by some means to be an excellent vermin-killer, though steady and staunch at game. As we were just leaving the wood a woodcock rose, which I killed. Our way took us up the rushy course of a burn. Both dogs came to a dead point near the stream, and then drew for at least a quarter of a mile, and just as my patience began to be exhausted, a brace of magnificent old blackcocks rose, but out of shot. One of them came back right over our heads at a good height, making for the wood. As he flew quick down the wind, I aimed nearly a

---

[1] The modern practice and science of grouse-driving was still undiscovered in the days of Mr. St. John. Readers who wish to become acquainted with the literature of this subject are referred to the Badminton Library, and to Mr. Speedy's *Sport in the Highlands and Lowlands of Scotland*.

yard ahead of him as he came towards me, and down he fell, fifty yards behind me, with a force that seemed enough to break every bone in his body. Another and another blackcock fell to my gun before we had left the burn, and also a hare, who got up in the broken ground near the water. Our next cast took us up a slope of hill, where we found a wild covey of grouse. Right and left at them the moment they rose, and killed a brace; the rest went over the hill. Another covey on the same ground gave me three shots. From the top of the hill we saw a dreary expanse of flat ground, with Loch A-na-caillach in the centre of it, a bleak cold-looking piece of water, with several small grey pools near it. Donald told me a long story of the origin of its name, pointing out a large cairn of stones at one end of it. The story was, that some few years ago—" Not so long either, Sir (said Donald); for Rory Beg, the auld smuggler, that died last year, has often told me that he minded the whole thing weel "—there lived down below the woods an old woman, by habit and repute a witch, and one possessed of more than mortal power, which she used in a most malicious manner, spreading sickness and death among man and beast. The minister of the place, who came, however, but once a month to do duty in a building called a chapel, was the only person who, by dint of prayer and Bible, could annoy or resist her. He at last made her so uncomfortable by attacking her with holy water and other spiritual weapons, that she suddenly left the place, and no one knew where she went to. It soon became evident, however, that her abode was not far off, as cattle and people were still taken ill in the same unaccountable manner as before. At last, an idle fellow, who was out poaching deer near Loch A-na-caillach late one evening, saw her start through the air from the cairn of stones towards the inhabited part of the country. This put people on the lookout, and she was constantly seen passing to and fro on her unholy errands during the fine moonlight nights. Many a time was she shot at as she flew past, but without success. At last a pot-valiant and unbelieving old fellow, who had long been a sergeant in some Highland regiment, determined to free his neighbours from the witch; and having loaded his gun with a double charge of gunpowder, put in, instead of shot, a crooked sixpence and some silver buttons, which he had made booty of somewhere or other in war time. He then, in the most foolhardy manner, laid himself down on the hill, just where we were then standing when Donald told me the story, and, by the light of the moon, watched the witch leave her habitation in the cairn of stones. As soon as she was gone, he went to the very place which she had just left, and there lay down in ambush to await her return. "'Deed did he, Sir; for auld Duncan was a mad-like deevil of a fellow, and was feared of nothing." Long he waited, and many a pull he took at his bottle of smuggled whisky, in order to keep out the cold of a September night. At last, when the first grey of the morning began to appear, "Duncan hears a sough, and a wild uncanny kind of skirl over his head, and he sees the witch hersel, just coming like a muckle bird right towards him,—'deed, Sir, but he wished himsel at hame; and his finger was so stiff with cold and fear that he could na scarce pull the trigger. At last, and long, he did put out (Anglicé, shoot off) just as she was hovering over his head, and going to light down on the cairn." Well, to cut the story short, the next morning Duncan was found lying on the cairn in a deep slumber, half sleep and half swoon, with his gun burst, his collar-bone nearly broken, and a fine large heron shot through and through lying beside him, which heron, as every one felt assured, was the caillach herself. "She has na done much harm since yon (concluded Donald); but her ghaist is still to the fore, and the loch side is no canny after the gloaming. But, Lord guide us, Sir, what's that?" and a large long-legged hind rose from some hollow close to the loch, and having stood for a minute with her long ears standing erect, and her gaze turned intently on us, she trotted slowly off, soon disappearing amongst the broken ground. But where are the dogs all this time? There they are, both standing, and evidently at different packs of grouse. I killed three of these birds, taking a right and left shot at one dog's point, and then going to the other.

Off went Old Shot now, according to his usual habit, straight to a rushy pool. I had him from a friend in Ireland, and being used to snipe-shooting, he preferred it to everything else. The cunning old fellow chose not to hear my call, but made for his favourite spot. He immediately stood, and now for the first time seemed to think of his master, as he looked back over his shoulder at me, as much as to say, "Make haste down to me, here is some game." And sure enough up got a snipe, which I killed. The report of my gun putting up a pair of mallards, one of which I winged a long way off, "Hie away, Shot," and Shot, who was licensed to take such liberties, splashed in with great glee, and after being lost to sight for some minutes amongst the high rushes, came back with the mallard in his mouth. "A bad lesson for Carlo that, Master Shot," but he knows better than to follow your example. We now went up the opposite slope leaving Loch A-na-caillach behind us, and killing some grouse, and a mountain hare,[1] with no white about her as yet. We next came to a long stony ridge, with small patches of high heather. A pair of ravens rising from the rocks, soared croaking over us for some time. A pair or two of old grouse were all we killed here. But the view from the summit was splendidly wild as we looked over a long range of grey rocks, beyond which lay a wide and extensive lake, with several small islands in it. The opposite shore of the lake was fringed with birch-trees, and in the distance were a line of lofty mountains whose sharp peaks were covered with snow. Human habitation or evidence of the presence of man was there not, and no sound broke the silence of the solitude excepting the croak of the ravens and the occasional whistle of a plover. "Yon is a fine corrie for deer," said Donald, making me start, as he broke my reverie, and pointing out a fine amphitheatre of rocks just below us. Not being on the look-out for deer, however, I did not pay much attention to what he said, but allowed the dogs to range on where they liked. Left to themselves, and not finding much game, they hunted wide, and we had been walking in silence for some time, when on coming round a small rise between us and the dogs, I saw two fine stags standing, who, intent on watching the dogs, did not see us. After standing motionless for a minute, the deer walked deliberately towards us, not observing us until

---

[1] *Lepus albus*, commonly known as the white or blue hare, has increased in numbers considerably in many parts of Scotland, mainly owing to the destruction of vermin.

This hare has increased of late years to a wonderful extent in some of the higher parts of Scotland, becoming quite a nuisance both to the sheep-farmer and the grouse-shooter, tainting the whole ground. Occasionally it descends from the high grounds, and I have known it killed not only in the woods, but even as far from its home as the seashore near Covesea, Spynie, etc. Change of dress in autumn caused by an actual change of colour in the hair itself, without the shedding of the fur.—C. St. J.

they were within forty yards; they then suddenly halted, stared at us, snorted, and then went off at a trot, but soon breaking into a gallop, fled rapidly away, but were in sight for a long distance. Shot stood watching the deer for some time, but at last seeing that we took no steps against them, looked at me, and then went on hunting. We killed several more grouse and a brace of teal. Towards the afternoon we struck off to the shepherd's house. In the fringe of a birch that sheltered it, we killed a blackcock and hen, and at last got to the end of our walk with fifteen brace of grouse, five black game, one mallard, a snipe, a woodcock, two teal, and two hares; and right glad was I to ease my shoulder of that portion of the game which I carried to help Donald, who would at any time have preferred assisting me to stalk a red deer than to kill and carry grouse. Although my day's sport did not amount to any great number, the variety of game, and the beautiful and wild scenery I had passed through, made me enjoy it more than if I had been shooting in the best and easiest muir in Scotland, and killing fifty or sixty brace of birds.

In preserving and increasing a stock of grouse, the first thing is to kill the vermin of every kind, and none more carefully than the grey crows,[1] as these keen-sighted birds destroy an immense number of eggs. The grouse should also be well watched in the neighbourhood of any small farms or corn-fields that may be on the ground, as incredible numbers are caught in horsehair snares on the sheaves of corn.

A system of netting grouse has been practised by some of the poachers lately, and when the birds are not wild

---

[1] Gray says (*Birds of Scotland*, p. 178) that the hooded invariably breeds with the carrion crow in almost every district of Western Scotland where the two are found. It is a permanent resident in the Inner and Outer Hebrides and St. Kilda, and particularly mischievous to lambs and poultry on the west side of the Long Island. If it gets a chance it will even rob eagles' nests.

The Gaelic name of the bird is "flannag," which means to skin or flay. A Morayshire proverb said—

    The guile, the Gordon, and the hooded craw,
    Were the three worst things Moray ever saw.

The guile is a common corn-weed; the Gordon, the plundering Lord Lewis Gordon. "It is now, however, but seldom that Moray ever sees a hooded crow, at least at a time when its presence is really injurious, strychnine and gunpowder having cleared the country of it as a pest." Cf. note on p. 48.

A large case containing specimens of variations between the hooded and carrion crow may be seen at the Natural History Museum, Kensington, and is well worthy of inspection by all who are interested in these birds.

they catch great numbers in this manner; and as in nine cases out of ten the shepherds are in the habit of assisting and harbouring the poachers, as well as allowing their dogs to destroy as many eggs and young birds as they like, these men require as much watching as possible. I have generally found it entirely useless to believe a word that they tell me respecting the encroachments of poachers, even if they do not poach themselves. With a clever sheep-dog and a stick I would engage to kill three parts of every covey of young grouse which I found in July and the first part of August; and, in fact, the shepherds generally do kill great numbers in this noiseless and destructive manner. As the black game for the most part breed in plantations, where sheep and shepherds have no business to be found, they are less likely to be killed in this way. But the young ones, till nearly full grown, lie so close, that it is quite easy to catch half the brood.

When able to run, the old hen leads them to the vicinity of some wet and mossy place in or near the woodlands, where the seeds of the coarse grass and of other plants, and the insects that abound near the water, afford the young birds plenty of food. The hen takes great care of her young, fluttering near any intruder as if lame, and having led him to some distance from the brood takes flight, and making a circuit returns to them. The cock bird sometimes keeps with the brood, but takes good care of himself, and running off leaves them to their fate. Wild and wary as the blackcock usually is, he sometimes waits till you almost tread on him, and then flutters away, giving as easy a shot to the sportsman as a turkey would do. At other times, being fond of basking in the sun, he lies all day enjoying its rays in some open place where it is difficult to approach him without being seen.

In snowy weather the black game perch very much on the fir-trees, as if to avoid chilling their feet on the colder ground: in wet weather they do the same.

During the spring, and also in the autumn, about the time the first hoar-frosts are felt, I have often watched the blackcocks in the early morning, when they collect on some rock or height, and strut and crow with their curious note not unlike that of a wood-pigeon. On these occasions they often have most desperate battles. I have seen five or six blackcocks all fighting at once, and so intent and eager were they, that I approached within a few yards before they rose. Usually there seems to be a master-bird in these assemblages, who takes up his position on the most elevated spot, crowing and strutting round and round with spread-out tail like a turkey-cock, and his wings trailing on the ground. The hens remain quietly near him, whilst the smaller or younger male birds keep at a respectful distance, neither daring to crow, except in a subdued kind of voice, nor to approach the hens. If they attempt the latter, the master-bird dashes at the intruder, and often a short melee ensues, several others joining in it, but they soon return to their former respectful distance. I have also seen an old blackcock crowing on a birch-tree with a dozen hens below it, and the younger cocks looking on in fear and admiration. It is at these times that numbers fall to the share of the poacher, who knows that the birds resort to the same spot every morning.

Strong as the blackcock is, he is often killed by the peregrine falcon and the hen-harrier. When pursued by these birds, I have known the blackcock so frightened as to allow himself to be taken by the hand. I once caught one myself who had been driven by a falcon into the garden, where he took refuge under a gooseberry bush and remained quiet till I picked him up. I kept him for a day or two, and then, as he did not get reconciled to his prison, I turned him loose to try his fortune again in the woods. Like some other wary birds, the blackcock, when flushed at a distance, if you happen to be in his line of flight, will pass over your head without turning off, as long as you remain motionless. In some places, apparently well adapted for these birds, they will never increase, although left undisturbed and protected, some cause or other preventing their breeding. Where they take well to a place, they increase very rapidly, and, from their habit of taking long flights, soon find out the corn-fields, and are very destructive, more so, probably, than any other kind of winged game.

A bold bird by nature, the blackcock, when in confinement, is easily tamed, and soon becomes familiar and attached to his master. In the woods instances are known of the blackcock breeding with the pheasant.[1] I saw a hybrid of this kind at a bird-stuffer's in Newcastle: it had been killed near Alnwick Castle. The bird was of a beautiful bronzed-brown colour, and partaking in a remarkable degree of the characteristics of both pheasant and black game. I have heard also of a bird being killed which was supposed to be bred between grouse and black game, but I was by no means satisfied that it was anything but a peculiarly dark-coloured grouse.

The difference of colour in grouse is very great, and on different ranges of hills is quite conspicuous. On some ranges the birds have a good deal of white on their breasts, on others they are nearly black: they also vary very much in size.

Our other species of grouse, the ptarmigan,[2] as every sportsman knows, is found only on the highest ranges of the Highlands. Living above all vegetation, this bird finds its scanty food amongst the loose stones and rocks that cover the summits of Ben Nevis and some other mountains. It is difficult to ascertain indeed what food the ptarmigan can find in sufficient quantities on the barren heights where they are found. Being visited by the sportsman but rarely, these birds are seldom at all shy or wild, but, if the day is fine, will come out from among the scattered stones, uttering their peculiar croaking cry, and running in flocks near the intruder on their lonely domain, offer, even to the worst shot, an easy chance of filling his bag.

When the weather is windy and rainy, the ptarmigan are frequently shy and wild; and when disturbed, instead of

---

[1] For a celebrated instance see White's *Selborne* (ed. Bell, i. p. 430), and the notes on this hybrid, which are accompanied by a figure from Elmer's painting of it, in Sir W. Jardine's edition of White, p. 274.
With regard to black game breeding with grouse, see Colquhoun, *The Moor and the Loch*, vol. i. p. 169, 4th ed. An accurate likeness of such a hybrid forms the frontispiece to that volume.

[2] "The ptarmigan seems never to descend from the summits of the mountains, and is never found in heather, keeping always to the loose stony tracts which are found above all vegetable growth, with the exception of the plants and mosses that can exist 3000 feet above the level of the sea in this country" (*Natural History and Sport in Moray*, p. 188).
"Ptarmigan, in both sexes, have a triple moult: after the breeding season is over into a grey suit; then again, as autumn passes on, into their snowy winter clothing; in spring they put on again another distinctive dress—the wings and tail, however, do not partake of these changes" (Art. "Birds," *Encyc. Britan.* vol. iii. 1875). The contrast of white feathers in a ptarmigan's wing with the delicately pencilled grey feathers, as the bird is passing into the winter change, is exquisite. Perhaps no other bird exhibits such snow-white plumage.

running about like tame chickens, they fly rapidly off to some distance, either round some shoulder of the mountain, or by crossing some precipitous and rocky ravine get quite out of reach. The shooting these birds should only be attempted on fine, calm days. The labour of reaching the ground they inhabit is great, and it often requires a firm foot and steady head to keep the sportsman out of danger after he has got to the rocky and stony summit of the mountain.

In deer-stalking I have sometimes come amongst large flocks of ptarmigan, which have run croaking close to me, apparently conscious that my pursuit of nobler game would prevent my firing at them. Once, on one of the highest mountains of Scotland, a cold, wet mist suddenly came on. We heard the ptarmigan near us in all directions, but could see nothing at a greater distance than five or six yards. We were obliged to sit down and wait for the mist to clear away, as we found ourselves gradually getting entangled amongst loose rocks, which frequently, on the slightest touch, rolled away from under our feet, and we heard them dashing and bounding down the steep sides of the mountain, sometimes appearing, from the noise they made, to be dislodging and driving before them large quantities of debris; others seemed to bound in long leaps down the precipices, till we lost the sound far below us in the depths of the corries. Not knowing our way in the least, we agreed to come to a halt for a short time, in hopes of some alteration in the weather. Presently a change came over the appearance of the mist, which settled in large fleecy masses below us, leaving us as it were on an island in the midst of a snow-white sea, the blue sky and bright sun above us without a cloud. As a light air sprang up, the mist detached itself in loose masses, and by degrees drifted off the mountain side, affording us again a full view of all around us.

The magnificence of the scenery, looking down from some of these mountain heights into the depths of the rugged and steep ravines below, is often more splendid and awfully beautiful than pen or pencil can describe; and the effect is often greatly increased by the contrast between some peaceful and sparkling stream and green valley seen afar off, and the rugged and barren foreground of rock and ravine, where no living thing can find a resting-place save the eagle or raven.

I remember a particular incident of that day's ptarmigan-shooting; which, though it stopped our sport for some hours, I would not on any account have missed seeing. Most of the mist had cleared away, excepting a few cloud-like drifts, which were passing along the steep sides of the mountain. These, as one by one they gradually came into the influence of the

MOUNTAIN SCENERY.

currents of air, were whirled and tossed about, and then disappeared; lost to sight in the clear noonday atmosphere, as if evaporated by wind and sun.

One of these light clouds, which we were watching, was suddenly caught in an eddy of wind, and, after being twisted into strange fantastic shapes, was lifted up from the face of the mountain like a curtain, leaving in its place a magnificent stag, of a size of body and stretch of antler rarely seen; he was not above three hundred yards from us, and standing in full relief between us and the sky. After gazing around him, and looking like the spirit of the mountain, he walked slowly on towards a ridge which connected two shoulders of the mountain together. Frequently he stopped, and scratched with his hoof at some lichen-covered spot, feeding slowly (quite unconscious of danger) on the moss which he separated from the stones. I drew my shot, and put bullets into both barrels, and we followed him cautiously, creeping through the winding hollows of the rocks, sometimes advancing towards the stag, and at other times obliged suddenly to throw ourselves flat on the face of the stony mountain, to avoid his piercing gaze, as he turned frequently round to see that no enemy was following in his track.

He came at one time to a ridge from which he had a clear view of a long stretch of the valley beneath. Here he halted to look down either in search of his comrades or to see that all was safe in that direction. I could see the tops of his horns as they remained perfectly motionless for several minutes on the horizon. We immediately made on for the place, crawling like worms over the stones, regardless of bruises and cuts. We were within about eighty yards of the points of his horns; the rest of the animal was invisible, being concealed by a mass of stone behind which he was standing. I looked over my shoulder at Donald, who answered my look with a most significant kind of silent chuckle; and, pointing at his knife, as if to say that we should soon require its services, he signed to me to move a little to the right hand, to get the animal free of the rock, which prevented my shooting at him. I rolled myself quietly a little to one side, and then silently cocking both barrels, rose carefully and slowly to one knee. I had already got his head and neck within my view, and in another instant would have had his shoulder. My finger was already on the trigger, and I was rising gradually an inch or two higher. The next moment he would have been mine, when, without apparent cause, he suddenly moved, disappearing from our sight in an instant behind the rocks. I should have risen upright, and probably should have got a shot; but Donald's hand was laid on my head without ceremony, holding me down. He whispered, "The muckle brute has na felt us; we shall see him again in a moment." We waited for a few minutes, almost afraid to breathe, when Donald, with a movement of impatience, muttered, "'Deed, Sir, but I'm no understanding it,"—and whispered to me to go on to look over the ridge, which I did, expecting to see the stag feeding, or lying close below it. When I did look over, however, I saw the noble animal at a considerable distance, picking his way down the slope to join some half-dozen hinds who were feeding below him, and who occasionally raised their heads to take a good look at their approaching lord and master. "The Deil tak the brute," was all that Donald said, as he took a long and far-sounding pinch of snuff, his invariable consolation and resource in times of difficulty or disappointment. When the stag had joined the hinds, and some ceremonies of recognition had been gone through, they all went quietly and steadily away, till we lost sight of them over the shoulder of the next hill. "They'll no stop till they get to Alt-na-cahr," said Donald, naming a winding rushy burn at some distance off; "Alt-na-cahr" meaning the "Burn of many turns," as far as my knowledge of Gaelic goes. And there we were constrained to leave them and continue our ptarmigan-shooting, which we did with but little success and less spirit.

Soon afterwards a magnificent eagle suddenly rose almost at our feet, as we came to the edge of a precipice, on a shelf of which, near the summit, he had been resting. Bang went one barrel at him, at a distance of twenty yards. The small shot struck him severely, and, dropping his legs, he rose into the air, darting upwards nearly perpendicularly, a perfect cloud of feathers coming out of him. He then came wheeling in a stupefied manner back over our heads. We both of us fired together at him, and down he fell with one wing broken, and hit all over with our small shot. He struggled hard to keep up with the other wing, but could not do so, and came heavily to the ground within a yard of the edge of the precipice. He fell over on his back at first, and then rising up on his feet, looked round with an air of reproachful defiance. The blood was dropping slowly out of his beak, when Donald foolishly ran to secure him, instead of leaving him to die where he was; in consequence of his doing so, the eagle fluttered back a few steps, still, however, keeping his face to the foe. But, coming to the edge of the precipice, he fell backwards over it, and we saw him tumbling and struggling downwards, as he strove to cling to the projections of the rock—but in vain, as he came to no stop till he reached the bottom, where we beheld him, after regaining his feet for a short time, sink gradually to the ground. It was impossible for us to reach the place where he lay dead without going so far round that the daylight would have failed us. I must own, notwithstanding the reputed destructiveness of the eagle, that I looked with great regret at the dead body of the noble bird, and wished that I had not killed him, the more especially as I was obliged to leave him to rot uselessly in that inaccessible place.

PTARMIGAN

WILD CAT

CHAPTER IV

The Wild Cat: Strength of; Rencontre with—Trapping tame Cats: Destructiveness of—Poisoning vermin—Trapping vermin

THE true wild cat [1] is gradually becoming extirpated, owing to the increasing preservation of game; and though difficult to hold in a trap, in consequence of its great strength and agility,

---

[1] The Duke of Sutherland, as head of the Clan Chattan, naturally protects the wild cat to a certain extent. Mr. F. Buckland states that a striking difference exists between it and tame cats in the length of intestines. They were only five feet in two specimens of the wild cat, whereas they would be probably three times the length in the domesticated cat (*Log-Book of a Fisherman*, p. 252). The wild cat is certainly not the parent stock of our household cats. Its period of gestation is sixty-eight days, twelve days longer than that of the domestic animal, yet they have been known to breed together (St. G. Mivart, *The Cat*, Murray, 1881, p. 6 note).

it is by no means difficult to deceive, taking any bait readily, and not seeming to be as cautious in avoiding danger as many other kinds of vermin. Inhabiting the most lonely and inaccessible ranges of rock and mountain, the wild cat is seldom seen during the daytime; at night (like its domestic relative) it prowls far and wide, walking with the same deliberate step, making the same regular and even track, and hunting its game in the same tiger-like manner; and yet the difference between the two animals is perfectly clear, and visible to the commonest observer.

The wild cat has a shorter and more bushy tail, stands higher on her legs in proportion to her size, and has a rounder and coarser look about the head. The strength and ferocity of the wild cat when hemmed in or hard pressed are perfectly astonishing. The body when skinned presents quite a mass of sinew and cartilage.

I have occasionally, though rarely, fallen in with these animals in the forests and mountains of this country; once, when grouse-shooting, I came suddenly, in a rough and rocky part of the ground, upon a family of two old ones and three half-grown young ones. In the hanging birch-woods that border some of the Highland streams and lochs, the wild cat is still not uncommon, and I have heard their wild and unearthly cry echo far in the quiet night as they answer and call to each other. I do not know a more harsh and unpleasant cry than that of the wild cat, or one more likely to be the origin of superstitious fears in the mind of an ignorant Highlander.

These animals have great skill in finding their prey, and the damage they do to the game must be very great, owing to the quantity of food which they require. When caught in a trap, they fly without hesitation at any person who approaches them, not waiting to be assailed. I have heard many stories of their attacking and severely wounding a man, when their escape has been cut off. Indeed, a wild cat once flew at me in the most determined manner. I was fishing at a river in Sutherland, and in passing from one pool to another had to climb over some rock and broken kind of ground. In doing so, I sank through some rotten heather and moss up to my knees, almost upon a wild cat, who was concealed under it. I was quite as much startled as the animal herself could be, when I saw the wild-looking beast so unexpectedly rush out from between my feet, with every hair on her body standing on end, making her look twice as large as she really was. I had three small Skye terriers with me, who immediately gave chase, and pursued her till she took refuge in a corner of the rocks, where, perched in a kind of recess out of reach of her enemies, she stood with her hair bristled out, and spitting and growling like a common cat. Having no weapon with me, I laid down my rod, cut a good-sized stick, and proceeded to dislodge her. As soon as I was within six or seven feet of the place, she sprang straight at my face over the dogs' heads. Had I not struck her in mid-air as she leaped at me, I should probably have got some severe wound. As it was, she fell with her back half broken amongst the dogs, who, with my assistance, despatched her. I never saw an animal fight so desperately, or one which was so difficult to kill. If a tame cat has nine lives, a wild cat must have a dozen.

Sometimes one of these animals takes up its residence at no great distance from a house, and entering the hen-houses and outbuildings, carries off fowls or even lambs in the most audacious manner. Like other vermin, the wild cat haunts the shores of the lakes and rivers, and it is therefore easy to know where to lay a trap for them. Having caught and killed one of the colony, the rest of them are sure to be taken if the body of their slain relative is left in some place not far from their usual hunting-ground, and surrounded with traps, as every wild cat who passes within a considerable distance of the place will to a certainty come to it. The same plan may be adopted successfully in trapping foxes, who also are sure to visit the dead body of any other fox which they scent during their nightly walk.

There is no animal more destructive than a common house-cat, when she takes to hunting in the woods. In this case they should always be destroyed, as when once they have learned to prefer hares and rabbits to rats and mice, they are sure to hunt the larger animals only. I believe, however, that by cropping their ears close to the head, cats may be kept from hunting, as they cannot bear the dew or rain to enter these sensitive organs.

Tame cats who have once taken to the woods soon get shy and wild, and then produce their young in rabbit-holes, decayed trees, and other quiet places; thus laying the foundation of a half-wild race. It is worthy of notice, that whatever colour the parents of these semi-wild cats may have been, those bred out of them are almost invariably of the beautiful brindled grey colour, as the wild cats.

A shepherd, whose cat had come to an untimely end—by trap or gun, I forget which—in lamenting her death to me, said it was a great pity so valuable an animal should be killed, as she brought him every day in the year either a grouse, a young hare, or some other head of game. Another man told me that his cat brought to the house during the whole winter a woodcock or a snipe almost every night, showing a propensity for hunting in the swamps and wet places near which the cottage was situated, and where these birds were in the habit of feeding during the night. A favourite cat of my own once took to bringing home rabbits and hares, but never winged game. Though constantly caught in traps, she could never be cured of her hunting propensities. When caught in an iron trap, instead of springing about and struggling, and by this means breaking or injuring her legs, she used to sit quietly down and wait to be let out. There is a cat at the farm now, who is caught at least twice a week, but from adopting the same plan of waiting quietly and patiently to be liberated, she seldom gets her foot much hurt.

The animal that requires the greatest care in trapping is the fox. If the trap is too smooth, he slips his foot out; if too sharp, he cuts off his foot, and escapes, leaving it behind him. I consider the best manner of having fox-traps made is to get them without teeth, but with about three spikes of an inch in length on each side of the trap; these entering the animal's leg without cutting it, hold him firmly and securely.

The surest way, however, of destroying foxes (I am speaking of course of foxes of the Highlands, where no hounds are kept) is by poison. But then the rabbit or bait in which the poison is laid should not be touched by the hand, so suspicious is this animal of the slightest taint of man. The most artistic way is to catch a rabbit or crow in a trap, and having killed it with a stick, a small slit should be cut in the head, without however touching the animal with the hand; into this hole three or four grains of the poison called strychnia should be dropped. So powerful is this poison, that a fox having eaten the above quantity seldom goes thirty yards before he dies. Strychnia is the concentrated part of nux vomica. Though frequently much adulterated, it can generally be obtained of sufficient strength from any respectable druggist. The strychnia is, I believe, mixed with a little alkali, to prevent its power being destroyed by exposure to the air. In poisoning crows with it, a very small quantity is sufficient, and it should be put into a slit in the skin or the eye of a dead animal. Before a carrion crow has taken three or four pecks at the poisoned carrion he falls backwards perfectly dead. Weasels, stoats, and all vermin are destroyed by it with equal ease. The drug having no smell, these animals are not shy of eating a dead rabbit or bird on which it has been placed. Foxes and large vermin always commence at the head of their prey, while for smaller vermin and birds a hole should be cut in the skin to receive the poison, as they generally begin their operations whenever they see an opening where the flesh is exposed to view.

It is needless to give a warning against using this powerful drug rashly, as no man in his senses would place it anywhere but in the most secure situations. It is worth remembering that foxes, carrion crows, and many other destructive animals will eat a dead rat, whereas no dog will do so. By poisoning the dead bodies of this animal, therefore, no risk is run of destroying your dogs. An equally good way of applying strychnia is in the body of a wild duck or a wood-pigeon. Many a fox, whose worldly experience nearly ensures him safety from trap or gin, will fall a victim to this poison; for so small a quantity is necessary, and so scentless is it, that a sufficient dose is swallowed before the animal discovers its presence in anything which he is eating. From the extreme rapidity with which it acts, destroying life almost instantaneously, it is perhaps as merciful a way of putting an end to noxious and troublesome animals as can be devised, and no method can be more certain. I have always been of opinion that nine keepers out of ten who carry guns are of but little use in destroying vermin. The grand desideratum in preserving game is, that the animals should be left in perfect quiet. A man walking about with a gun in his hand, shooting at magpies and crows, does nearly as much mischief to the preserves as if he shot at the game itself.

A quiet intelligent trapper does more good in killing vermin than a dozen men with guns. The former sees a pair of crows,[1] or a stoat; if he is well skilled in his profession, the creatures are dead by the next day, having been caught without noise and without disturbing a single head of those animals which are required to be kept in peace and quiet.

The shooting keeper in making his way through woods and coverts to get shots at vermin, often fails in killing it, but is sure to disturb and molest the game, driving it here and there, and exposing it to the view and attacks of hawks and poachers. I have always a far better opinion of the usefulness of a keeper when I see him with a number of traps on his shoulder, than when he carries his gun always with him. It is no bad amusement occasionally to accompany an intelligent and experienced trapper on his rounds, and see his plans to deceive and entice the fox and the otter, the hawk or the raven.

In catching all these animals, the spot to be selected for trapping should not be near their abodes or nests, but in that part of the outskirts of the covers where they wander during the night-time in pursuit of prey. Almost every kind of vermin hunts in the open country and fields, wherever they may lie concealed during the day: for knowing that rabbits, hares, and the other animals which form their principal food, resort to the pastures, the corn-fields, or the waterside to feed during the night; to these same places do their hungry enemies follow them. Hawks and crows, too, who feed in the daytime, are

---

[1] *C. cornix*, the hooded crow, feeds on almost everything and even kills young lambs, first picking out their eyes. Eats grain. I have killed this bird of every variety and shade of grey and black, sometimes quite black, at other times marked as described [in histories of birds], and in every intermediate variety. There appears to be no internal difference between the hooded crow and the common carrion crow of the south; the hooded crow being a northern bird.—C. St. J.

C. frugilegus (rook) eats eggs.—C. St. J.

The hooded crow is the most numerous of all the vermin in the north of Scotland with which a keeper has to contend. Ravens too maintain themselves in fair numbers in the northern mountainous districts owing to their nests being so difficult of access. But the black-backed gulls are believed by Mr. J. Smith of Assynt to destroy as many eggs of game as do the hooded crows.

perfectly aware that they have a better chance of seeing and catching their prey in the open country than in the woods and covers. Besides which, a hungry fox or hawk, hunting for game, is less on his guard than when prowling quietly and cautiously through the woods.

THE RIGHT SORT OF GAMEKEEPER

AFFRAY WITH POACHERS

CHAPTER V

Poaching in the Highlands—Donald—Poachers and Keepers—Bivouac in Snow—
Connivance of Shepherds—Deer killed—Catching a Keeper—Poaching in the
Forests—Shooting Deer by Moonlight—Ancient Poachers.

I HAD a visit last week from a Highland poacher of some notoriety in his way. He is the possessor of a brace of the finest deer-hounds in Scotland, and he came down from his mountain home to show them to me, as I wanted some for a friend. The man himself is an old acquaintance of mine, as I had fallen in with him more than once in the course of my rambles. A finer specimen of the genus Homo than Ronald I never saw. As he passes through the streets of a country-town, the men give him plenty of walking room; while not a girl in the street but stops to look after him, and says to her companions—"Eh, but yon's a bonnie lad." And indeed Ronald is a "*bonnie lad*"—about twenty-six years of age—his height more than six feet, and with limbs somewhat between those of a Hercules and an Apollo—he steps along the street with the good-natured, self-satisfied swagger of a man who knows all the women are admiring him. He is dressed in a plain grey kilt and jacket, with an otter-skin purse and a low skull-cap with a long peak, from below which his quick eye seems to take in at a glance everything which is passing around him. A man whose life is spent much in hunting and pursuit of wild animals, acquires unconsciously a peculiar restless and quick expression of eye, appearing to be always in search of something. When Ronald doffs his cap, and shows his handsome hair and short curling beard, which covers all the lower part of his face, and which he seems to be something of a dandy about, I do not know a finer-looking fellow amongst all my acquaintance—and his occupation, which affords him constant exercise without hard labour, gives him a degree of strength and activity seldom equalled. As he walked into my room, followed by his two magnificent dogs, he would have made a subject worthy of Landseer in his best moments—and it would have been a picture which many a fair damsel of high, as well as low degree, would have looked upon with pleasure. Excepting when excited, he is the most quiet, good-natured fellow in the world; but I have heard some stories of his exploits, in defence of his liberty, when assailed by keepers, which proved his immense strength, though he has always used it most good-naturedly. One feat of his is worth repeating. He was surprised by five men in a shealing, where he had retired to rest after some days' shooting in a remote part of the Highlands. Ronald had a young lad with him, who could only look on, in consequence of having injured one of his hands.

Ronald was awoke from his sleep in the wooden recess of the shealing (which is called a bed), by the five men coming in,—and saying that they had tracked him there, that he was caught at last, and must come along with them. "'Deed, lads," said Ronald, without rising, "but I have had a long travel to-day, and if I am to go, you must just carry me." "Sit quiet, Sandy," he added to his young companion. "They'll no fash us, I'm thinking." The men, rather surprised at such cool language from only one man with nobody to assist him but a boy, repeated their order for him to get up and go with them; but receiving no satisfactory answer, two of them went to his bed to pull him out. "So I just pit them under me" (said

Ronald in describing it), "and kept them down with one knee. A third chiel then came up, with a bit painted wand, and told me that he was a constable, but I could na help laughing at the man, he looked so frightened like;—and I said to him, 'John Cameron, my man, you'd be better employed making shoes at home than coming here to disturb a quiet lad like me, who only wants to rest himself': and then I said to the rest of them, still keeping the twa chiels under my knee, 'Ye are all wrong, lads; I'm no doing anything against the law; I am just resting myself here, and rest myself I will: and you have no right to come here to disturb me; so you'd best just mak off at once.' They had not caught me shooting, sir," he added, "and I was sure that no justice would allow of their seizing me like an outlaw. Besides which, I had *the licence* with me, though I didn't want to have to show it to them, as I was a stranger there, and I didn't wish them to know my name. Weel, we went on in this way, till at last the laird's keeper, who I knew well enough, though he didn't know me, whispered to the rest, and all three made a push at me, while the chiels below me tried to get up too. The keeper was the only one with any pluck amongst them, and he sprang on my neck, and as he was a clever-like lad, I began to get sore pressed. Just then, however, I lifted up my left hand, and pulled one of the sticks that served for rafters, out of the roof above me, and my blood was getting quite mad like, and the Lord only knows what would have happened if they hadn't all been a bit frightened at seeing me get the stick, and when part of the roof came falling on them, and so they all left me and went to the other end of the shealing. The keeper was but ill pleased though—as for the bit constable body, his painted stick came into my hand somehow, and he never got it again! One of the lads below my knee got hurt in this scuffle too, indeed one of his ribs was broken, so I helped to lift him up, and put him on the bed. The others threatened me a great deal, but did na like the looks of the bit constable's staff I had in my hand. At last, when they found that they could do nothing, they begged me, in the Lord's name, to leave the shealing and gang my way in peace. But I did na like this, as it was six hours at least to the next bothy where I could get a good rest, so I just told them to go themselves—and as they did na seem in a hurry to do so, I went at them with my staff, but they did na bide my coming, and were all tumbling out of the door in a heap, before I was near them: I could na help laughing to see them. It was coming on a wild night, and the poor fellow in the bed seemed vera bad, so I called to them and told them they might just come back and sleep in the shealing if they would leave me in peace—and after a little talk they all came in, and I laid down in my plaid at one end of the bothy, leaving them the other. I made the lad who was with me watch part of the night to see they didn't get at me when I was asleep, though I didn't want him to join in helping me, as they knew his name, and it might have got him into trouble. In the morning I made my breakfast with some meal I had with me, and gave them the lave of it. They would have been right pleased to have got me with them,—but as they could na do it, like wise chiels, they didn't try—so I wished them a good day, and took the road. I had my gun and four brace of grouse, which they looked at very hard indeed, but I did not let them lay hands on anything. When I had just got a few hundred yards away, I missed my shot belt, so I went back and found that the keeper had it, and would not give it up. 'You'll be giving me my property, lad, I'm thinking,' I said to him; but he was just mad like with rage, and said that he would not let me have it. However, I took him by the coat and shook him a bit, and he soon gave it me, but he could na keep his hands off, and as I turned away, he struck me a sair blow with a stick on my back; so I turned to him, and 'deed I was near beating him weel, but after all I thocht that the poor lad was only doing his duty, so I only gave him a lift into the burn, taking care not to hurt him; but he got a grand ducking—and, Lord! how he did swear. I was thinking, as I travelled over the hills that day, it was lucky that these twa dogs were not with me, for there would have been wild work in the shealing. Bran there canna bide a scuffle but what he must join in it, and the other dog would go to help him; and the Lord pity the man they took hold of—he would be in a bad way before I could get this one off his throat—wouldn't he, poor dog?"—and Bran looked up in Ronald's face with such a half leer, half snake-like expression, that I thought to myself, that I would about as soon encounter a tiger as such a dog, if his blood was well roused.

The life of a Highland poacher is a far different one from that of an Englishman following the same profession. Instead of a sneaking night-walking ruffian, a mixture of cowardice and ferocity, as most English poachers are, and ready to commit any crime that he hopes to perpetrate with impunity, the Highlander is a bold fearless fellow, shooting openly by daylight, taking his sport in the same manner as the Laird, or the Sassenach who rents the ground. He never snares or wires game, but depends on his dog and gun. Hardy and active as the deer of the mountain, in company with two or three comrades of the same stamp as himself, he sleeps in the heather wrapped in his plaid, regardless of frost or snow, and commences his work at daybreak.[1] When a party of them sleep out on the hill side, their manner of arranging their couch is as follows:—If snow is on the ground, they first scrape it off a small space; they then all collect a quantity of the driest heather they can find. The next step is for all the party excepting one to lie down close to each other, with room between one couple for the remaining man to get into the rank when his duty is done; which is, to lay all the plaids on the top of his companions, and on the plaids a quantity of long heather; when he has sufficiently thatched them in, he creeps into the vacant place, and they are made up for the night. The coldest frost has no effect on them when bivouacking in this manner. Their guns are laid dry between them, and their dogs share their masters' couch.

With the earliest grouse-crow they rise and commence operations. Their breakfast consists of meal and water. They generally take a small bag of meal with them; but it is seldom that there is not some good-natured shepherd living near their day's beat, who, notwithstanding that he receives pay for keeping off or informing against all poachers, is ready to give them milk and anything else his bothy affords. If the shepherd has a peculiarly tender conscience, he vacates the hut himself on

---

[1] Times have changed since Mr. St. John's day, and the romantic sporting poacher of the type of Ronald is a thing of the past. The organisation of an efficient police force and more careful watching have rendered his life an impossible one. But of poaching generally there is no decrease, especially in the neighbourhood of manufacturing towns and by operatives out of work. With increase of game preserving, and of facilities of locomotion and transport, has come an increase of the more unsportsmanlike class of poachers. The Ground Game Act, moreover, and the large number of itinerant surreptitious game dealers, have led to an increased amount of illicit destruction of game by farmers and farm servants.

seeing them approach, leaving his wife to provide for the guests. He then, if accused of harbouring and assisting poachers, can say in excuse, " 'Deed, your honour, what could a puir woman do against four or five wild Hieland lads with guns in their hands?" In fact, the shepherds have a natural fellow-feeling with the poachers, and, both from policy and inclination, give them any assistance they want, or leave their wives and children to do so; and many a side of red deer or bag of grouse they get for this breach of promise to their masters. In the winter season a poacher calls on the shepherd, and says, "Sandy, lad, if you look up the glen there, you'll see a small cairn of stones newly put up; just travel twenty paces east from that, and you'll find a bit venison to yoursel' "—some unlucky deer having fallen to the gun of one of the poaching fraternity. This sort of argument, as well as the fear of " getting a bad name," is too strong for the honesty of most of the shepherds, who are erroneously supposed to watch the game, and to keep off trespassers. The keepers themselves in the Highlands, as long as the poachers do not interfere too much with their master's sport, so as to make it imperative on them to interfere, are rather anxious to avoid a collision with these "Hieland lads." For, although they never ill-use the keepers in the savage manner that English poachers so frequently do, I have known instances of keepers, who (although they were too smart gentlemen to carry their master's game) have been taken prisoners by poachers on the hill, and obliged to accompany them over their master's ground, and carry the game killed on it all day. They have then either been sent home, or, if troublesome, the poachers have tied them hand and foot, and left them on some marked spot of the muir, sending a boy or shepherd to release them some hours afterwards. Going in large bodies on well-preserved ground, these men defy the keepers, and shoot in spite of them. If pursued by a party stronger than themselves, they halt occasionally, and fire bullets either over the heads of their pursuers or into the ground near them, of course taking care not to hurt them. The keepers go home, protesting that they have been fired upon and nearly killed, while the Highlanders pursue their sport. The grand object of the poachers being to keep out of the fangs of the law, they never uselessly run the risk of being identified, and although they frequently have licences, they always avoid showing them if possible, in order that their names may not be known. If they shoot on ground where the watchers know them, they take great care to avoid being seen. If they think there is any likelihood of a prosecution occurring, they betake themselves to a different part of the country till the storm is blown over. In some of the wide mountain districts, a band of poachers can shoot the whole season without being caught, and I fancy that many of the keepers, and even their masters, rather wish to shut their eyes to the trespassing of these gangs as long as they keep to certain districts, and do not interfere with those parts of the grouse-ground which are the most carefully preserved.

Some proprietors or lessees of shooting-grounds make a kind of half-compromise with the poachers, by allowing them to kill grouse as long as they do not touch the deer; others, who are grouse-shooters, let them kill the deer to save their birds. I have known an instance where a prosecution was stopped by the aggrieved party being quietly made to understand, that if it was carried on, "a score of lads from the hills would shoot over his ground for the rest of the season."

In the eastern part of the Highlands and on the hills adjoining the Highland roads, the grand harvest of the poachers arises from grouse, which are shipped by the steamers, and sent by the coaches southwards, in numbers that are almost incredible. Before the 12th of August, hundreds of grouse are shipped, to be ready in London on the first day that they become legal food for her Majesty's subjects. In these districts the poachers kill the deer only for their amusement, or to repay the obliging blindness and silence of shepherds and others. Many a fine stag is either shot or killed by dogs during the winter season;—the proprietor, or person who rents the forest, supposing that his paying half-a-dozen watchers and foresters ensures the safety of his deer.

"Indeed, his lordship has seven foresters," said a Highlander to me; "but they are mostly old men, and not that fit for catching the likes of me; besides which, if we leave the forest quiet during the time his lordship's down, they are not that over hard on us; nor are we sair on their deer either, for they are all ceevil enough, except the head forester, who is an

Englishman, and we wouldna wish to get them to lose their bread by being turned away on our account. So it's not often we trouble the forest, unless, maybe, we have a young dog to try, and we canna get a run at a deer on the marches of the ground, where it would harm no one."

"And how do you manage not to be caught?" was my question.

"Why, we sleep at some shepherd's house or shealing; and if there is not one convenient, we *lay out* somewhere on the ground, going to our sleeping-place after nightfall; and so we are ready to get at the deer by daylight; and maybe we have killed one and carried him off before the foresters have found out that we are out."

It is not so easy, however, for the poachers to kill deer undiscovered with dogs, as it is with the gun; for in the event of the greyhounds getting in chase of a young stag or a hind, they may be led away to a great distance, and in the course of the run move half the deer in the forest; and there is no surer sign of mischief being afloat than seeing the deer passing over the hills in a startled manner. No man, accustomed to them, can mistake this sign of an enemy having disturbed them; and one can judge pretty well the direction the alarm comes from by taking notice of the quarter in which the wind is, and from which part of the mountain the deer are moving. With a rifle, however, in the hand of a good shot, the business is soon over, without frightening the rest of the herd a tenth part so much, or making them change their quarters to such a distance; and even if the shot is heard by the keepers, which is a great chance, it is not easy to judge exactly from which direction it comes amongst the numerous corries and glens which confuse and mislead the listener.

Ronald told me that one day his dogs brought a fine stag to bay, in a burn close to the house of the forester on the ground where he was poaching: "The forester luckily was no at hame, sir; but the dogs made an awful noise, *yowling* at the stag; and a bit lassie came out and tried to stone them off the beast: so I was feared they might turn on her, and I just stepped down from where I was looking at them, and putting my handkerchief over my face, that the lassie mightn't ken me, took the dogs away, though it was a sair pity, as it was a fine beast; and one of the dogs was quite young at the time, and it would have been a grand chance for blooding him."

Many a deer is killed during the bright moonlight nights. The poacher in this case finds out some grassy burn or spot of ground, where the deer are in the habit of feeding. Within shot of this, and with his gun loaded with three pistol-balls, or a bullet and two slugs, he lies ensconced, taking care to be well concealed before the time that the deer come to feed, and keeping to leeward of the direction in which they will probably arrive. Many an hour he may pass in his lonely hiding-place, listening to every cry and sound of the different animals that are abroad during the night-time, and peering out anxiously to see if he can distinguish the object of his vigil approaching him. Perhaps, although he may hear the deer belling or clashing their horns together in the distance, none come within reach of his gun during the whole night; and the call of the grouse-cock just before daybreak, as he collects his family from their roosting-places in the heather, warns him that it is time to leave his ambuscade, and betake himself home, chilled and dispirited. It often, however, happens that he hears the tramp of the deer as they descend from the more barren heights to feed on the grass and rushes near his place of concealment. On they come, till he can actually hear their breathing as they crop the herbage; and can frequently distinguish their ghostlike forms as they pass to and fro, sometimes grazing, and sometimes butting at each other in fancied security. His own heart beats so that he almost fears the deer will hear him. Often his finger is on the trigger; but he still refrains, as no deer has come into full view which he thinks worth killing. At last a movement amongst the herd apprises him that the master stag is probably approaching. And suddenly the gaunt form of the animal appears in strong relief between him and the sky, standing on some rising bit of ground, within thirty yards of the muzzle of his gun. The next instant the loud report is echoing and rolling along the mountain side, till it gradually dies away in the distance. The stag, on receiving the shot, utters a single groan, partly of affright and partly of pain, and drops to the ground, where he lies plunging and floundering, but unable to rise from having received three good-sized pistol-balls in his shoulder. The rest of the herd, frightened by the report and the flash of the gun, dart off at first in all directions; but soon collecting together, they can be heard in the still night, for some time after they are lost to view, going up the hill side at a steady gallop. The poacher rushes up to the stag, who is now nearly motionless, only showing symptoms of life by his loud, deep breathing, and an occasional quiver of his limbs, as his life is oozing rapidly away in streams of blood. The skene dhu, plunged into the root of his neck, and reaching to his heart, soon ends his struggles; and before the next morning the carcass is carried off and cut up. Many a noble stag falls in this way. Near the Caledonian Canal, which affords great facility of carriage, the Lochaber poachers kill a considerable number during the season, sending them to Edinburgh, Glasgow, or other large towns, where they have some confidential friend to receive and sell them. In Edinburgh, there are numbers of men who work as porters, etc., during the winter, and poach in the Highlands during the autumn. When in town, these men are useful to their friends on the hills in disposing of their game, which is all killed for the purpose of being sent away, and not for consumption in the country.

Many poachers of the class I have here described are of respectable origin, and are well enough educated. When my aforesaid acquaintance Ronald called on me, he had a neat kind of wallet with his dry hose, a pair of rather smart worsted-worked slippers (he did not seem disposed to tell me what fair hands had worked them), and clean. linen, etc. He wore also a small French gold watch, which had also been given him. Several of the Highlanders who have lived in this way emigrate to Canada, and generally do well; others get places as foresters and keepers, making the best and most faithful servants. Their old allies seldom annoy them when they take to this profession, as there is a great deal of good feeling amongst them, and a sense of right, which prevents their thinking the worse of their quondam comrade because he does his duty in his new line of life.

There is another class of hill poacher—the old, half worn-out Highlander, who has lived and shot on the mountain before the times of letting shooting-grounds and strict preserving had come in. These old men, with their long single-barrelled gun, kill many a deer and grouse, though not in a wholesale manner, hunting more from ancient habit and for their own use than for the market. I have met some quaint old fellows of this description, who make up by cunning and knowledge of the ground for want of strength and activity. I made acquaintance with an old soldier, who after some years' service had returned to his native mountains, and to his former habits of poaching and wandering about in search of deer. He lived in the midst of plenty of them too, in a far-off and very lonely part of Scotland, where the keepers of the property seldom came. When they did so, I believe they frequently took the old man out with them to assist in killing a stag for their master. At other times he wandered through the mountains with a single-barrelled gun, killing what deer he wanted for his own use, but never selling them. I never in my life saw a better shot with a ball: I have seen him constantly kill grouse and plovers on the ground. His occupation, I fear, is at last gone, owing to changes in the ownership and the letting of the shooting, for the last time I heard of him he was leading an honest life as cattle-keeper.

When this man killed a deer far from home, he used to go to the nearest shepherd's shealing, catch the horse, which was sure to be found feeding near at hand, and make use of it to carry home the deer. This done, he turned the horse's head home, and let it loose, and as all Highland ponies have the bump of locality strongly developed, it was sure to find its way home. I have known one of these old poachers coolly ride his pony up the mountain from which he intended to take a deer, turn it loose, and proceed on his excursion. The pony, as cunning and accustomed to the work as his master, would graze quietly near the spot where he was left, till his services were required to take home the booty at night. The old man never went to the hill till he had made sure of the whereabouts of the forester, by which means he always escaped detection.

The principal object of pursuit of the Highland poacher, next to grouse and deer, are ptarmigan, as these birds always bring a high price, and by making choice of good weather and knowing where to find the birds, a man can generally make up a bag that repays him for his day's labour, as well as for his powder and shot. Being sportsmen by nature, as well as poachers, they enjoy the wild variety of a day's ptarmigan-shooting as much as the more legal shooter does. In winter, when a fresh fall of snow has taken place, a good load of white hares is easily obtained, as this animal is found in very great numbers on some mountains, since the destruction of vermin on so large a scale has taken place. What with the sale of these different kinds of game, and a tolerable sum made by breaking dogs, a number of young men in the Highlands make a very good income during the shooting-season, which enables them to live in idleness the rest of the year, and often affords them the means of emigrating to America, where they settle quietly down and become extensive and steady farmers.

BIVOUAC ON THE HILLS UNDER THE HEATHER

SPEARING SALMON OR BURNING THE WATER

CHAPTER VI

Salmon-fishing—Salmon ascending Fords—Fishers—Cruives—Right of Fishing—Anecdote—Salmon-leaps—History of the Salmon—Spearing Salmon—River Poaching—Angling—Fly-making—Eels—Lampreys.

During the spring and summer it is an amusing sight to watch the salmon making their way up the river. Every high tide brings up a number of these fish, whose whole object seems to be to ascend the stream. At the shallow fords, where the river spreading over a wide surface has but a small depth of water, they are frequently obliged to swim, or rather wade (if such an expression can be used), for perhaps twenty yards in water of two inches in depth, which leaves more than half the fish exposed to view. On they go, however, scrambling up the fords, and making the water fly to the right and left, like ducks at play. When the fish are numerous, I sometimes see a dozen or more at once. They might be killed in these places by spears, or even a stick, and indeed many a salmon does come to his death in this way. The fishermen (when the river is low) save a great deal of useless fatigue, and of injury to their nets, by working in some pool immediately above a shallow place, where they station one of their number, who watches for the fish ascending, giving a signal to his companions whenever he sees one. They then immediately put out their nets, and are nearly sure to catch the salmon. In this way very few of the fish can escape as long as the water is low, but when a slight flood comes they can get up unperceived. It is as easy to see them in the night-time as in the day, the water glancing and shining as they struggle up. Indeed on the darkest night the noise they make is easily heard, and distinguished by the accustomed ear of the fishermen.

There is something wild and interesting in listening during the night to the shout of the man stationed to watch, when he sees fish, and the sound of the oars and boat immediately afterwards, though the object of pursuit is but a fish after all. Sometimes a silent otter suddenly shows himself on the ford, having slipped quietly and unobserved through the deeper parts of the stream till he is obliged to wade, not having water enough to cover him. His appearance is the signal of a general outcry, and if he returns to the deep water where the net is, the fishermen occasionally manage to entangle him, and dragging him to shore, soon despatch him. He is one of their worst enemies. More often, however, he slips noiselessly to the side of the river, and half ensconced behind some broken bank, remains quiet and concealed till the danger is past, and then glides away unperceived. There is no animal more difficult to get the advantage of than the otter, as long as he is on ground that he knows. The fish which escape the nets, and those which go up during floods and on Sundays, on which day they are allowed to have a free passage, seldom stop until they get to the deep quiet pools amongst the rocks some four or five miles up the water, where they rest till fresh water and opportunity enable them to continue their upward progress. Neither sea-trout nor salmon ever seem happy excepting when making their way up a stream. It is wonderful, too, against what difficulties, in the shape of falls and rapids, they will ascend a river. In the Findhorn, owing to the impetuosity of the stream, the frequent and sudden floods it is subject to, and the immense quantity of shingle and gravel, which is always shifting its place, and changing the course of the lower part of the water, there are no cruives made use of. They would probably be destroyed as fast as they were built. In the Spey, however, and many other rivers, large cruives are built, which quite prevent the ascent of the fish, excepting on Sundays and on floods. To describe a cruive minutely would be tedious. It is, however, merely a kind of dam built across the river, with openings here and there, allowing the water to pass through in a strong stream, and through which the fish ascend and get into a kind of wooden cage, out of which they cannot find their way again, the entrance being made after the fashion of a wire mouse-trap, affording an easier ingress than egress. Much do the anglers on the upper part of the Spey pray for a furious flood, or spate, as it is called, which may break down these barriers, and enable the salmon to ascend to the higher pools before the fishermen can repair the damage done.

The right of fishing in many of the Scotch rivers is vested in a very singular manner; as, for instance, in the Findhorn, where the proprietor of many miles of land along the river banks has no right to throw a line in the water, but is obliged to pay a rent for fishing on his own ground. Indeed, this kind of alienation of the right of fishing from the person who would seem to be the natural proprietor of it is very common. I remember an anecdote told me by an old Highlander as to the cause of the fishing in a particular river in Sutherland being out of the hands of the proprietor of the land on its banks. The story is as follows:—The laird of the property higher up on the water was also the possessor of a small island in the river. He was a deep, long-headed fellow, and grudged his neighbour the profit he made out of the fishing just below him, the water on the upper part not being so good. He therefore commenced building a fort on the island, and falling in with his neighbour, asked him in an off-hand way to give him, merely, he said, for the convenience of his workmen, a right of fishing the whole river until his building was completed, salmon in those days being used as a means of feeding the numerous retainers and servants who lived upon and followed every laird and chieftain. Indeed, but a few years back it was often made a stipulation by servants on being hired by a

Highland master that they should not be fed on salmon above a certain number of days in the week. But to continue my story. The permission was granted; and, to save all dispute about the matter, even a legal written document was given over to the wily laird, granting him exclusive right of fishing and netting the river, "until his house was finished." The building was immediately stopped, and the right of fishing still belongs to the proprietor of the little islet, who will probably never finish his building, as doing so would put an end to his valuable rights on the river. So runs the tale, which does more credit to the acuteness than to the honesty of the inventor of the ruse. The jumping of the salmon up a fall is a curious and beautiful sight, and the height they leap, and the perseverance which they show in returning again and again to the charge, after making vain efforts to surmount the fall, are quite wonderful. Often on a summer evening, when the river is full of fish, all eager to make their way up, have I watched them for hours together, as they sprang in rapid succession, looking like pieces of silver as they dashed up the falls with rapid leaps. The fish appear to bend their head to their tail, and then to fling themselves forward and upwards, much as a bit of whalebone whose two ends are pinched together springs forward on being released. I have often watched them leaping, and this has always seemed the way in which they accomplish their extraordinary task. Both salmon and sea-trout, soon after they enter the fresh water, from the sea, make wonderful leaps into the air, shooting perpendicularly upwards, to the height of some feet, with a quivering motion, which is often quite audible. This is most likely to get rid of a kind of parasitical insect which adheres to them when they first leave the sea. The fishermen call this creature the sea-louse: it appears to cause a great deal of irritation to the fish. It is a sure sign that the salmon is in good condition, and fresh from the sea, when these insects are found adhering to him.

Though the natural history of the salmon is daily being searched into, and curious facts connected with it are constantly ascertained, I fancy that there is much still to be learnt on the subject, as some of the statements advanced seem so much at variance with my own frequent though unscientific observations, that I cannot give in to all that is asserted. But as I have not opportunities of proving many points, I will leave the whole subject in the abler hands of those who have already written on it, and whose accounts, though they may err here and there, are probably in the main correct. As long as the salmon are in the river water they seem to lose condition, and become lean and dark coloured. By the time that they have ascended to within a dozen miles or so of the source of the river they are scarcely fit to eat. Nevertheless vast numbers are killed by poachers and shepherds in the autumn, even after the legal season is over. I once fell in with a band of Highlanders, who were employed busily in the amusing but illegal pursuit of spearing salmon by torchlight. And a most exciting and interesting proceeding it was. The night was calm and dark. The steep and broken rocks were illuminated in the most brilliant manner by fifteen or sixteen torches, which were carried by as many active Highlanders, and glanced merrily on the water, throwing the most fantastic light and shade on all around as they moved about. Sometimes one of them would remain motionless for a few moments, as its bearer waited in the expectation that some fish which had been started by his companions would come within reach of his spear, as he stood with it ready poised, and his eager countenance lighted up by his torch as he bent over the water. Then would come loud shouts and a confused hurrying to and fro, as some great fish darted amongst the men, and loud and merry peals of laughter when some unlucky fellow darting at a fish in too deep water, missed his balance, and fell headlong into the pool. Every now and then a salmon would be seen hoisted into the air, and quivering on an uplifted spear. The fish, as soon as caught, was carried ashore, where it was knocked on the head and taken charge of by some man older than the rest, who was deputed to this office. Thirty-seven salmon were killed that night; and I must say that I entered into the fun, unmindful of its not being quite in accordance with my ideas of right and wrong; and I enjoyed it probably as much as any of the wild lads who were engaged in it. There was not much English talked amongst the party, as they found more expressive words in Gaelic to vent their eagerness and impatience. All was good humour, however; and though they at first looked on me with some slight suspicion, yet when they saw that I enjoyed their torchlight fishing, and entered fully into the spirit of it, they soon treated me with all consideration and as one of themselves. I happened to know one or two of the men; and after it was over, and we were drying our drenched clothes in a neighbouring bothy, it occurred to me to think of the river bailiffs and watchers, several of whom I knew were employed on that part of the stream, and I asked where they were, that they did not interfere with the somewhat irregular proceeding in which we had all been engaged. "'Deed ay, sir, there are no less than twelve bailies and offishers on the water here, but they are mostly douce-like lads, and don't interfere much with us, as we only come once or twice in the season. Besides which, they ken well that if they did they might get a wild ducking amongst us all, and they would na ken us again, as we all come from beyont the braes yonder. Not that we would wish to hurt the puir chiels," continued my informer, as he took off a glass of whisky, "as they would be but doing their duty. They would as lave, however, I am thinking, be taking a quiet dram at Sandy Roy's down yonder as getting a ducking in the river; and they are wise enough not to run the risk of it." Not bad reasoning either, thought I; nor can I wonder that the poor water-bailiffs would prefer a quiet bowl of toddy to a row with a party of wild Badenoch poachers, who, though good-natured enough on the whole, were determined to have their night's fun out in spite of all opposition. There are worse poachers, too, than these said Highlanders, who only come down now and then more for the amusement than the profit of the thing; and whom it is generally better policy to keep friends with than to make enemies of.[1]

The ponderous lexicographer, who describes a fishing-rod as a stick with a fool at one end, and a worm at the other, displays in this saying more wit than wisdom. Not that I quite go the whole length of my quaint and amiable old friend, Isaac Walton, who implies in every page of his paragon of a book, that the art of angling is the *summum bonum* of happiness, and that an angler must needs be the best of men. I do believe, however, that no determined angler can be naturally a bad or vicious man. No man who enters into the silent communings with Nature, whose beauties he must be constantly

---

[1] For a delightful account of a "leistering" expedition on the Tweed in which Sir Walter Scott's old keeper Tom Purdie took part, we refer our readers to the last chapter of Mr. Scrope's well-known *Days and Nights of Salmon Fishing*.

surrounded by, and familiar with during his ramblings as an angler, can fail to be improved in mind and disposition during his solitary wanderings amongst the most lovely and romantic works of the creation, in the wild Highland glens and mountains through which the best streams take their course. I do not include in my term angler, the pond or punt fisher, however well versed he may be in the arts of spitting worms and impaling frogs, so learnedly discussed by Isaac—notwithstanding the kindliness and simplicity of heart so conspicuous in every line he writes. Angling, in my sense of the word, implies wandering with rod and creel in the wild solitudes, and tempting (or endeavouring to do so) the fish from their clear water, with artificial fly or minnow. Nothing can be more unlike the "*worm*" described as forming one end of the thing called a fishing-rod, than the gay and gaudy collection of feathers and tinsel which form the attraction of a Findhorn fly. Let us look at the salmon-fly, which I have just finished, and which now lies on the table before me, ready for trial in some clear pool of the river. To begin: I tie with well-waxed silk a portion of silkworms' intestines on a highly-tempered and finished Limerick-made hook. Here are three different substances brought into play already. I next begin at the tail of the fly: first come two turns of gold thread, then a tenth part of an inch of red floss-silk ; next comes the tail, consisting of a bright gold feather from the crest of the golden pheasant. The body is now to be made of, alternately, a stripe of green, a stripe of blue, and the remainder of orange-coloured floss-silk, with a double binding of gold thread and silver tinsel; the legs are made of a black barn-door cock's hackle, taken from him, in winter, when the bird is in full plumage; next to the wing comes a turn of grouse's feather, and two or three turns of the purple-black feather which is pendent on the breast of an old cock heron. Now for the wing, which is composed of a mixture of feathers from the mallard killed in this country ; from the teal drake, also a native ; from the turkey-cock ; the bustard, from India ; a stripe or two of green parrot ; a little of the tippet of the gold pheasant ; a thread or two from the peacock's tail ; a bit from the Argus pheasant, and from the tail of a common hen pheasant : all these mixed and blended together form an irresistible wing. Round the shoulder of the wing a turn of the blue and black feather off a jay's wing. For the head, a small portion of that substance called pig's wool, so mysterious to the uninitiated, pigs not being the usual animals from which wool is supposed to be derived; then finished off with a few turns of black ostrich feather; not forgetting that finish to the whole, two horns of red and blue macaw's feather. Now, all this makes a fly, either of the dragon or some other species, which no salmon who is in a taking mood (one can hardly suppose he swallows it out of hunger) can resist. See the gallant fish, as he rises suddenly up from the dark depths of the pool, poises himself for a moment, as the fly hovers before him, in the twirling eddy, then darts forward, seizes the gaudy bait, and retreats again, apparently well satisfied with his skill in fly-catching, till he suddenly finds himself pulled up, and held fast by the unexpected strength of the insect. I suspect that a salmon, after a quarter of an hour's struggle on a line, would scarcely call the fisherman at the other end "a fool," even if he took the fly to be some newly-discovered glittering worm. Skill in fly-fishing can only be acquired by practice, and no directions can make a good angler. And even when fairly hooked, a salmon is only to be held by a happy mixture of the *suaviter in modo* and *fortiter in re*, which keeps the line at a gentle but firm stretch, from which he cannot escape by dint of straightforward pulling—to which the skilful fisher must gradually yield, to prevent too much strain on his slight line. Nor, on the other hand, ought the fish to be allowed, by the angler slackening the line, to get a sudden jerk at it, by means of a fresh rush, as few lines or hooks can stand this. In fishing for sea-trout, I always kill the largest fish, and the greatest number, by using small flies, though certainly too small hooks are apt to lead to disappointment, by not taking sufficient hold of this tender-skinned fish. As all rivers require different flies for sea-trout, no general rule can be given, but I never find myself unable to catch trout, if there are any in the water, and I use either a small palmer, red, black, or white, and if these do not succeed, I try a small fly with black or blue body, a turn or two of silver twist, no hackle round the body, but a little black hackle immediately under the wings, which latter consist of lark's or hen blackbird's feather, or that of some other bird of a similar pale grey colour. I have often been amused by being told gravely by some fishing-tackle maker in a country-town, when showing him one of these simple flies, "Why, sir, that fly *may* do now and then, but it is not fit for *this* river, and I am afraid, sir, you will catch nothing with it." His own stock of flies, which he wants to sell, being all of one kind probably, which he has managed to convince himself and others are the only sort the fish in the neighbouring stream will rise at. I remember one day on the Findhorn when the fish would not rise at a fly, although they were leaping in all directions. I put on a small white fly and filled my basket, to the astonishment of two or three *habitués* of the river, who could catch nothing. Having watched me some time, and not being able to make out why I had such good sport, they begged to look at my fly. They scarcely believed their own eyes when I showed them my little white moth, which the sea-trout were rising at so greedily; it being so unlike the flies which from habit and prejudice they had been always accustomed to use.

I was much interested one day in May, in watching the thousands of small eels which were making their way up the river. It was some distance from the mouth, and where the stream, confined by a narrow rocky channel, ran with great strength. Nevertheless these little eels, which were about six inches long, and as large round as a quill, persevered in swimming against the stream. When they came to a fall, where they could not possibly ascend, they wriggled out of the water, and gliding along the rock close to the edge, where the stone was constantly wet from the splashing and spray of the fall, they made their way up till they got above the difficulty, and then again slipping into the water, they continued their course. For several hours there was a continued succession of these little fish going up in the same way; and, for more than a week, the same thing was to be seen every day. The perseverance they displayed was very great, for frequently, although washed back several times, an eel would always continue its efforts till it managed to ascend. Towards winter they are said to descend the river again, in equal numbers. Trout and many birds feed constantly on these small eels, catching them with great ease in the shallows.

One summer day I was amused by watching the singular proceedings of two lampreys[1] in a small ditch of clear running water near my house. They were about six inches in length,

---

[1] The Lamprey (*Petromyzon marinus*) ascends the Scottish rivers to breed about the end of June, and remains until August. T. Edward notes that it is a common fish in Banffshire, and Yarrell quotes a passage from Sir W. Jardine which illustrates Mr. St. John's anecdote: "They are not furnished with the elongation of the jaw, afforded to

and as large round as a pencil. The two little creatures were most busily and anxiously employed in making little triangular heaps of stones, using for the purpose irregularly-shaped bits of gravel about the size of a large pea. When they wished to move a larger stone, they helped each other in endeavouring to roll it into the desired situation: occasionally they both left off their labours and appeared to rest for a short time, and then to return to the work with fresh vigour. The object of their building I am not sufficiently learned in the natural history of the lamprey to divine; but I conclude that their work had something to do with the placing of their spawn. I had, however, a good opportunity of watching them, as the water was quite clear and shallow, and they were so intent upon what they were at, that they took no notice whatever of me. I had intended to examine the little heaps of stones which they had made, but going from home the next day put it out of my recollection, and I lost the opportunity. It seems, however, so singular a manœuvre on the part of fish to build up regular little pyramids of gravel, bringing some of the stones from the distance of two feet against the current and rolling them to the place with evident difficulty, that the lampreys must have some good reason which induces them to take this trouble. It is a great pity that the habits of fish and animals living in water are so difficult to observe with any degree of exactness.

most of our fresh-water fish, to form the receiving furrows at this important season; but the want is supplied by the sucker-like mouth, by which they individually remove each stone. Their power is immense. Stones of a very large size are transported, and a large furrow is soon formed. The *P. marinus* remains, in a pair, on each spawning-place; and, while there employed, retain themselves affixed by the mouth to a large stone" (*History of British Fishes*, i. p. 36).

RAPIDS ON THE FINDHORN

THE LONG-EARED OWL.

CHAPTER VII

Short-eared Owl: Habits of—Long-eared Owl—Tame Owl—White Owl—Utility of Owls—Mice—Rats: Destructiveness of—Water Rats: Food of—Killing Rats—Ratcatchers.

AMONGST the migratory birds that pass the winter in this country is the short-eared owl,[1] *Strix brachyotus*: it arrives in

[1] The short-eared owl comes over in small flocks to this country, many being often seen together in a turnip-field, or other low cover on their first arrival. Some few, however, remain to breed in this country, building on the ground in rough heather, etc. It hunts earlier in the evening than other owls.—C. St. J.

It is found in summer in North Europe; eastwards it occurs throughout Siberia, wintering in the southern countries, Persia, Burmah, and South China. On the American continent it breeds in various parts of Canada and the United States, and in winter has been found as far south as Chili and the Falkland Isles.—Seebohm, *Siberia in Europe*, p. 118.

October, sometimes in flights of some number. I have heard from perfectly good authority of sixteen or seventeen of these birds having been found in one turnip-field on the east coast, evidently having just arrived. It is a long-winged bird, and more active in its manner of flight than most of the other owls, nor is it so completely nocturnal. I saw one of this kind hunting a rushy field and regularly beating it for prey at mid-day. The owl was so intent on his pursuit that he flew straight in my direction and nearly close to me before he observed me. When he did so, he darted off with great quickness and with a most hawk-like flight, but too late to escape. I killed him (though it is against my usual rule to shoot at an owl) because he appeared to me to be of a different species from any with which I was acquainted. Before I shot him he had put up and made a dash at a snipe, but did not follow up his pursuit, probably perceiving that it would be useless. I have very frequently flushed this kind of owl in rushes, furze, and other low cover. When put up, instead of being distressed and confused by the light of the sun, he flies boldly and steadily away. Sometimes I have seen one, when put up, rise high in the air and fly straight away until I could no longer distinguish him.

The owls that breed here are the long-eared owl, the tawny owl, and the barn-owl: the latter, though so common in England, is by far the rarest in this country.

The long-eared owl [1] is a fine bold bird, and his bright yellow eye gives him a peculiarly handsome appearance: altogether he is of a lighter make and more active than the other owls; they are very common in the shady fir-woods. I often see this bird sitting on a branch close to the stem of the tree, and depending on the exact similitude of his colour to that of the bark, he sits motionless with his bright golden eye watching earnestly every movement I make. If he fancies himself observed, and likely to be molested, down he dashes, flies a hundred yards or so, and then suddenly pitches again.

---

[1] This owl is common enough in the fir-woods. It generally takes possession of the deserted nest of the crow or some other large bird. When it has young it hunts and destroys a great number of birds.—C. St. J.

The habits of pouting noticed in the text are common to this bird and the tawny owl. I have seen the latter on the top of a farm-house in the moonlight, puffing out its throat as it hooted. Virgil, no mean ornithologist, had probably noticed this habit—

Solaque culminibus ferali carmine bubo
Saepe queri, et longas in fletum ducere voces.—Aen. 4. 462.

His long ears and bright eyes give him a most unbirdlike appearance as he sits watching one. As soon as evening comes on, the owl issues forth in full life and activity, and in the woods here may be seen and heard in all directions, sitting on the topmost branch of some leafless tree, generally a larch or ash (these two being his favourites), where he hoots incessantly for an hour together, swelling his throat out, and making the eccentric motions of a pouter pigeon. They breed in rocks, ivy, or in the deserted nest of a magpie.

I do not know why, but I never could succeed in rearing one of these birds—they have invariably died, without any apparent cause, before their first year was over. Not so with the tawny owl.[1] One of these birds has been in my kitchen-garden for three years. Though his wing is sometimes cut, he can fly sufficiently to get over the wall, but seldom ventures beyond the adjoining flower-garden or orchard. From habit or tameness this bird seems to pay little regard to sunshine or shade, sitting during the daytime as indifferently in the most open and exposed places as in the more shaded corners: he is quite tame too, and answers to the call of the children. He hoots as vigorously at mid-day as at night, and will take a bird from my hand when offered to him. Although his flight has been impeded by his wing being cut, he seems to have entirely cleared the garden of mice, with which it was much overrun. Though a light bird, and not apparently very strongly built, his sharp claws and bill enable him to tear to pieces any crow or sea-gull that is offered to him. When he has had his meal off some large bird of this kind, and has satisfied his appetite, he carries away and carefully hides the remainder, returning to it when again hungry. I do not know whether the owl, when at liberty in his native woods, has the same fox-like propensity to hide what he cannot eat. I have frequently heard this kind of owl hoot and utter another sharp kind of cry during the daytime in the shady solitudes of the pine-woods.

The white or barn-owl[2] is rare here, and very seldom seen. I believe him to have been almost eradicated by traps and keepers.

---

[1] The tawny owl is common enough, building in old crows' nests, in clefts of rocks, old ruins, etc., sometimes in rabbit-holes, in which latter situation I have found the eggs.—C. St. J.

[2] This owl lives almost wholly on mice. It is not common at all in this part of the country, though I have seen them about the rocks of the Findhorn and elsewhere, and on

With regard to the mischief done by owls, all the harm they do is amply repaid by their utility in destroying a much more serious nuisance in the shape not only of the different kinds of mice, but of rats also, these animals being their principal food and the prey which they are most adapted for catching.

I knew an instance where the owls having been nearly destroyed by the numerous pole-traps placed about the fields for the destruction of them and the hawks, the rats and mice increased to such an extent on the disappearance of these their worst enemies, and committed such havoc among the nursery-gardens, farm-buildings, etc., that the proprietor was obliged to have all the pole-traps taken down, and the owls having been allowed to increase again, the rats and mice as quickly diminished in number. When the long-eared owls have young, they are not particular as to what they prey upon, and I have found the remains of many different kinds of game about their nests.

The wings of the owl are peculiarly adapted for seizing their sharp-eared prey with silence: were it otherwise, from not having the rapidity of the hawk and other birds of prey, the owl would have little chance of catching the active little mouse. As it is, he comes silently and surely near the ground, and dropping down on the unfortunate mouse, surrounds it with his wings, and grasping it in his sharp and powerful claws, soon puts an end to the little animal. The wings are fringed with a downy texture, which makes his flight quite inaudible on the calmest night. The numbers of mice destroyed by a breeding pair of owls must be enormous, and the service they perform by so doing very great to the farmer, the planter, and the gardener. Though neither cats nor owls ever eat the little shrew-mouse,[1] they always strike and kill it when opportunity offers, leaving the animal on the spot. What there is so obnoxious to all animals of prey in this little creature it is impossible to say. Besides the shrew we have the common

Elgin Cathedral. But they are comparatively rare. It is on the whole very useful in destroying so many mice.—C. St. J.

Mr. C. Innes, who edited St. John's *Natural History and Sport in Moray*, 1863, adds as a note to that book (p. 298), on the barn-owl : "This is one of the few birds I have known transplanted and breed and thrive in its new country. A pair of white owls were brought from England by a school-boy more than twenty years ago to the banks of the Nairn, where their descendants are now in good numbers. Their first independent settlement was in the tower of Kilravock."

[1] *Sorex araneus* and *S. fodiens*, water-shrew, Moray.—C. St. J.

house-mouse, the short-eared mouse, and that beautiful bright-eyed kind the long-tailed field-mouse. The last is very destructive to the garden-seeds, and without the assistance of the owls would be kept under with great difficulty. The large-headed, short-eared mouse is not so pretty an animal, but equally destructive, taking great delight in sweet peas and other seeds: they also climb the peach-trees and destroy great quantities of the fruit. A fig-tree this year, when its winter covering of straw was taken off, was found to be entirely barked and all the shoots eaten off by these mice. The shrew-mouse has the same propensity for barking trees. I have known the former kind, indeed, destroy Scotch fir-trees of the height of fifteen or sixteen feet by nibbling and peeling the topmost shoot till the tree gradually withered away. The quantities of acorns and other seeds that the long-tailed field-mice hoard up for their winter use show that, were they allowed to increase, the mischief they would do would be incalculable; and undoubtedly the best way of getting rid of all mice is to preserve and encourage owls. The long-tailed field-mouse[1] has great capabilities as a digger, and in making his hole carries up an incredible quantity of earth and gravel in a very short time. When the weather is cold they close up the mouth of their hole with great care. They seem to produce their young not underground, but in a comfortable, well-built nest, formed in the shape of a ball, with a small entrance on one side. As it is built of the same material as the surrounding herbage, and the entrance is closed up, it is not easily seen.

Everybody must be glad to encourage any animal that kills a rat,[2] and the owls are the most determined enemies to this, the most disgusting and obnoxious animal which we have in this country. For what can be so sickening as to know that these animals come direct from devouring and revelling in the foulest garbage in the drains of your house, to the larder where your own provisions are kept; and, fresh from their stinking and filthy banquet, run over your meat with their clammy paws, and gnaw at your bread with their foul teeth? what

---

[1] This mouse is very fond of flesh, frequently eating the dead rabbits, etc., used for bait to vermin-traps. The dormouse frequently builds a nest in the branches of copse-wood.—C. St. J.

[2] *Mus rattus* (black rat) I believe is extinct in Moray. Twenty years ago plentiful (1850).—C. St. J.

cleansing and washing can wipe away their traces? Nothing will keep out these animals when they have once established themselves in a house. They gnaw through stone, lead, or almost anything. They may be extirpated for a time, but you suddenly find yourself invaded by a fresh army. Some old rats, too, acquire such a carnivorous appetite, that fowls and ducks, old or young, pigeons, rabbits,—all fall a prey to them. Adepts in climbing as well as in undermining, they get at everything, dead or alive. They reach game, although hung most carefully in a larder, by climbing the wall, and clinging to beam or rope till they get at it; they then devour and destroy all that can be reached. I have frequently known them in this manner destroy a larder full of game in a single night. They seem to commence with the hind-legs of the hares, and to eat downwards, hollowing the animal out as it hangs up, till nothing but the skin is left. In the fields, to which the rats betake themselves in the summer time, not only corn, but game, and eggs of all kinds, fall to their share.

Mr. Waterton says that no house in England has more suffered from the Hanoverian rats than his own; I don't doubt it—in every sense. The poor water-rat[1] is a comparatively harmless animal, feeding principally upon herbage, not refusing, however, fish, or even toads, when they come in its way. The succulent grasses that grow by the sides of ditches, seem to form its chief food during the summer season. Early in the spring, before these grasses are well grown, the water-rat preys much on toads. I have found little piles of the feet, and remains of several of these animals, near the edge of water frequented by these rats, which they seem to have collected together in certain places, and left there. I have known the water-rat do great damage to artificial dams and the heads of ponds, by undermining them, and boring holes in every direction through them, below the water-mark, as well as above it. The water-rat has peculiarly sensitive organs of scent, and it is therefore almost impossible to trap him, as he is sure to discover the taint of the human hand. Cunning as the house-rat is, this kind is much more so. Though the former may be in a measure kept down by constant trapping, it is a trouble-

---

[1] *Arvicola amphibia.* Of its two varieties, in Morayshire the black water-rat is most common, though the brown is also found. *A. agrestis* (field vole), Moray.—C. St. J.

some method, and there are sure to be some cunning old patriarchs who will not enter any kind of trap.[1] I believe that the best kind of trap in a house is the common gin, laid open and uncovered in their runs. They then do not seem to suspect any danger, but when the trap is covered they are sure to detect its presence, and, like all wild animals, they are much more cautious in avoiding a concealed danger than an open one. Poison is the best means of getting rid of them, and the manner of applying it is as follows:—For the space of a fortnight feed the rats with good wholesome meal and water in some quiet room or cellar accessible to all these troublesome inmates of your house. At first two or three rats may find it out; these are sure to lead others to the place, till the whole company of freebooters go for their share. As soon as you see that they seem to have collected in numbers in your feeding-room, season your meal with plenty of arsenic, and you may be pretty sure of its being all devoured. Continue giving them this till you find no more come, and by that time probably there are none left alive in the house. The only danger is, that some of them may die behind the wainscots of your rooms, in which case you must either open the place and search till you find the dead animal, or you must vacate that room till the dreadful stench is over. That rats carry off hens' and even turkeys' eggs to some considerable distance is a fact; how they accomplish this feat I should like to known, as they do it without breaking the shell, or leaving any mark upon it.[2] A crow or magpie, Columbus-like, shortens the difficulty by sticking the lower mandible of his bill into a hen's egg when he wants to carry it off, but this is beyond a rat's capabilities; nevertheless, eggs form one of their favourite repasts. The increase of rats, if left to breed in peace, would exceed that of almost any other animal, as they produce broods of six or eight young ones in rapid succession, throughout the greatest part of the year. In building a nest for her young, the female carries off every

---

[1] Readers who wish to become acquainted with the habits of rats, and the best methods of exterminating them, should read Barkley's *Studies in the Art of Ratcatching*.

[2] Mr. Speedy in his *Sport in the Highlands and Lowlands of Scotland* writes: "From personal observation I can testify how one was carried. Going hurriedly into a stable where hens were in the habit of dropping their eggs, I witnessed a huge rat bearing an egg along the manger towards its hole at the end. It hugged it with one of its fore feet, holding it against its breast, and in this manner was travelling along the outer beam of the manger."

soft substance which she can find; pieces of lace, cloth, and above all, paper, seem to be her favourite lining.

The natural destroyers in this country of this obnoxious animal seem to be, the hen-harrier, the falcon, the long-eared and the tawny owls, cats, weasels, and stoats; and, *ante omnes*, boys of every age and grade wage war to the knife against rats, wherever and whenever they can find them.

As for rat-catchers—find me an honest one, and I will forfeit my name. I would as soon admit a colony of rats themselves, as one of these gentry to my house,—not but what I have amused myself by learning slight tricks of the trade from one of these representatives of roguery and unblushing effrontery, but, *fas est et ab hoste doceri*. Rats swarm about the small towns in this country where the herrings are cured, living amongst the stones of the harbours and rocks on the shore, and issuing out in great numbers towards nightfall, to feed on the stinking remains of the fish.

They have been seen migrating from these places at the end of the fishing-season in compact bodies and in immense numbers. They then spread themselves, an invading host, amongst the farm-houses and stack-yards in the neighbourhood; repairing again to the coast for the benefit of a fish diet and sea air, when their wonderful instinct tells them that the fishing-season has again commenced. But I really must finish the subject, or my reader will be as tired as I am myself of these accounts of the unprincipled greediness and voracity of the Hanoverian or Grey Rat, who has made for itself a home in this country, after nearly extirpating the original indigenous and much less vile race of British rats.

RATS CARRYING OFF EGG

THE SNOWY OWL.

CHAPTER VIII

Crossbills: Habits of; Nest—Snowy Owl—Great-eared Owl—Hoopoe—Shrike—Tawny and Snow Bunting—Lizards—Singular Pets—Toads: Utility of; Combats of—Adders—Dog and Snakes—Large Snake—Blind-Worm.

WHILST walking through the extensive fir and larch woods in this neighbourhood, I am often much amused by the proceedings of those curious little birds the crossbills.[1] They pass incessantly from tree to tree with a jerking quick flight in

---

[1] The Common Crossbill. The bill of the young is not crooked when they first leave the nest. The male crossbill loses its red plumage, and returns to a plain olive green. I have seen it during the whole year in Morayshire, where it breeds at Dulsie. I have also obtained nest and eggs from Balnagowan in Ross-shire. The eggs are like those of the greenfinch, but larger and more oval. The nest is also like that of the greenfinch, but built more loosely. The only *authentic* nests that I know of are belonging to Mr. Hancock at Newcastle (C. St. J.) For another excellent account of the crossbill's habits, breeding, nests, etc., see *Natural History and Sport in Moray*, p. 124. It is not uncommon in Ross-shire and the eastern districts of Sutherland, but, of course, owing to the paucity of trees, is unknown in Assynt. Mr. Knox (*Autumns on the Spey*, p. 33) gives a charming narrative of the feeding of a party of crossbills in the woods.

search of their food, which consists of the seeds of the fir and larch. They extract these from the cones with the greatest skill and rapidity, holding the cone in one foot, and cutting it up quickly and thoroughly with their powerful beak, which they use much after the manner of a pair of scissors. When the flock has stripped one tree of all the sound cones, they simultaneously take wing, uttering at the same time a sharp harsh chattering cry. Sometimes they fly off to a considerable height, and after wheeling about for a short time, suddenly alight again on some prolific-looking tree, over which they disperse immediately, hanging and swinging about the branches and twigs, cutting off the cones, a great many of which they fling to the ground, often with a kind of impatient jerk. These cones, I conclude, are without any ripe seed. They continue uttering a constant chirping while in search of their food on the branches. I have never succeeded in finding the nest of the crossbill, though I am confident that they breed in this country, having seen the birds during every month of the year, so that either some barren ones must remain, or they hatch their young here. The nest has been described to me as placed at a considerable height from the ground, at the junction of some large branch with the main stem.

The crossbill itself is a busy, singular-looking little fellow, as he flits to and fro, or climbs, parrot-like, up and down the branches; and the cock, with his red plumage shining in the sun, has more the appearance of some Eastern or tropical bird than any other of our sober northern finches. When engaged in feeding, these birds are often so intent on their occupation that they will allow a horsehair snare, attached to the end of a long twig, to be slipped round their necks before they fly away. In captivity they are very tame, but restless, and are constantly tearing with their strong mandibles at the woodwork and wires of their cage.

Altogether the crossbill is a gay, lively bird, and, I hope, likely to increase and become a regular inhabitant of this country, as the numerous plantations of fir and larch which are daily being laid out, afford them plenty of their favourite and natural food.[1]

---

[1] This forecast has been in a great measure verified. Crossbills are now fairly abundant in many districts, especially of the west coast.

The eastern coast of Scotland, owing to its proximity to Sweden and Norway, and also to the great prevalence of easterly winds, is often visited by foreign birds. Amongst these is that splendid stranger the snowy owl,[1] who occasionally is blown over to our coast from his native fastnesses amongst the mountains and forests of the north of Europe. Now and then one of these birds is killed here, and I was told of one having been seen two or three years back on part of the ground rented by me. He was sitting on a high piece of muirland, and at a distance looked, said my informant, "like a milestone." This bird was pursued for some hours, but was not killed. The snowy owl has been also seen, to the astonishment of the fisherman or bent-puller, on the sand-hills, where he finds plenty of food amongst the rabbits that abound there. One was winged in that district a few years ago, and lived for some time in confinement. He was a particularly fine old bird, with perfect plumage, and of a great size. I am much inclined to think that the great-eared owl, *Strix bubo*,[2] is also occasionally a visitor to the wildest parts of this district. A man described to me a large bird, which he called an eagle. The bird was sitting on a fir-tree, and his attention was called to it by the grey crows uttering their cries of alarm and war. He went up to the tree, and close above his head sat a great bird, with large staring yellow eyes, as bright (so he expressed it) as two brass buttons. The man stooped to pick up a stone or stick, and the bird dashed off the tree into the recesses of the wood, and was not seen again. I have no doubt that, instead of an eagle, as he supposed it to be, it was the great *Strix bubo*. The colour of its eyes, the situation the bird was in on the branch of a tall fir-tree, and its remaining quiet until the man approached so close to it, all convince me that it must have been the great owl, whose loud midnight hootings disturb the solitude of the

---

[1] The snowy owl is an occasional visitor on the east coast, apparently driven over by continued severe gales from the north-east.—C. St. J.

Continental skins of this bird are worth a pound each in London. About 1845 a friend was shooting a wild-duck in a snowstorm in the north of Caithness, when a snowy owl swooped upon the falling duck, and carried it off in its claws. The sportsman's second barrel laid the owl low, and they have been both stuffed and set up together.

Tengmalm's owl (*N. Tengmalmi*) was killed at Spinningdale, Sutherland, by Mr. Dunbar.—C. St. J.

[2] *Bubo maximus*, Gray. It "has almost become extinct in the British Islands, but is still a resident in the mountainous districts of most parts of Europe."—Seebohm, *Siberia in Europe*, p. 84.

German forests, giving additional weight to the legends and superstitions of the peasants of that country, inclined as they are to belief in supernatural sounds and apparitions.

The hoopoe[1] has been killed in the east of Sutherland, on the bent-hills near Dornoch, and so also has the rose-coloured ousel.[2] These birds must have been driven over by the east winds, as neither of them are inhabitants of Britain. Indeed, many a rare and foreign bird may visit the uninhabited and desert tracts of bent and sand along the east coast without being observed, excepting quite by chance; and the probability is, that nine persons out of ten who might see a strange bird would take no notice of it.

Last winter I saw a great ash-coloured shrike[3] or butcher-bird in my orchard. The gardener told me that he had seen it for some hours in pursuit of the small birds, and I found lying about the walls two or three chaffinches, which had been killed and partly eaten, in a style unlike the performance of any bird of prey that I am acquainted with; so much so, indeed, that before I saw the butcher-bird, my attention was called to their dead bodies by the curious manner in which they seemed to have been pulled to pieces. Having watched the bird for a short time as he sat perched on an apple-tree very near me, I went in for my gun, but did not see him again. The tawny bunting and the snow-bunting[4] visit us in large

---

[1] The hoopoe (*Upupa epops*) has been seen once or twice in Shetland by Dr. Saxby, but "can only be regarded as a straggler in any part of Scotland" (Gray, p. 198). One was killed in the west woods of Moncreiff.

[2] *Pastor roseus.* The rose-coloured pastor (or ousel). A very rare visitor. I have killed it in Morayshire in June: the bird at the time was flying over my head. I saw one which had just been killed near Inverness in July; also near Dornoch.—C. St. J.

[3] A rare visitor. I once or twice have seen it near Forres.—C. St. J.

[4] "I have seen the snow-bunting on 4th September on a high mountain near Loch Rannoch while ptarmigan-shooting. They appeared to be a family of two old and three or four young birds" (C. St. J.) "The snow-bunting (*Plectrophanes nivalis*) is a circumpolar bird, breeding principally on the tundras of the Arctic regions beyond the limit of forest growth. It is an irregular migrant driven southwards in severe seasons in larger or smaller flocks to Central Europe, South Siberia, North China, Japan, and the Northern States of America. These birds seem to lead a roving, gipsy life during winter, perpetually trying to migrate northwards with every appearance of milder weather, and perpetually driven southwards with each recurring frost" (Seebohm, p. 50). It has long been suspected by ornithologists that the snow-bunting bred in Scotland. It was reserved for Mr. B. N. Peach and Mr. L. N. Hinxman of the Geological Survey of Scotland to verify this surmise. On 3rd July 1886 a nest with five young birds was discovered by them 2800 feet above sea-level on the eastern face of one of the wildest corries on the highest mountains of Sutherland. A most interesting description of this nest and an account of the old ones feeding the little ones may be seen in Harvie-Brown and Buckley's *Vertebrate Fauna of Sutherland and Caithness* (Douglas, 1887), p. 138 *seq.*

flocks, especially the latter, which birds remain here during the whole winter, appearing in greater or lesser flocks according to the temperature. In severe weather the fields near the seashore, and the shore itself, are sometimes nearly covered by them. When the snow-buntings first arrive, in October and November, they are of a much darker colour than they are afterwards as the winter advances. If there is much snow, they put on a white plumage immediately. I do not know how this change of colour is effected, but it is very visible, and appears to depend entirely on the severity of the season. They feed a great deal on the shore. When flying they keep in close rank, but as soon as they alight the whole company instantly disperse, and run (not jump, like many small birds) quickly about in search of their food, which consists principally of small insects and minute seeds. They often pitch to look for these on the barest parts of the sand-hills, the dry sands always producing a number of small flies and beetles. So fine and dry is the sand which composes the hillocks and plains of that curious district, that every beetle and fly that walks or crawls over its surface in calm and dry weather leaves its track as distinctly marked on the finely-pulverised particles, as the rabbit or hare does on snow. The footprints of the lizards, which abound there, are very neatly and distinctly marked, till the first breath of wind drifting the sand erases the impressions. One of my children brought home a large lizard one day, and put it into a box, intending to keep it as a pet; boys having strange tastes in the animals which they select as favourites. I remember that when I was a boy at school, I was the owner of three living pets—a rat, a bat, and a snake, all of which lived and flourished for some months under my tender care, notwithstanding the occasional edicts sent forth from headquarters against any living animal whatever being kept in the schoolroom. But to return to the lizard in the box. The next morning, to the children's great delight, the lizard had become much reduced in circumference, but had produced four young ones, who were apparently in full and vigorous enjoyment of life. They were voted, at a consultation of the children, to be entitled to, and worthy of liberty, and were all (mother and children) carefully put into the garden, in a sunny corner under the wall. For my own part, I can see nothing more disgusting in animals usually called reptiles, such as lizards and toads, than in any other living creatures. A toad is a most useful member of society, and deserves the freedom of all floricultural societies, as well as entire immunity from all the pains and penalties which he undergoes at the hands of the ignorant and vulgar. In hotbeds and hothouses he is extremely useful, and many gardeners take great care of toads in these places, where they do good service by destroying beetles and other insects. In the flower-beds too they are of similar use. Of quiet and domestic habits, the toad seldom seems to wander far from his seat or form under a loose stone, or at the foot of a fruit-tree or box-edging. There are several *habitués* of this species in my garden, whom I always see in their respective places during the middle of the day. In the evening they issue out in search of their prey. I found a toad one day caught by the leg in a horse-hair snare which had been placed for birds. The animal, notwithstanding the usual placid and phlegmatic demeanour of its race, seemed to be in a perfect fury, struggling and scratching at everything within his reach, apparently much more in anger than fear. Like many other individuals of quiet exterior, toads are liable to great fits of passion and anger, as is seen in the pools during April, when five or six will contend for the good graces of their sultanas with a fury and pertinacity that is quite wonderful, fighting and struggling for hours together. And where a road intervenes between two ditches, I have seen the battle carried on even in the dry dust, till the rival toads, in spite of their natural aquatic propensities, became perfectly dry and covered with sand, and in this powdered state will they continue fighting, regardless of the heat, which shrivels up their skin, or of passers-by, who may tread on them and maim them, but cannot stop their fighting. There is more character and energy in a toad than is supposed. After the young ones have acquired their perfect shape, they appear to leave the water, and frequently the roads and paths are so covered with minute but well-formed toadlings, that it is impossible to put your foot down without crushing some of them.

In some of the drier banks and hills in this country, there are numerous adders; like most other snakes, however, they never willingly fly at people, only biting when trod upon or taken hold of. I have had my dogs occasionally, but rarely, bitten by adders. The swelling is very severe, and only reduced after several hours' rubbing with oil and laudanum. A retriever of mine, having been bitten by an adder, conceived the most deadly hatred against them ever after, and killed a great number of them without being again bitten; his method was to snap quickly at the adder, biting it in two almost instantaneously, and before the reptile could retaliate. A favourite amusement of this dog, when he was in Sussex with me some time afterwards, used to be hunting the hedgerows for snakes and adders. He made a most marked distinction between the two, killing the former quietly and without hurry, but whenever he found an adder, he darted on it with a perfect frenzy of rage, at the same time always managing to escape the fangs of the venomous reptile, quickly as it can use them. The poisonous teeth of the adder greatly resemble the talons of a cat in shape, and can be raised or laid flat on the jaw according to the wish of their owner; indeed, the fangs of the adder, which are hollow throughout, are only raised when he is angry, and in self-defence. The common snake, which is quite harmless, has no such teeth. There are stories among the peasants, of adders being seen in Darnaway Forest, of great size and length, measuring five or six feet, but I do not believe that there are any larger than the usual size.

I have never seen the *Anguis fragilis*, or blind-worm, as it is called, but once in this country, though I am told it is not uncommon; a man brought me one last year which he had found floating down the river after a flood, as if swept off some rock by the sudden rise of the water. I mentioned the circumstance to some of my acquaintance, but could find no one who had either seen or heard of such a creature in this country. This one was alive when brought to me, but had received a cut which nearly divided its body in two, so that it did not long survive.

Amongst the rare feathered visitors to these woods, I forgot to mention the spotted woodpecker,[1] *Picus medius*, which bird I killed in Inverness-shire; I was attracted to the spot, where he was clinging to the topmost shoot of a larch-tree, by hearing his strange harsh cry.

---

[1] This was probably *Picus major*, the greater spotted woodpecker (see Newton's Yarrell, ii. p. 484). It has even been known to breed in limited numbers in North-East Scotland (Gray).

YELLOW-HAMMER'S NEST

CHAPTER IX

On the Peculiarities and Instinct of different Animals—Eggs of Birds—Nests—The Fox—Red-Deer Hind

THERE are two birds which, although wild and unapproachable at every other time, throw themselves during the breeding-season on the mercy and protection of man: these are the wood-pigeon and the missel-thrush. Scarcely any bird is more wary than the wood-pigeon at other times, yet in the spring there are generally half-a-dozen nests in the most exposed places close to my house, while the old birds sit tamely, and apparently devoid of all fear, close to the windows; they seem to have an instinctive knowledge of places where they are allowed to go through the business of incubation without being molested. In like manner, the missel-thrush, though during the rest of the year it is nearly impossible to get within a hundred yards of it, forms its nest in the apple-trees close to the house: they build at a height of six or seven feet, in the fork of the tree where the main limbs branch off; and although their nest is large, it is so carefully constructed of materials resembling in colour the bark of the tree, and is made to blend itself so gradually with the branches, as to show no distinct outline of a nest, and to render it very difficult to discover; and this bird, at other times so shy and timid, sits so close on her eggs that she will almost allow herself to be taken by the hand. The missel-thrushes on the approach of a hawk give a loud cry of alarm, and then collecting all their neighbours, lead them on to attack the common enemy, swooping and striking fearlessly at him, till he is driven out of the vicinity of their nests.

The observation of the different plans that birds adopt to avoid the discovery and destruction of their eggs, is by no means an uninteresting study to the naturalist. There is far more of art and cunning design in their manner of building, than the casual observer would suppose, and this, even amongst the commonest of our native birds. The wren, for instance, always adapts her nest to the colour and appearance of the surrounding foliage, or whatever else may be near the large and comfortable abode which she forms for her tiny family. In a beech-hedge near the house, in which the leaves of the last year still remain at the time when the birds commence building, the wrens form the outside of their nests entirely of the withered leaves of the beech, so that, large as it is, the passer-by would never take it for anything more than a chance collection of leaves heaped together, and though the nest is as firm and strong as possible, they manage to give it the look of a confused mass of leaves, instead of a round and compact ball, which it really is. The wren also builds near the ground, about the lower branches of shrubs which are overgrown and surrounded with long grass: in these situations she forms her nest of the long withered grass itself, and twines and arches it over her roof, in a manner which would deceive the eyes of any animal, excepting those of boys. When her nest is built, as it often is, in a spruce fir tree, she covers the outside with green moss, which of all the substances she could select is the one most resembling the foliage of the spruce: the interior of the wren's nest is a perfect mass of feathers and soft substances.

The chaffinch builds usually in the apple-trees, whose lichen-covered branches she imitates closely, by covering her nest with the lichens and moss of a similar colour. Even her eggs are much of the same hue. Sometimes this bird builds in the wall fruit trees, when she collects substances of exactly the same colour as the wall itself.

The greenfinch, building amongst the green foliage of trees, covers her nest with green moss, while her eggs resemble in colour the lining on which they are laid. The yellow-hammer, again, builds on or near the ground, and forming her nest outwardly of dried grass and fibres, like those by which it is surrounded, lines it with horsehair; her eggs too are not unlike in colour to her nest—while the greenish-brown of the bird herself closely resembles the colour of the grass and twigs about her.

The little whitethroat builds her nest on the ground, at the root of a tree or in long withered grass, and carefully arches it over with the surrounding herbage, and to hide her little white eggs, places a leaf in front of the entrance whenever she leaves her nest. When the partridge quits her eggs for the purpose of feeding, she covers them in the most careful manner, and even closes up her run by which she goes to and fro through the surrounding grass. The same plan is adopted by the wild duck, who hides her eggs and nest by covering them with dead leaves, sticks, and other substances, which she afterwards smooths carefully over so as entirely to conceal all traces of her dwelling. There are several domesticated wild ducks, who build their nests about the flower-beds and lawn near the windows—a privilege they have usurped rather against the will of my gardener. Tame as these birds are, it is almost impossible to catch them in the act of going to or from their nests. They take every precaution to escape observation, and will wait for a long time rather than go to their nests if people are about the place.

The pewits, who lay their eggs on the open fields with scarcely any nest, always manage to choose a spot where loose stones or other substances of the same colour as their eggs are scattered about. The terns lay their eggs in the same manner amongst the shingle and gravel. So do the ring-dotterel, the oyster-catcher, and several other birds of the same description: all of them selecting spots where the gravel resembles their eggs in size and colour. Without these precautions, the grey crows and other egg-eating birds would leave but few to be hatched.

The larger birds, the size of whose nests does not admit of their concealment, generally take some precautions to add to their safety. A raven, which builds in a tree, invariably fixes on the one that is most difficult to climb. She takes up her abode in one whose large size and smooth trunk, devoid of branches, set at defiance the utmost efforts of the most expert climbers of the village school. When she builds on a cliff, she fixes on a niche protected by some projection of the rock from all attacks both from above and below, at the same time choosing the most inaccessible part of the precipice. The falcon and eagle do the same. The magpie seems to depend more on the fortification of brambles and thorns with which she surrounds her nest than the situation which she fixes upon. There is one kind of swallow which breeds very frequently about the caves and rocks on the sea-shore here. It is almost impossible to distinguish the nest of this bird, owing to her choosing some inequality of the rock to hide the outline of her building, which is composed of mud and clay of exactly the same colour as the rock itself.

In fine, though some birds build a more simple and exposed nest than others, there are very few which do not take some precaution for their safety, or whose eggs and young do not resemble in colour the substances by which they are surrounded. The care of the common rabbit, in concealing and smoothing over the entrance of the hole where her young are deposited, is very remarkable, and doubtless saves them from the attacks of almost all their enemies, with the exception of the wily fox, whose fine scent enables him to discover their exact situation, and who in digging them out, instead of following the hole in his excavations, discovers the exact spot under which they are, and then digs down directly on them, thus saving himself a great deal of labour.

The fox chooses the most unlikely places and holes to produce her young cubs in; generally in some deep and inaccessible earth, where no digging can get at them, owing to the intervention of rocks or roots of trees. I once, however, two years ago, found three young foxes about two days old, laid in a comfortable nest in some long heather, instead of the usual subterraneous situation which the old one generally makes choice of. Deer and roe fix upon the most lonely parts of the mountain or forest for the habitation of their fawns, before they have strength to follow their parents. I one day, some time ago, was watching a red-deer hind with my glass, whose proceedings I did not understand, till I saw that she was engaged in licking a newly-born calf. I walked up to the place, and as soon as the old deer saw me she gave her young one a slight tap with her hoof. The little creature immediately laid itself down; and when I came up I found it lying with its head flat on the ground, its ears closely laid back, and with all the attempts at concealment that one sees in animals which have passed an apprenticeship to danger of some years, whereas it had evidently not known the world for more than an hour, being unable to run or escape. I lifted up the little creature, being half inclined to carry it home in order to rear it. The mother stood at the distance of two hundred yards, stamping with her foot, exactly as a sheep would have done in a similar situation. I, however, remembering the distance I had to carry it, and fearing that it might get hurt on the way, laid it down again, and went on my way, to the great delight of its mother, who almost immediately trotted up, and examined her progeny carefully all over, appearing, like most other wild animals, to be confident that her young and helpless offspring would be a safeguard to herself against the attacks of her otherwise worst enemy. I have seen roe throw themselves in the way of danger, in order to take my attention from their young. No animal is more inclined to do battle for her young ones than the otter; and I have known an instance of an old female otter following a man who was carrying off her young for a considerable distance, almost disputing the way with him; leaving the water, and blowing at him in their peculiar manner; till at last, having no stick or other means of defence, he actually got so frightened at her threats that he laid down the two young ones and went his way. He returned presently with a stick he had found, but both old and young had disappeared. Even a partridge will do battle for her young. A hen partridge one day surprised me by rushing out of some cover (through which I was passing by a narrow path) and flying at a large dog which accompanied me; she actually spurred and pecked him, driving him several yards along the road; and this done, she ran at my heels like a barn-door hen. As I passed, I saw her newly-hatched brood along the edge of the path. I have known a pheasant do exactly the same thing. Wild ducks, snipes, woodcocks, and many other shy birds, will also throw themselves boldly within the reach of destruction in defence of their young.

WHITETHROAT'S NEST

THE EAGLE AND MOUNTAIN HARE

CHAPTER X

The Eagle: Habits; Greediness; Anecdotes of; Killing Eagles; Trapping; Food of—The Peregrine Falcon: Manner of Hunting—Tame Falcon: Anecdotes of—Guinea-Hen and Ducks—The Osprey—The Kite: Trapping—The Buzzard: Nests and Habits of.

I SAW an eagle[1] to-day passing southwards, apparently on his way from the mountains of Sutherland or Caithness to the

---

[1] Rarely seen in Morayshire, excepting during its passage from the Grampians to the more northern mountains. The eggs, sometimes white, and sometimes spotted closely with light red brown. When taking its prey, such as a grouse or hare, on the ground,

more southern heights of the Grampians. The bird was flying very near the ground, making his way against the wind, and pursued by a whole squadron of grey crows, who had found out that he was a stranger, and taking advantage of the unconcerned contempt with which he treated their attacks, kept up a continual clamour and petty warfare against the royal bird. The eagle, as he came over the more enclosed part of the country, flew higher, as if suspicious of concealed foes amongst the hedges and enclosures. I have almost every year during my stay in Morayshire seen the eagles occasionally passing, at the beginning of winter invariably going southwards, and again early in the spring on their return northwards; in windy weather flying low, but when calm cleaving the air at a great height. The eagle's flight, when passing from one point to another, is peculiarly expressive of strength and vigour. He wends his way with deliberate strong strokes of his powerful wing, every stroke apparently driving him on a considerable distance, and in this manner advancing through the air as rapidly as the pigeon or any other bird which may appear to fly much more quickly.

Notwithstanding the facility with which he flies when once fairly launched, like many other heavy birds, a very slight wound disables him from rising into the air when on level ground. Even after having gorged himself to excess (and there is no greater glutton than this king of the air) the eagle is unable to rise, and falls a victim occasionally to his want of moderation in feeding. When in Sutherland I twice fell in with instances of eagles being knocked down when unable to rise from overeating. On one occasion a curious kind of character, who acted the part of hanger-on to me in my deer-shooting excursions, brought home an eagle, which he had killed with his stick

---

the eagle generally carries it off without stopping for a moment. To kill an animal it makes use only of its talons. The eagle, however, prefers the carcass of a large animal, such as a deer or sheep, to the trouble of hunting and taking smaller game.

The golden eagle *usually* breeds inland, and the white-tailed eagle *usually* on the cliffs overhanging the sea, though there are exceptions to both these rules. The white-tailed eagle (*A. albicilla*) also feeds on carrion as well as on fish. It is rare in Moray. —C. St. J.

The golden eagle still holds its own in the western districts of Scotland. It is preserved by the Duke of Sutherland and by almost all proprietors of land. Were it not for the demand for its eggs and the large price paid for them it would increase faster than, even as it is, it is said to do at present. It is a well-known bird in the Outer Hebrides, best known in Lewis and Harris. Its Gaelic name is "iolair dhubh" (black eagle).

before it could rise from the ground. This man, who was dumb, and was supposed (very erroneously) to be half-witted also, had a great *penchant* for assisting in beating the woods for roe or deer; and from long acquaintance with the country, and from a propensity (very common to people similarly afflicted) for wandering about, he had a perfect knowledge of every corner of the extensive woods on the property, and also a most shrewd guess as to where the deer would be lying, and in which direction they would break cover. Though generally of a most morose and even malicious temper, Muckle Thomas, as they called him, entertained a great affection, in his way, for me; and every morning was to be found seated in front of the windows, smoking a solitary pipe, and waiting to see if I wanted him. Though dumb, he was not deaf, and understanding what was said to him, could make himself quite intelligible by signs, assisting my comprehension by drawing, in a rude way, figures on the ground with the long staff which he invariably carried. One morning I had sent him to look in a certain part of the woods to see if any deer's tracks were visible. In an hour or two he returned with something large bundled up in his plaid, which he opened, and cast down his load at my feet with a look and grunt of triumph. After some explanatory signs, etc., I found out that he had come on the eagle, who had so completely gorged himself with a rotten sheep in the wood that he could not rise.

Another instance occurred in the same country. A shepherd's boy found an eagle gorging itself on some drowned sheep in a watercourse, and being, like all herd-boys, as skilful as David in the use of sling and stone, he had broken the eagle's pinion with a pebble, and had actually stoned the poor bird to death. In this case the eagle was taken at peculiar disadvantage, being surprised in a deep rocky burn, out of which he would have had difficulty in rising quickly, even if he had not dined so abundantly. When wounded by shot, or even after escaping (but maimed) from a trap, the eagle is often unable to rise. A curious anecdote was told me by a friend. An eagle had been caught in a vermin-trap, and, by his struggles, had drawn the peg by which the trap was fastened to the ground, and had flown away with it. Nothing was seen for some weeks of eagle or trap, till one day my friend, seeing some strange object hanging from the branch of a tree, went to examine what it was, and found the poor bird hanging by his leg, which was firmly held by the trap. The chain and peg had got fixed amongst the branches, and the poor eagle had died miserably from starvation in this position, suspended by the foot. Though certainly the eagles in some localities commit great havoc amongst the lambs, and also destroy the grouse when no larger game offers itself, it would be a great pity that this noble bird should become extinct in our Highland districts, who, notwithstanding his carnivorous propensities, should be rather preserved than exterminated. How picturesque he looks, and how perfectly he represents the *genius loci*, as, perched on some rocky point, or withered tree, he sits unconcerned in wind and storm, motionless and statue-like, with his keen, stern eye, however, intently following every movement of the shepherd or of the sportsman, who, deceived by his apparent disregard, attempts to creep within rifle-shot. Long before he can reckon on reaching so far with his bullet, the bird launches himself into the air, and gradually sweeping upwards, wheels high out of shot, leaving his enemy disappointed and vexed at having crept in vain through bog and over rock in expectation of carrying home so glorious a trophy of his skill. When intent on his game, the eagle frequently will venture within a short distance of the grouse-shooter or deer-stalker. I have seen him pounce (no, that is not the proper word, for he rather rushes) down on a pack of grouse, and, with outspread wings, he so puzzles and confuses the birds, that he seizes and carries off two or three before they know what has happened, and in the very face of the astonished sportsman and his dogs. The mountain hare, too, is carried off by the eagle with as much apparent ease as the mouse is borne away by the kestrel.

The marten and the wild cat are favourite morsels. A tame eagle which I kept for some time killed all the cats about the place. Sitting motionless on his perch, he waited quietly and seemingly unheeding till the unfortunate animal came within reach of his chain. Then down he flew, and surrounding the cat with his wings, seized her in his powerful talons, with one foot planted firmly on her loins, and the other on her throat; and nothing more was seen of poor Grimalkin except her skin, which the eagle left empty and turned inside out, like a rabbit-skin hung up by the cook, the whole of the carcass, bones and all, being stowed away in the bird's capacious maw. The quantity of meat taken from the stomach of an eagle killed on the mountain is sometimes perfectly incredible. I regret not having taken a note of the weight of mutton I once saw taken out of one I shot.

We are occasionally visited, too, by the peregrine falcon,[1] who makes sad havoc in the poultry-yard when he appears here. There is a nest of these birds always built in the inaccessible rocks of the Findhorn. Indeed, in the good old days of hawking, when a gentleman was known by his hawk and hound, and even a lady seldom went abroad without a hawk on her gloved hand, the Findhorn hawks were always in great request. The peregrine seems often to strike down birds for his amusement; and I have seen one knock down and kill two rooks, who were unlucky enough to cross his flight, without taking the trouble to look at them after they fell. In the plain country near the seashore the peregrine frequently pursues the pewits and other birds that frequent the coast. The golden-plover, too, is a favourite prey, and affords the hawk a severe chase before he is caught. I have seen a pursuit of this kind last for nearly ten minutes, the plover turning and doubling like a hare before greyhounds, at one moment darting like an arrow into the air, high above the falcon's head; at the next, sweeping round some bush or headland—but in vain. The hawk, with steady, relentless flight, without seeming to hurry herself, never gives up the chase, till the poor plover, seemingly quite exhausted, slackens his pace, and is caught by the hawk's talons in mid-air, and carried off to a convenient hillock or stone to be quietly devoured. Two years ago I brought a young peregrine falcon down from near the source of the Findhorn,

---

[1] The peregrine falcon, Moray. Does not breed in trees. *F. Islandicus* (German falcon) seen near Loch Spynie, March 1850.—C. St. J.

It is a common bird in many districts of West Scotland, and is generally found in pairs, each pair inhabiting a circle of some six or eight miles. The ravages of keepers and egg-collectors have of late years much thinned its numbers. Mr. Gray saw one strike off the head of a curlew on the seashore near Girvan. It was followed by its mate. A keeper on Loch Laggan told us he had often seen one swoop down on a flying covey of grouse, strike the head off one bird, wheel, and catch the dead bird in its talons. This he bore off while the head fell to the ground. Mr. Speedy says: "The falcon almost invariably strikes in the air, using his wing, with which he frequently decapitates his victim" (p. 358).

where I found her in the possession of a shepherd's boy, who fed her wholly on trout. For the first year the bird was of a dark brown colour above, with longitudinal spots on the feathers of her breast. On changing her plumage during the second autumn of her existence, she became of a most beautiful dark slate colour above, and the spots on her breast turned into cross-bars, every feather being barred with black; her throat became of a beautiful cream colour. With great strength, she is possessed of the most determined courage, and will attack any person or dog whom she takes a dislike to. Her poultry-killing propensities oblige me to keep her chained in the kitchen-garden, where no other bird, except a tame owl, resides. The owl she appears to tolerate with great good-nature, and even allows him to carry off any remains of pigeon or crow that she leaves after she has satisfied her hunger. One day an unfortunate duck strayed within reach of her chain, and was immediately pounced on and devoured, leaving a numerous family of ducklings to mourn her loss.

A curious stepmother took them in hand, however. A Guinea-fowl, whose mate had been condemned to death for killing young poultry, took compassion on the orphan ducklings, and led them about, calling them, and tending them with as much or more care than their deceased parent. It was a most singular sight to see the Guinea-fowl quite changing her natural habits, and walking about followed by a brood of young ducks. She never left them for a moment, excepting when she retired to her nest to lay; and even then, if the ducks uttered any cry of alarm, on the approach of dog or children, their stepmother came flying over bushes and fences in a most furious hurry. Indeed she became quite the terror of the children, running after them and pecking their legs if they came too near to her adopted brood; although at other times she was rather a wild and shy bird. The ducks had a habit of hunting for worms in the dusk of the evening, and the poor Guinea-hen, much against her inclination and natural propensities, thought it necessary always to accompany them. Frequently tired out, she used to fly up to roost, but always kept her eye on the young ducks, and on the least alarm came bustling down to protect them if she thought it necessary, at any hour of the night. A pugnacious cock at another time was rash enough to attack the hawk, and was not only killed, but devoured. Frequently unlucky pigeons came within reach of her chain, and were also eaten. In consequence of these depredations, she is exiled to the walled garden. One day I was altering her chain, and she flew away. After flying three or four times round the house and garden, she perched in a high tree and would not come down. I was obliged to leave her at night, and in the morning the hawk was nowhere to be found. For four days I saw nothing of her; but on going out early on the fifth morning, I saw her wheeling about at a great height, with some hooded crows giving battle to her. I stood out in an open place and whistled. As soon as she heard me, after two or three rapid sweeps round my head, she perched down on my arm, and immediately began caressing me, and as plainly as possible expressing her delight at having found me again; whether hunger or affection induced her to return, I know not; though I rather fear the former, as, on my giving her a rabbit, she commenced devouring it as if her fast had not been broken since she got away. In feeding on birds, I observe that she invariably begins by plucking them of almost all their feathers, however hungry she may be; and when I give her a rat or rabbit, she always pulls off most of the hair before commencing her meal. The only animal that she appears unwilling to eat is a mole, everything else is devoured without hesitation, and, when hungry, no bird is too large for her to attack. Black-backed gull or cormorant is instantly seized and plucked; and one day, a Skye terrier going too near her chain, she instantly flew at it, and, had I not come to the rescue, would probably have killed it, as, perching on the dog's back, the hawk commenced immediately tearing at its head and eyes. The male peregrine is considerably smaller than the female, and of a much lighter colour; their nest is built in some inaccessible niche or shelf of a lofty cliff or rock, and both birds assist in the business of incubation. The quantity of game killed by a pair of these birds to feed their young is immense; and, from their great courage and strength, no bird of the game kind in this country has any chance with them.

Occasionally an osprey [1] comes sailing down the course of

---

[1] The osprey rare in Moray. Seen near Spynie 1850 (C. St. J.) See *Natural History and Sport in Moray*, pp. 157-163, for an interesting account, probably the best in existence, of this bird's nest and habits while breeding. Sad to say, Mr. St. John and a friend, Mr.

the river, but does not breed anywhere in our immediate neighbourhood. This very beautiful bird drops like a stone on any unlucky fish that its sharp eye may detect in the clear pools of the river, and I believe she seldom pounces in vain. Having caught a trout or small salmon, she flies with it to land, or to some rock, and there tears it up. When the river is too high and black for the fish to be attainable, no dead carcass comes amiss to her; and in floods on the Findhorn there is seldom any dearth of food of this kind. Mountain sheep or wounded roe are frequently swept down its rapid course, when swollen with much rain or by the melting of snows on the higher mountains from whence this river derives its source. This winter, a young red deer (a calf of about eight months old) was found in the river. The animal had been shot with a slug through the shoulder, and had probably taken to the water (as wounded deer are in the habit of doing), and had been drowned and carried down the stream.

That beautiful bird, the kite,[1] is now very rare in this country. Occasionally I have seen one, wheeling and soaring at an immense height; but English keepers and traps have nearly extirpated this bird, as no greater enemy or more destructive a foe to young grouse can exist. Their large and ravenous young require a vast quantity of food, and the old birds manage to keep their craving appetite well supplied. Not only young grouse and black game, but great numbers of young hares are carried to the nest. Though a bird of apparently such powerful and noble flight, the kite appears not to be very destructive to old grouse, but to confine her attacks

---

Dunbar, shot probably the last ospreys in Sutherland on Loch Assynt. They used to build a huge nest, which from year to year had been added to until it attained size enough, as my informant said, to fill a cart, on the top of the ruined castle of Macleod by the edge of that loch, and formed a very noticeable feature on it by their sailing over and plunging into its waters for food.

The osprey (*Pandion haliætus*) is a rare visitor to the British Isles during the spring and autumn migration. It is a circumpolar bird, and may almost be said to be cosmopolitan in its range, breeding in Europe, Asia, Africa, America, and Australia. It has been recorded too from New Zealand (Seebohm, *Siberia in Europe*, p. 138). The osprey is now protected on several estates in Scotland.

[1] The kite is nearly extinct in this country, though tolerably numerous a few years back. A tame kite which I have feeds on almost anything that is dead, and also eats porridge, etc., with the hens and chickens, never touching the live poultry.—C. St. J. See *Natural History in Moray*, p. 254.

The kite (*Milvus vulgaris*) is now never seen in Assynt, and is hardly to be found in Scotland. Mr. J. Smith in 1879 had been told that a pair bred on Speyside, at Rothiemurchus.

to the young broods. During the season of the year, too, when she has no young ones to provide for, carrion of all kinds forms her principal food. In consequence of her greedy disposition, the kite is very easily trapped. From her habit of following the course of streams, and hunting along the shores of the loch in search of dead fish or drowned animals of any kind, one of the most successful ways of trapping the kite is to peg down the entrails of some animal in the shallow part of the water, and then to place the trap either on the shore immediately adjoining; or, what is often done, to form a small artificial promontory close to the bait, and to set the trap on this. The garbage catches the sharp eye of the bird, as she soars at a great height above it, and the clever trapper seldom fails in catching her in this manner.

The buzzard [1] is another of the hawk tribe which is gradually becoming rarer and rarer, and from the same cause. Like the kite, too, the buzzard is a carrion-feeding bird, and seldom kills anything but small birds, mice, or frogs, excepting during the breeding-season, when it is very destructive to game; at other times the buzzard lives an indolent, lazy life. After having satisfied her hunger, this bird will sit for hours perfectly motionless on some withered branch, or on a projecting corner of rock, whence she commands a good view of the surrounding country, and can easily detect the approach of danger. A cowardly bird, except when excited by hunger, she submits patiently to the attacks of the smaller birds, and flies from the magpie or jackdaw. Like the kite, the raven, the eagle, and all birds who feed much on carrion, the buzzard has a lofty flight when in search of food. Soaring high up in the air, and wheeling in circles, she appears to examine the surface of the land for miles and miles, in hopes of detecting some dead sheep or other carcass. The buzzard evinces little cunning in avoiding traps, and is easily caught. I have found their nests, containing from three to four large and nearly white eggs, in different situations; sometimes built on rocks, and at other times in the branches of a tree, at no great height from the ground. She sits close, and will allow the near approach of a passer-by before she leaves her eggs. Though she is one of the most ignoble of the hawk kind, I have a lingering affection for this bird, in consequence of her

---

[1] The buzzard (*Buteo vulgaris*).

being connected in my remembrances with the rocky burns and hanging woods of the most romantic glens in the Highlands, where I have frequently fallen in with her nest and young. In this part of the country the buzzard has become very rare, and is only seen as an occasional visitor.

MY PUGNACIOUS PEREGRINE

THE SPARROWHAWK

CHAPTER XI

The Hen-Harrier : Destructiveness to Game ; Female of ; Trapping—The Sparrowhawk : Courage of ; Ferocity ; Nest—The Kestrel : Utility of—The Merlin : Boldness—The Hobby—Increase of Small Birds.

IN the autumn my partridges suffer much from the hen-harrier.[1] As soon as the corn is cut this bird appears, and hunts the whole of the low country in the most determined and systematic manner. The hen-harrier, either on the hill-side or in the turnip-field, is a most destructive hunter. Flying at the height of only a few feet from the ground, he quarters the ground as regularly as an old pointer, crossing the field in every direction ; nor does he waste time in hunting useless ground, but tries turnip-field after turnip-field, and rushy field after rushy field, passing quickly over the more open ground, where he thinks his game is not so likely to be found. The moment he sees a

[1] The hen-harrier is fond of hunting about farm-yards, where it kills rats, etc. It also is a great frequenter of marshes, where it hunts later in the evening than any other hawk. Feeds on grouse, partridges, rats, reptiles. During summer the hen-harrier generally frequents the moors and high grounds, killing great numbers of grouse, etc. ; in the winter it hunts more in the lower part of the country. When hunting it flies low, and quarters the ground as carefully as an old pointer.—C. St. J.

bird, the hawk darts rapidly to a height of about twenty feet, hovers for a moment, and then comes down with unerring aim on his victim, striking dead with a single blow partridge or pheasant, grouse or black-cock, and showing a strength not to be expected from his light figure and slender though sharp talons.

I saw on a hill-side in Ross-shire a hen-harrier strike a heath hen. I instantly drove him away, but too late, as the head of the bird was cut as clean off by the single stroke as if done with a knife. On another day, when passing over the hill in the spring, I was attended by a hen-harrier for some time, who struck down and killed two hen grouse that I had put up. Both these birds I contrived to take from him; but a third grouse rose, and was killed and carried off over the brow of a hill before I could get up to him. There is no bird more difficult to shoot than this. Hunting always in the open country, though appearing intent on nothing but his game, the wary bird, with an instinctive knowledge of the range of shot, will keep always just out of reach, and frequently carry off before your very face the partridge you have flushed, and perhaps wounded.

There is a diversity of opinion whether the hawk commonly called the ringtail is the female of the hen-harrier. I have, however, no doubt at all on the subject. The ringtail is nothing more than the female or young bird. The male does not put on his blue and white plumage till he is a year old. I have frequently found the nest both on the mountain, where they build in a patch of rough heather, generally by the side of a burn, and also in a furze-bush. Though very destructive to grouse and other game, this bird has one redeeming quality, which is, that he is a most skilful rat-catcher. Skimming silently and rapidly through a rickyard, he seizes on any incautious rat who may be exposed to view; and from the habit this hawk has of hunting very late in the evening, many of these vermin fall to his share. Though of so small and light a frame, the hen-harrier strikes down a mallard without difficulty; and the marsh and swamp are his favourite hunting-grounds. Quick enough to catch a snipe, and strong enough to kill a mallard, nothing escapes him. Although so courageous in pursuit of game, he is a wild, untameable bird in captivity; and though I have sometimes endeavoured to tame one, I could never succeed in rendering him at all familiar. As he disdains to eat any animal not killed by himself, he is a very difficult bird to trap. The best chance of catching him is in what is called a pole-trap, placed on a high post in the middle of an open part of the country; for this hawk has (in common with many others) the habit of perching on upright railings and posts, particularly as in the open plains, where he principally hunts, there are but few trees, and he seldom perches on the ground. His flight is leisurely and slow when searching for game; but his dart, when he has discovered his prey, is inconceivably rapid and certain.

There is another most destructive kind of hawk who frequently pays us a visit—the sparrowhawk.[1] Not content with the partridges and other *feræ naturæ*, this bold little freebooter invades the poultry-yard rather too frequently. The hens scream, the ducks quack, and rush to the cover of the plantations; whilst the tame pigeons dart to and fro amongst the buildings, but in vain. The sparrowhawk darts like an arrow after one of the latter birds, and carries it off, though the pigeon is twice or three times his own weight. The woman who takes care of the poultry runs out, but is too late to see anything more than a cloud of white feathers, marking the place where the unfortunate pigeon was struck. Its remains are, however, generally found at some little distance; and when this is the case, the hawk is sure to be caught, as he invariably returns to what he has left, and my boys bring the robber to me in triumph before many days elapse. Sometimes he returns the same day to finish picking the bones of the bird, but often does not come back for two or three. In the meantime, whatever part of the pigeon he has left is pegged to the ground, and two or three rat-traps are set round it, into one of which he always contrives to step. When caught, instead of seeming frightened, he flies courageously at the hand put down to pick him up, and fights with beak and talons to the last. Occasionally, when standing still amongst the trees, or even when passing

---

[1] *Accipiter nisus.* In the remoter districts of the west of Scotland it is not nearly so numerous as the merlin or kestrel, owing to the lack of wooded localities, in which it delights. It is a great foe to partridges and domestic poultry. "The female sparrowhawk would be the game-preserver's worst enemy did it not vary its diet by an occasional wood-pigeon or some such heavy bird of little consequence" (Gray, p. 41).

the corner of the house, I have been startled by a sparrowhawk gliding rapidly past me. Once one came so close to me, that his wing actually brushed my arm; the hawk being in full pursuit of an unfortunate blackbird. On another occasion, a sparrowhawk pursued a pigeon through the drawing-room window, and out at the other end of the house through another window, and never slackened his pursuit, notwithstanding the clattering of the broken glass of the two windows they passed through. But the most extraordinary instance of impudence in this bird that I ever met with, was one day finding a sparrowhawk deliberately standing on a very large pouter-pigeon on the drawing-room floor, and plucking it, having entered in pursuit of the unfortunate bird through an open window, and killed him in the room.[1]

The sparrowhawk sometimes builds on rocks, and sometimes in trees. Like all rapacious birds, he is most destructive during the breeding-season. I have found a great quantity of remains of partridges, wood-pigeons, and small birds about their nests; though it has puzzled me to understand how so small a bird can convey a wood-pigeon to its young ones. There is more difference in size between the male and female sparrowhawk than between the different sexes of any other birds of the hawk kind, the cock bird being not nearly so large or powerful a bird as the hen. Supposing either male or female sparrowhawk to be killed during the time of incubation, the survivor immediately finds a new mate, who goes on with the duties of the lost bird, whatever stage of the business is being carried on at the time, whether sitting on the eggs or rearing the young.

The kestrel breeds commonly with us about the banks of the river, or in an old crow's nest.[2] This is a very beautifully marked hawk, and I believe does much more good than harm. Though occasionally depriving us of some of our lesser singing birds, this hawk feeds principally, and indeed almost wholly, on

---

[1] My own windows have more than once been broken by sparrowhawks pursuing pigeons and blackbirds from the shrubbery. On one occasion an unfortunate sparrowhawk thus broke its back in darting through the glass of my drawing-room window, yet when found some little time afterwards lying on the floor it fought vigorously with beak and talons and resisted every attempt to take it up or succour it. At another time I know of one breaking the glass of a nursery window and striking the bare arm of a little girl who was sitting close to the window. It probably mistook the child's arm for a small bird, dimly visible as it was through the glass.

[2] On rocks and rarely in trees.—C. St. J.

mice. Any person who knows a kestrel-hawk by sight must have constantly observed them hovering nearly stationary in the air, above a grass-field, watching for the exit from its hole of some unfortunate field-mouse. When feeding their young, a pair of kestrels destroy an immense number of these mischievous little quadrupeds, which are evidently the favourite food of these birds. Being convinced of their great utility in this respect, I never shoot at, or disturb a kestrel. It is impossible, however, to persuade a gamekeeper that any bird called a hawk can be harmless; much less can one persuade so opinionated and conceited a personage (as most keepers are) that a hawk can be useful; therefore the poor kestrel generally occupies a prominent place amongst the rows of bipeds and quadrupeds nailed on the kennel, or wherever else those trophies of his skill are exhibited. It is a timid and shy kind of hawk, and therefore very difficult to tame, never having an appearance of contentment or confidence in its master when kept in captivity.

Another beautiful little hawk is common here in the winter, the merlin.[1] This bird visits us about October, and leaves us in the spring. Scarcely larger than a thrush, the courageous little fellow glides with the rapidity of thought on blackbird or fieldfare, sometimes even on the partridges, and striking his game on the back of the head, kills it at a single blow. The merlin is a very bold bird, and seems afraid of nothing. I one day winged one as he was passing over my head at a great height. The little fellow, small as he was, flung himself on his back when I went to pick him up, and gave battle most furiously, darting out his talons (which are as sharp and hard as needles) at everything that approached him. We took him home, however, and I put him into the walled garden, where he lived for more than a year. He very soon became quite tame, and came on being called to receive his food, which consisted of birds, mice, etc. So fearless was he, that he flew instantly at

---

[1] The merlin breeds on the heather generally; sometimes in a tree. It has four eggs.—C. St. J.

The merlin is a regular summer migrant to the moors of South Yorkshire and North Derbyshire. These moors are the constant breeding-place of three species of hawk—the kestrel, the sparrowhawk, and the merlin. The kestrel hovers over the ground at a considerable height, and pounces down on a mouse, and occasionally a lizard or a young grouse. The sparrowhawk skims over hill-tops or hedges, or round rocks, and comes upon its prey unawares. The merlin, on the contrary, fairly flies it down. The merlin lays its eggs about the middle of May, so that the voracious young may be fed upon young grouse.—Seebohm, *Siberia in Europe,* p. 83.

the largest kind of sea-gull or crow that we gave him. When hungry, and no other food was at hand, he would attend the gardener when digging, and swallow the large earthworms as they were turned up. To my great regret, we found the little bird lying dead under the tree in which he usually roosted; and though I examined him carefully, I could not find out the cause of his death.

Although all these small hawks which frequent this country destroy a certain quantity of game, their principal food consists of thrushes, blackbirds, and other small birds. In the winter, when the greenfinches collect in large flocks on the stubble fields, I have frequently seen the merlin or sparrowhawk suddenly glide round the angle of some hedgerow or plantation, and taking up a bird from the middle of the flock, carry it off almost before his presence was observed by the rest of the greenfinches.

Sometimes two merlins hunt together, and, as it were, course a lark, or even swallow, in the air, the two hawks assisting each other in the most systematic manner. First one hawk chases the unfortunate bird for a short time, while his companion hovers quietly at hand; in a minute or so, the latter relieves his fellow-hunter, who in his turn rests. In this way they soon tire out the lark or swallow; and catching the poor bird in mid-air, one of the hawks flies away with him, leaving his companion to hunt alone till his return from feeding their young brood.

The hobby,[1] a beautiful little hawk, like a miniature peregrine falcon, is not very common here, though I have occasionally killed it. This kind of hawk leaves us before the winter. I have seen its nest in a fir or larch tree; but they seem to be very rare here. A strong courageous bird, the hobby attacks and preys on pigeons and partridges, though so much larger than himself.

Since the introduction of English traps and keepers, all birds of prey are gradually decreasing in this country, whilst blackbirds, thrushes, and other singing birds increase most rapidly. In the highland districts of Moray, where a few years back a blackbird or thrush was rather a rare bird, owing to the skill and perseverance of gamekeepers and vermin-trappers in extermi-

---

[1] The hobby (*Falco subbuteo*) is a regular summer migrant to temperate Europe and Asia, and still breeds in the British Islands. A few winter in South Europe, but most appear to migrate into Africa, occasionally straying as far as the Cape. Eastwards it winters in India and South China.—Seebohm, *Siberia in Europe*, p. 139.

nating their enemies, they now abound, devastating our fruit-gardens, but amply repaying all the mischief they do by enlivening every glade and grove with their joyous songs. This year (1846) the thrushes and blackbirds were in full voice in January, owing to the mildness of the winter; and I knew of a thrush who was sitting on eggs during the most severe storm of snow that we have had the whole season.

KESTRELS

THE OTTER IN HIS HAUNTS

CHAPTER XII

The Otter: Habits—Catching of—Shooting—Attachment to each other—Anecdotes—Fish killed by

HAVING lately seen the tracks of three or four otters[1] about the edge of the burn, I had some strong traps placed on a sandbank where they were in the nightly habit of landing. For

---

[1] In severe frosts, etc., the otter (*Lutra vulgaris*) catches and eats rabbits, hares, and any animal which it can surprise, or in some situations takes to the sea-shore, living on flounders, crabs, etc.; produces its young at different seasons of the year. —C. St. J.

some unknown reason of their own, they appeared to leave the water at this bank, and, after going round some alder bushes, to return again to the pool. We placed the traps with great care, fastening them strongly, and covering them with sand. Before setting the trap for an otter, both the hands of the person who sets it and the trap itself should be well washed and rubbed with sand, in order to take away the human scent as much as possible. After setting the trap, a small branch of a tree should be used to smooth the ground and obliterate all footmarks, and then dipping the branch in the water, the whole place should be well sprinkled, which generally does away with all marks of people having been about it. As otters invariably have some particular points at which they leave the water, it is easy to know where to place the trap. They do not, however, always haunt the same part of a stream, so the trapper must have some patience. After our traps had been set for two nights, we found, on going to them in the morning, that an otter had been caught, and by twisting the chain round the root of a tree had contrived to break it, and escape with the trap on its leg. I sent home for my retriever, who, from having been severely bitten by other otters, was very eager in pursuing them. We hunted up and down the burn for some time in vain; at last we found his track and that of the trap in the sand at a shallow place of the water. This encouraged us, and we renewed our search. At last, nearly a mile from where the trap had been set, the dog began to run up and down the bank, whining and showing evident symptoms of perceiving, or, as my old keeper called it, "feeling" the smell of the otter. He could not make out exactly where it was, till at last coming to a dead stop opposite a quantity of floating branches and roots that had collected at a turn of the water, he pointed for a moment, and then springing in, pulled out a large otter with the trap still on him. It was rather difficult to know whether the otter was bringing the dog, or the dog the otter, so vehemently did they fight and pull at each other; but we ran up, and soon put an end to the battle. The next morning I found another otter in the traps. Nothing could keep the dog from him; the moment he came within three hundred yards of the place he smelt him, and rushed off to attack him. A few nights afterwards, the moon being bright and the air quite still, my keeper determined to lay wait for the remaining otter.

His track showed that he was a very large one, and he seemed too cunning for the traps. The man's plan was to make himself a small hiding-place, opposite a shoal in the burn, where the otter must needs wade instead of swimming. We had come to the conviction from the tracks that the otters remained concealed during the daytime a considerable way up the water, and hunted down the burn during the night to where it joined the river.

It was a fine calm December night, with a full moon. The old man, wrapped in a plaid, and with a peculiar head-dress made of an old piece of drugget, which he always wore on occasions of this kind, took up his position at six o'clock. Before nine the otter was killed, having appeared, as he had calculated, on its way down to the river.

This is one of the surest ways of killing this animal when he frequents a river or brook which in parts is so shallow as to oblige the otter to show himself in his nightly travels. They appear to go a considerable distance, generally hunting down the stream, and returning up to their place of concealment before dawn. At certain places they seem to come to land every night, or, at any rate, every time that they pass that way. In solitary and undisturbed situations I have sometimes fallen in with the otter during the day. In a loch far on the hills, I have seen one raise itself half out of the water, take a steady look at me, and then sink gradually and quietly below the surface, appearing again at some distance, but next time showing only part of its head. At other times I have seen one floating down a stream, with no exertion of its own which could attract notice; but passing with the current, showing only the top of its head and its nose, with its tail floating near the surface, and waving to and fro as if quite independent of all restraint from its owner. If he fancies that he is observed on these occasions, down he sinks to the bottom, where he lies quietly as long as he can do without air; and when obliged to rise to breathe, he comes up close to the bank, or amongst weeds, with only his nose above water. If, however, the water is clear, and you persist in watching him, and by quickly approaching him, oblige him constantly to dive, the poor beast will at last in sheer despair crawl out on the bank, concealing himself in the best manner he can. But it takes some time to oblige him to do this.

Otters are very affectionate animals. If you shoot an old one who has young in the vicinity, they very soon appear searching anxiously for their mother; and if you kill the young ones, the parent will come boldly to the surface, and hover about the place till she is killed herself. When a pair of otters frequent a place, if one is killed, the other will hunt for its lost mate in the most persevering manner. If one is caught in a trap, the other remains all night near her, running round and round, in vain trying to get her away. Though usually so noiseless and quiet, on these occasions they make a great hubbub, blowing and snorting almost like a swimming horse.

Sometimes they lie all day on some small island or bank covered with rushes, ready to slip down into the water on the approach of danger. I was one day in August looking for young wild ducks in a swamp covered with rushes and grass, when my dog, who was running and splashing through the shallow water, suddenly stood still, sometimes whining as if caught in a trap, and then biting furiously at something in the water. I could not imagine what had happened to him, and he either would not or could not come to me when called, so I waded over to see what was the matter. I found a large otter firmly holding on by his powerful jaws to the dog's shoulder, and had he not had a good covering of curly hair, I believe the brute would have broken his leg, so severe was the bite: even when I came up, the otter seemed very little inclined to let go; but at last did so, and I shot him as he splashed away.

When one of these animals is surprised in an open place, he will for some time trust to being concealed, remaining flat on the ground, with his sharp little eyes, which are placed very high on the head, intently fixed on you. Like all other wild animals, he has an instinctive knowledge of how long he is unperceived, for the moment he sees that your eye is on him, he darts off, but not till then. During the winter many of the river and lake otters take to the coast,[1] travelling a long way for

---

[1] The otter is plentiful in some localities in the Hebrides, frequenting the sea-shore for the most part, until the salmon and sea trout begin to "run" in July, when it follows them up the streams, and frequents the fresh-water lochs. A forester in Harris showed me a small rock in Loch Resort where he once killed two at one shot. A shepherd in North Uist, on his own beat alone, had shot over seventy otters during a residence of twenty-five years.—"On the Mammalia of the Outer Hebrides," by J. Harvie-Brown, F.Z.S., *Proceedings of the Nat. Hist. Soc. of Glasgow*, 29th April 1879, p. 93.

this purpose, sometimes keeping the course of the streams, but occasionally going across the country. I have seen their tracks in places at a very great distance from water, where they evidently had been merely passing down to the sea.

When on the coast, they frequent the caves and broken masses of rock. The otters that live wholly on the coast grow very large. It is easy to turn them out of their holes with terriers, as long as you remain quiet and unobserved by the otter yourself. If he once has found out that you are waiting to receive him at the mouth of his hole, he will fight to the last rather than leave it. I have been told that they bolt more readily to a white-coloured dog than to any other. All courageous dogs who have been once entered at otters, hunt them with more eagerness and animosity than they do any other kind of vermin.

The otters here are very fond of searching the shallow pools of the sea at the mouth of the river for flounders, and I often find their tracks, where they have evidently been so employed. If surprised by the daylight appearing too soon to admit of their returning to their usual haunts, they will lie up in any broken bank, furze bush, or other place of concealment.

At some of the falls of the Findhorn, where the river runs so rapidly that they cannot stem it, they have to leave the water to go across the ground; and in these places they have regularly-beaten tracks. I was rather amused at an old woman living at Sluie, on the Findhorn, who, complaining of the hardness of the present times, when "a puir body couldna get a drop smuggled whisky, or *shot* a rae without his lordship's sportsman finding it out," added to her list of grievances that even the otters were nearly all gone, "puir beasties." "Well, but what good could the otters do you?" I asked her. "Good, your honour? why scarcely a morn came but they left a bonny grilse on the scarp down yonder, and the *vennison* was none the waur of the bit the puir beasts eat themselves." The people here call every eatable animal, fish, flesh, or fowl, venison, or as they pronounce it, "vennison." For instance they tell you that the snipes are "good vennison," or that the trout are not good "vennison" in the winter.

It seems that a few years ago, before the otters had been so much destroyed, the people on particular parts of the river were never at a loss for salmon, as the otters always take them ashore, and generally to the same bank or rock, and when the fish are plentiful, they only eat a small piece out of the shoulder of each, leaving the rest. The cottagers, aware of this, were in the habit of looking every morning for these remains.

THE OTTER'S ATTACK.

THE WEASEL'S VICTIM

CHAPTER XIII

Weasels—Ferrets: Fierceness of—Anecdotes—Food of Weasels—Manner of hunting for Prey—The Stoat: Change of Colour; Odour of; Food of; their catching Fish—Polecat—The Marten Cat: Habits; Trapping; Eating Fruit; Activity of; Different Species.

THE bloodthirstiness and ferocity of all the weasel tribe is perfectly wonderful. The proverb "*L'appétit vient en mangeant*" is well applied to these little animals. The more blood they spill, the more they long for, and are not content till every animal that they can get at is slain. A she-ferret, with a litter of young ones, contrived to get loose a few nights back, and instinctively made her way to the henhouse, accompanied by her six kittens, who were not nearly half grown, indeed their eyes were not quite open. Seven hens and a number of tame rabbits were killed before they were discovered; and every animal that they killed, notwithstanding its weight and size, was dragged to the hutch in which the ferrets were kept, and as they could not get their victims through the hole by which they had escaped themselves, a perfect heap of dead bodies was collected round their hutch. When I looked out of my window in the morning, I had the satisfaction of seeing four of the young ferrets, covered with blood, dragging a hen (which I had flattered myself was about to hatch a brood of young pheasants) across the yard which was between the henhouse and where these ferrets were kept; the remainder of them were assisting the old one in slaughtering some white rabbits. Their eagerness to escape again, and renew their bloody attacks, showed the excited state the little wretches were in, from this their first essay in killing.

In the same way the wild animals of the tribe must be wofully destructive when opportunity is afforded them. Sitting opposite a rabbit-hole, I one day saw a tiny weasel bring out four young rabbits one after the other, and carry, or rather drag them away one by one towards her own abode in a cairn of loose stones; and, a few days ago, I saw one bring three young landrails in as many minutes out of a field of high wheat. In fact, as long as she can find an animal to kill, so long will a weasel hunt, whether in want of food or not. I have frequently seen a weasel, small as he is, kill a full-grown rabbit. The latter is sometimes so frightened at the persevering ferocity of its little enemy, that it lies down and cries out before the weasel has come up. Occasionally these animals join in a company of six or eight, and hunt down rabbit or hare, giving tongue and tracking their unfortunate victim like a pack of beagles.

There is no doubt that in some degree they repay the damage done to game, by the number of rats and mice which they destroy (the latter being their favourite food). The weasel will take up its abode in a stack-yard, living on the mice and small birds that it catches for some time, and the farmer looks on it as a useful ally; till, some night, the mice begin to grow scarce, and then the chickens suffer. Eggs, fresh and rotten, are favourite dainties with the weasel.

I once witnessed a very curious feat of this active little animal. I saw a weasel hunting and prying about a stubble field in which were several corn-buntings flying about, and every now and then alighting to sing on the straggling thistles that rose above the stubble. Presently the little fellow disappeared at the foot of a thistle, and I imagined he had gone into a hole. I waited, however, to see what would happen, as, from the way he had been hunting about, he evidently had some mischief in his head. Soon a corn-bunting alighted on the very thistle near which the weasel had disappeared, and which was the highest in the field. The next moment I saw something spring up as quick as lightning, and disappear again along with the bird. I then thought it time to interfere, and found that the weasel had caught and killed the bunting, having, evidently guided by his instinct or observation, waited concealed at the foot of the plant where he had expected the bird to alight. A friend of mine, who was a great naturalist, assured me that, tracking a weasel in snow on the hill-side, he found where the animal had evidently sprung upon a grouse; and, on carrying on his observation, he had convinced himself that the bird had flown away with the quadruped, and had fallen to the ground about thirty yards off, where he found it with its throat cut; and the tracks of the weasel again appeared, as if he had come down with the bird, and having sucked its blood, had gone on his way, looking for a new victim.

The stoat is also very common here, and equally destructive and sanguinivorous—if I may use such a word. Being larger, too, he is more mischievous to game and poultry, and not so useful in killing mice. I often see the stoat hunting in the middle of an open field: its activity is so great that few dogs can catch it. When pursued, it dives into any rat's or mole's hole that lies in its way. I find that a sure mode of driving all animals of this kind out of a hole, is to smoke tobacco into it. They appear quite unable to stand the smell, and bolt out immediately in the face of dog or man, rather than put up with it. Tobacco-smoke will also bring a ferret out of a rabbit-hole, when everything else fails to do so. In winter the stoat changes its colour to the purest white, with the exception of the tip of the tail, which always remains black.[1] The animal is then very beautiful, with its shining black eyes and white body. The fur is very like that of the ermine, but is quite useless, owing to the peculiar odour of the animal, which can never be got rid of. It is worthy of note that the stoat does not emit this odour excepting when hunted or wounded.

[1] The weasel never turns white, but only the stoat.—C. St. J.

When I have shot one, killing it on the spot, before he has seen me, no smell is to be perceived. The same thing I have also observed when it has been caught in a large iron trap, which has killed it instantaneously, before there has been time for fear or struggling. When, however, I have had some chase after a stoat before shooting it, or have caught one alive in a trap, the stench of the little animal is insupportable,—and sticks to the skin, in spite of every attempt to get rid of it.

The attachment of the stoat and weasel to their young is very great. I chased a weasel into a hollow tree: she was carrying some animal in her mouth, and though I was on the very point of catching her before she got to her refuge, she would not drop it. I fancied that it was a newly-born rabbit that she was carrying off. I applied smoke to the hole, and out came the weasel again, still carrying the same burden. She ran towards a stone wall, but was met by a terrier half-way, who killed her, catching her with the greater facility in consequence of her obstinacy in carrying away what I still thought was some prey. On picking it up, however, I found that it was a young weasel, unable to run, which its mother was endeavouring to carry to a place of safety, her former hole in an adjoining field having been ploughed over. I cannot express my regret at the fate of this poor creature, when I saw that her death was caused wholly by her maternal affection. Notwithstanding the havoc which these animals make among my rabbits, nothing would have induced me to molest her, had I known what she was carrying.

The track of the stoat is very like that of a young rabbit, and may be easily mistaken for it. They travel over an amazing extent of ground in their nocturnal rambles, as their marks in the snow can testify. The edges of rivers and brooks seem their favourite hunting-places. By some means or other they manage to catch eels. I tracked a stoat from the edge of a ditch to its own hole, at the distance of several hundred yards. He had been carrying some heavy body, as I could plainly see by the marks in the snow; and this, on digging out the hole, I found to be an eel about nine inches long. No bait is better for all kinds of the weasel tribe than fish, which they seem to have a great liking for, and evidently feed upon whenever they inhabit a neighbourhood where they can procure them.

The polecat is now comparatively rare in this country, in consequence of the number of gamekeepers and vermin-trappers: they still, however, frequent the banks of the river, where they take shelter among the loose stones and rocks. There is no difference in appearance between the polecat and the brown ferret, which also partakes very frequently of the shyness of his wild relative, being much more apt to become cross-tempered and ready to return to a state of nature than the tamer white ferret. The polecat is extremely destructive—nothing comes amiss to it.[1] I found in the hole of a she-polecat, besides her young ones, three kittens that had been drowned at the distance of at least a quarter of a mile. Besides these, her larder contained the remains of hares, rabbits, and of an infinity of birds and several eels.

There was a wood-pigeon that had young ones nearly full-grown in an ivy-covered tree close to the window of my dressing-room. One morning I saw the old birds flying about in distress, but I could see no hawk or bird of prey about. Presently down fell one of the young birds, and in a moment afterwards the other young one also fell to the ground, both bleeding at the throat. I immediately loaded my gun, and had the satisfaction of shooting a large polecat, which came climbing down the tree and was just preparing to carry away one of the young pigeons.

Like the stoat, the polecat has a beautiful fur, rendered useless by the strong odour of the animal. Notwithstanding the quantity of game and other creatures killed by the polecat, he does not appear to be very quick on the ground, and must owe his success in hunting more to perseverance and cunning than to activity. Like the stoat and weasel, this animal is easily caught in box-traps, and is attracted in an extraordinary manner by the smell of musk, which they appear quite unable to resist.

In trapping all these small beasts with iron traps the bait should be suspended at some little height above the trap, to oblige them to jump up, and by so doing there is a better chance that, notwithstanding their light weight, the trap will be sprung.

Formerly I frequently mistook the track of the marten-cat for that of a hare, when seen in the snow. Its way of placing its feet, and of moving by a succession of leaps, is quite similar

---

[1] The polecat is very fond of fish, eels, etc.—C. St. J.

to that of the more harmless animal, which so often serves it for food. The general abode of the marten is in woods and rocky cairns. He is a very beautiful and graceful animal, with a fine fur quite devoid of all smell, but owing to its great agility it must be one of the most destructive of the tribe. When hunting, their movements are quick and full of elegance, the effect of which is much heightened by their brilliant black eyes and rich brown fur, contrasted with the orange-coloured mark on their throat and breast. The marten, when disturbed by dogs, climbs a tree with the agility of a squirrel,[1] and leaps from branch to branch, and from tree to tree. I used frequently to shoot them with my rifle on the tall pine-trees in Sutherland. In this part of the country they are now seldom seen. This animal is not wholly carnivorous, being very fond of some fruits —the strawberry and raspberry, for instance. I found in my garden in Inverness-shire that some animal came nightly to the raspberry-bushes; the track appeared like that of a rabbit or hare, but as I also saw that the animal climbed the bushes, I knew it could be neither of these. Out of curiosity, I set a trap for the marauder; the next morning, on going to look at it very early, I could see nothing on the spot where I had put my trap but a heap of leaves, some dry and some green; I was just going to move them with my hand, when I luckily discerned a pair of bright eyes peering sharply out of the leaves, and discovered that I had caught a large marten, who, finding that he could not escape, had collected all the leaves within his reach, and had quite concealed himself under them. The moment he found that he was discovered, he attacked me most courageously, as the marten always does, fighting to the last. I had other opportunities of satisfying myself that this animal is a great fruit-eater, feeding much on the wild raspberries, and even blackberries, that grow in the woods. Though generally inhabiting cairns of stones, the marten sometimes takes possession of some large bird's nest, and relining it, there brings up her young, which are remarkably pretty little creatures. I endeavoured once to rear and tame a litter of young martens which I found in an old crow's nest, and I believe I should have succeeded had not a terrier got at them in my absence, and revenged himself on them for the numerous bites he had felt from martens

---

[1] The squirrel is not uncommon near the Spey.—C. St. J.

and polecats in his different encounters with them. I have more frequently seen this animal abroad during the daytime than any of the other weasels.

I remember starting one amongst the long heather in the very midst of a pack of dogs of a Highland fox-hunter: though all the dogs, greyhounds, fox-hounds, and terriers, were immediately in full pursuit, the nimble little fellow escaped them all, jumping over one dog, under another, through the legs of a third, and finally getting off into a rocky cairn, whence he could not be ejected. "It's the evil speerit hersel'," said the old man, as, aiming a blow at the marten, he nearly broke the back of one of his best lurchers. Nor did he get over his annoyance at seeing his dogs so completely baffled, till after many a Gaelic curse at the beast and many a pinch of snuff. The marten-cat is accused by the shepherds of destroying a great many sheep. His manner of attack is said to be by seizing the unfortunate sheep by the nose, which he eats away, till the animal is either destroyed on the spot or dies a lingering death. I have been repeatedly told this by different Highland shepherds and others, and believe it to be a true accusation. They kill numbers of lambs, and when they take to poultry-killing, enter the henhouse fearlessly, committing immense havoc; in fact seldom leaving a single fowl alive—having the same propensity as the ferret for killing many more victims than they can consume.

The eagle is said to prey frequently on the marten-cat, but I never happened to witness an encounter between them; my tame eagle, however, always seemed to prefer them to any other food. I have no doubt that the eagle on its native mountain pounces on any living creature that it can conquer, and therefore must frequently kill both marten and wild cat, both which animals frequent the rocks and high ground where this bird hunts.

From the strength and suppleness of the marten, he cannot fall a very easy prey to any eagle of this country, and probably when pounced upon he does not die without a severe battle.

There are said to be two kinds of martens here,[1] the pine-

---

[1] Mr. J. Smith, keeper in Assynt, informs me that he believes there is only one kind of marten in that district, the yellow-breasted variety. About 1869 it was very numerous. Now it is all but exterminated, owing to the premium paid for shooting it, and the price its skin commands, viz. from ten to fifteen shillings. In the Shin valley, I heard of two or three pairs in 1879.

marten[1] and the beech-marten; the former having a yellow mark on the breast, and the latter a white one. I do not, however, believe that they are of a distinct species, but consider the variety of shade in the colour of the breast to be occasioned by difference of age, or to be merely accidental—having frequently killed them in the same woods with every intermediate shade, from yellow to white, on their breasts; the animals being perfectly alike in every other particular. The oldest-looking martens had generally a whiter mark than the others, but this rule did not apply to all.

[1] The pine-marten is still not uncommon in the wilder districts of Scotland, as in the Sutherland and Ross-shire deer forests, and also in the North of England, where it is occasionally killed by fox-hounds. When pursued, it generally makes for the rocks. It is very destructive to birds, lambs, and even sheep.

The late Mr. Blyth, it may be added, told Mr. Alston that his own investigations led him to agree with the latter's conclusion on the single species of marten now to be found in the British Isles.

A HUNTING BULLDOG

CHAPTER XIV

Anecdotes and Instinct of Dogs—Anecdotes of Retriever—Shepherds' Dogs—Sagacity—Dogs and Monkey—Bulldog—Anecdotes of Shooting a Stag—Treatment of Dogs.

So much has been written, and so many anecdotes told, of the cleverness and instinct of dogs, that I am almost afraid to add anything more on the subject, lest I should be thought tedious. Nevertheless I cannot refrain from relating one or two incidents illustrating the instinct, almost amounting to reason, that some of my canine acquaintances have evinced, and which have fallen under my own notice. Different dogs are differently endowed in this respect, but much also depends on their education, manner of living, etc. The dog that lives with his master constantly, sleeping before his fire, instead of in the kennel, and hearing and seeing all that passes, learns, if at all quick-witted, to understand not only the meaning of what he sees going on, but also, frequently in the most wonderful manner, all that is talked of. I have a favourite retriever, a black water-spaniel, who for many years has lived in the house, and been constantly with me; he understands and notices everything that is said, if it at all relates to himself or to the sporting plans for the day: if at breakfast-time I say, without addressing the dog himself, " Rover must stop at home to-day, I cannot take him out," he never attempts to follow me; if, on the contrary, I say, however quietly, " I shall take Rover with me to-day," the moment that breakfast is over he is all on the *qui vive*, following me wherever I go, evidently aware that he is to be allowed to accompany me. When left at home, he sits on the step of the front door, looking out for my return, occasionally howling and barking in an ill-tempered kind of voice; his great delight is going with me when I hunt the woods for roe and deer. I had some covers about five miles from the house, where we were accustomed to look for roe: we frequently made our plans over night while the dog was in the room. One day, for some reason, I did not take him: in consequence of this, invariably when he heard us at night forming our plan to beat the woods, Rover started alone very early in the morning, and met us up there. He always went to the cottage where we assembled, and sitting on a hillock in front of it, which commanded a view of the road by which we came, waited for us: when he saw us coming, he met us with a peculiar kind of grin on his face, expressing, as well as words could, his half doubt of being well received, in consequence of his having come without permission: the moment he saw that I was not angry with him, he threw off all his affectation of shyness, and barked and jumped upon me with the most grateful delight.

As he was very clever at finding deer, I often sent him with the beaters or hounds to assist, and he always plainly asked me on starting, whether he was to go with me to the pass, or to accompany the men. In the latter case, though a very exclusive dog in his company at other times, he would go with any one of the beaters, although a stranger to him, whom I told him to accompany, and he would look to that one man for orders as long as he was with him. I never lost a wounded roe when he was out, for once on the track he would stick to it.

the whole day if necessary, not fatiguing himself uselessly, but quietly and determinedly following it up. If the roe fell and he found it, he would return to me, and then lead me up to the animal, whatever the distance might be. With red-deer he was also most useful. The first time that he saw me kill a deer he was very much surprised; I was walking alone with him through some woods in Ross-shire, looking for woodcocks; I had killed two or three, when I saw such recent signs of deer, that I drew the shot from one barrel, and replaced it with ball. I then continued my walk. Before I had gone far, a fine barren hind sprang out of a thicket, and as she crossed a small hollow, going directly away from me, I fired at her, breaking her backbone with the bullet; of course she dropped immediately, and Rover, who was a short distance behind me, rushed forward in the direction of the shot, expecting to have to pick up a woodcock; but on coming up to the hind, who was struggling on the ground, he ran round her with a look of astonishment, and then came back to me with an expression in his face plainly saying, "What have you done now?—you have shot a cow or something." But on my explaining to him that the hind was fair game, he ran up to her and seized her by the throat like a bulldog. Ever afterwards he was peculiarly fond of deer-hunting, and became a great adept, and of great use. When I sent him to assist two or three hounds to start a roe—as soon as the hounds were on the scent, Rover always came back to me and waited at the pass: I could enumerate endless anecdotes of his clever feats in this way.

Though a most aristocratic dog in his usual habits, when staying with me in England once, he struck up an acquaintance with a ratcatcher and his curs, and used to assist in their business when he thought that nothing else was to be done, entering into their way of going on, watching motionless at the rats' holes when the ferrets were in, and as the ratcatcher told me, he was the best dog of them all, and always to be depended on for showing if a rat was in a hole, corn-stack, or elsewhere; never giving a false alarm, or failing to give a true one. The moment, however, that he saw me, he instantly cut his humble friends, and denied all acquaintance with them in the most comical manner.

The shepherds' dogs in the mountainous districts often

show the most wonderful instinct in assisting their masters, who, without their aid, would have but little command over a large flock of wild blackfaced sheep. It is a most interesting sight to see a clever dog turn a large flock of these sheep in whichever direction his master wishes, taking advantage of the ground, and making a wide sweep to get round the sheep without frightening them, till he gets beyond them, and then rushing barking from flank to flank of the flock, and bringing them all up in close array to the desired spot. When, too, the shepherd wishes to catch a particular sheep out of the flock, I have seen him point it out to the dog, who would instantly distinguish it from the rest, and follow it up till he caught it. Often I have seen the sheep rush into the middle of the flock, but the dog, though he must necessarily have lost sight of it amongst the rest, would immediately single it out again, and never leave the pursuit till he had the sheep prostrate, but unhurt, under his feet. I have been with a shepherd when he has consigned a certain part of his flock to a dog to be driven home, the man accompanying me farther on to the hill. On our return we invariably found that he had either given up his charge to the shepherd's wife or some other responsible person, or had driven them, unassisted, into the fold, lying down himself at the narrow entrance to keep them from getting out till his master came home. At other times I have seen a dog keeping watch on the hill on a flock of sheep, allowing them to feed all day, but always keeping sight of them, and bringing them home at a proper hour in the evening. In fact it is difficult to say what a shepherd's dog would not do to assist his master, who would be quite helpless without him in a Highland district.

Generally speaking, these Highland sheepdogs do not show much aptness in learning to do anything not connected in some way or other with sheep or cattle. They seem to have been brought into the world for this express purpose, and for no other.

They watch their master's small crop of oats or potatoes with great fidelity and keenness, keeping off all intruders in the shape of sheep, cattle, or horses. A shepherd once, to prove the quickness of his dog, which was lying before the fire in the house where we were talking, said to me, in the middle of a sentence concerning something else—"I'm thinking, Sir, the cow is in the potatoes." Though he purposely laid no stress on these words, and said them in a quiet, unconcerned tone of voice, the dog, which appeared to be asleep, immediately jumped up, and leaping through the open window, scrambled up the turf roof of the house, from which he could see the potato-field. He then (not seeing the cow there) ran and looked into the byre where she was, and finding that all was right, came back to the house. After a short time the shepherd said the same words again, and the dog repeated his look-out; but on the false alarm being a third time given, the dog got up, and wagging his tail, looked his master in the face with so comical an expression of interrogation, that we could not help laughing aloud at him, on which, with a slight growl, he laid himself down in his warm corner, with an offended air, and as if determined not to be made a fool of again.

Occasionally a poaching shepherd teaches his dog to be of great service in assisting him to kill game. I remember one of these men, who was in the habit of wiring hares, and though the keepers knew of his malpractices, they were for some time unable to catch him in the act, in consequence of his always placing his three dogs as vedettes in different directions, to warn him of the approach of any person. A herd-boy at the farm near my house puts his dog to a curious use. A great part of his flock are sent to pasture on the carse-ground across the river, and when the boy does not want to go across to count them and see that they are all right, deterred from doing so by the water being flooded, or from any other reason, he sends his dog to swim across and collect the sheep on the opposite bank, where he can see them all distinctly. Though there are other sheep on the carse belonging to different people, the dog only brings his own flock. After they are counted and pronounced to be all right by the boy, the dog swims back again to his master.

Were I to relate the numberless anecdotes of dogs that have been told me, I could fill a volume.

I am often amused by observing the difference of temper and disposition which is shown by my own dogs—as great a difference, indeed, as would be perceived among the same number of human beings.

Having for many years been a great collector of living *pets* there is always a vast number of these hangers-on about the house—some useful, some ornamental, and some neither the one nor the other.

Opposite one window of the room I am in at present are a monkey and five dogs basking in the sun, a bloodhound, a Skye terrier, a setter, a Russian poodle, and a young Newfoundland bitch, who is being educated as a retriever; they all live in great friendship with the monkey, who is now in the most absurd manner searching the poodle's coat for fleas, lifting up curl by curl, and examining the roots of the hair. Occasionally, if she thinks that she has pulled the hair, or lifted one of his legs rather too roughly, she looks the dog in the face with an inquiring expression to see if he is angry. The dog, however, seems rather to enjoy the operation, and showing no symptoms of displeasure, the monkey continues her search, and when she sees a flea catches it in the most active manner, looks at it for a moment, and then eats it with great relish. Having exhausted the game on the poodle, she jumps on the back of the bloodhound bitch, and having looked into her face to see how she will bear it, begins a new search, but finding nothing, goes off for a game at romps with the Newfoundland dog. While the bloodhound bitch, hearing the voice of one of the children, whom she has taken a particular fancy to, walks off to the nursery, the setter lies dozing and dreaming of grouse; while the little terrier sits with ears pricked up, listening to any distant sounds of dog or man that she may hear; occasionally she trots off on three legs to look at the back door of the house, for fear any rat-hunt or fun of that sort may take place without her being invited. Why do Highland terriers so often run on three legs? particularly when bent on any mischief? Is it to keep one in reserve in case of emergencies? I never had a Highland terrier who did not hop along constantly on three legs, keeping one of the hind-legs up as if to rest it.

The Skye terrier has a great deal of quiet intelligence, learning to watch his master's looks, and understand his meaning in a wonderful manner. Without the determined blind courage of the English bull terrier, this kind of dog shows great intrepidity in attacking vermin of all kinds, though often his courage is accompanied by a kind of shyness and reserve; but when once roused by being bit or scratched in its attacks on vermin, the Skye terrier fights to the last, and shows a great deal of cunning and generalship, as well as courage. Unless well entered, when young, however, they are very apt to be noisy, and yelp and bark more than fight. The terriers which I have had of this kind show some curious habits, unlike most other dogs. I have observed that when young they frequently make a kind of seat under a bush or hedge, where they will sit for hours together, crouched like a wild animal. Unlike other dogs too, they will eat (though not driven by hunger) almost anything that is given them, such as raw eggs, the bones and meat of wild ducks, or wood-pigeons, and other birds, that every other kind of dog, however hungry, rejects with disgust. In fact, in many particulars, their habits resemble those of wild animals; they always are excellent swimmers, taking the water quietly and fearlessly when very young. In tracking wounded deer I have occasionally seen a Skye terrier of very great use, leading his master quietly, and with great precision, up to the place where the deer had dropped, or had concealed himself; appearing too to be acting more for the benefit of his master, and to show the game, than for his own amusement. I have no doubt that a clever Skye terrier would in many cases get the sportsman a second shot at a wounded deer with more certainty than almost any other kind of dog. Indeed, for this kind of work, a quiet though slow dog often is of more use than the best deer-hound. I at one time had an English bull-dog, which accompanied me constantly in deer-stalking; he learned to crouch and creep up to the deer with me, never showing himself, and seeming to understand perfectly what I wished him to do. When necessary I could leave him for hours together, lying alone on the hill, when he would never stir till called by me. If a deer was wounded, he would follow the track with untiring perseverance, distinguishing the scent of the wounded animal, and singling it out from the rest, never making a mistake in this respect; he would also follow the stag till he brought him to bay, when, with great address in avoiding the horns, he would rush in and seize him either by the throat or the ear, holding on till I came up, or, as he once did, strangling the animal, and then coming back to show me where he had left it.

In driving some woods one day in Ross-shire, a fine stag broke into a wide opening; two or three sportsmen were stationed at some distance above me; as the deer passed, I saw the light puffs of smoke, and heard the crack of their rifles as they fired. At every shot the poor animal doubled with the most extraordinary bounds; he tried to turn back to the cover from which he had been driven, but the shouts of the beaters deterred him, and after stopping for a moment to deliberate, he came back fully determined to cross the opening, in order to gain the shelter of some large woods beyond it. He was galloping across it, when crack went another rifle, the ball striking with a splash into a small pool of water close to him, this turned him towards me, and down he came in my direction as hard as he could gallop; he appeared to be coming directly at me: just as he was about a hundred yards from me, a shout from the beaters, who were coming in view, turned him again, and he passed me, going *ventre à terre*, with his head up and his horns back over his shoulders, giving me a good broadside shot; I fired, and he reeled, turning half round. Bang went my other barrel, and the stag rolled over like a rabbit, with a force and crash that seemed as if it would have broken every bone in his body. Up he got again, and went off, apparently as sound as ever, into the large wood, passing close to a sportsman who was loading; when in the wood, we saw him halt for a moment on a hillock and take a good steady look at us all, who were lost in astonishment at his escape after having been so fairly upset. He then went off at a steady swinging gallop, and we heard him long after he was out of view crashing through the dry branches of the young fir-trees. "Bring the dog," was the cry, and a very large animal, something between a mastiff and a St. Bernard, was brought; the dog went off for a little while, barking and making a great noise, but after rushing up against half a dozen trees, and tumbling over amongst the hidden stones, he came back limping and unwilling to renew the hunt. I had left my bulldog with a servant at a point of the wood some distance off, and I proposed sending for him; one of the sportsmen, who had never seen him engaged in this kind of duty, sarcastically said, "What, *that* dog who followed us to-day, as we rode up? He can be no use; he looks more fit to kill cats or pin a bull." Our host, however, who was better acquainted with his merits, thought otherwise; and when the bulldog came wagging his tail and jumping up on me, I took him to the track and sent him upon it; down went his nose and away he went as hard as he could go, and quite silently. The wood was so close and thick that we could not keep him in sight, so I proposed that we should commence our next beat, as the dog would find me wherever I was, and the strangers did not seem much to expect any success in getting the wounded stag. During the following beat we saw the dog for a moment or two pass an opening, and the next instant two deer came out from the thicket into which he had gone. "He is on the wrong scent, after all," said the shooter who stood next to me. "Wait, and we will see," was my answer.

We had finished this beat and were consulting what to do, when the dog appeared in the middle of us, appearing very well satisfied with himself though covered with blood, and with an ugly tear in his skin all along one side. "Ah!" said some one, "he has got beaten off by the deer." Looking at him, I saw that most of the blood was not his own, the wound not being at all deep; I also knew that once having had hold of the deer, he would not have let go as long as he had life in him. "Where is he, old boy? take us to him," said I; the dog, perfectly understanding me, looked up in my face, and set off slowly with a whine of delight. He led us through a great extent of wood, stopping every now and then that we might keep up with him; at last he came to the foot of a rock where the stag was lying quite dead with his throat torn open, and marks of a goodly struggle all round the place; a fine deer he was too, and much praise did the dog get for his courage and skill: I believe I could have sold him on the spot at any price which I had chosen to ask, but the dog and I were too old friends to part, having passed many years together, both in London, where he lived with my horses and used to run with my cab, occasionally taking a passing fight with a cat; and also in the country, where he had also accompanied me in many a long and solitary ramble over mountain and valley.

In choosing a young dog for a retriever, it is a great point to fix upon one whose ancestors have been in the same line of business. Skill and inclination to become a good retriever are hereditary, and one come of good parents scarcely requires any breaking, taking to it naturally as soon as he can run about. It is almost impossible to make some dogs useful in this way, no teaching will do it unless there be a natural inclination—a first-rate retriever *nascitur non fit*. You may break almost any dog to carry a rabbit or bird, but it is a different thing entirely to retrieve satisfactorily, or to be uniformly correct in distinguishing and sticking to the scent of the animal which is wounded.

In the same way pointing is hereditary in pointers and setters, and puppies of a good breed, and of a well-educated ancestry, take to pointing at game as naturally as to eating their food,—and not only do they, of their own accord, point steadily, but also back each other, quarter their ground regularly, and in fact instinctively follow the example of their high-bred and well-brought-up ancestors. For my own part, I think it quite a superfluous trouble crossing a good breed of pointers with fox-hound, or any other kind of dog, by way of adding speed and strength,—you lose more than you gain, by giving at the same time hard-headedness and obstinacy. It is much better, if you fancy your breed of pointers or setters to be growing small or degenerate, to cross them with some different family of pointers or setters of stronger or faster make, of which you will be sure to find plenty with very little trouble. It is a great point in all dogs to allow them to be as much at liberty as possible; no animal kept shut up in a kennel or place of confinement can have the same use of his senses as one which is allowed to be at large to gain opportunities of exerting his powers of observation and increase his knowledge in the ways of the world. Dogs which are allowed to be always loose are very seldom mischievous and troublesome, it is only those which are kept too long shut up and in solitude that rush into mischief the moment they are at liberty; of course it is necessary to keep dogs confined to a certain extent, but my rule is to imprison them as little as possible. Mine, therefore, seldom are troublesome, but live at peace and friendship with numerous other animals about the house and grounds, although many of those animals are their natural enemies and objects of chase: dogs, Shetland ponies, cats, tame rabbits, wild ducks, sheldrakes, pigeons, etc., all associate together and feed out of the same hand; and the only one of my pets whose inclination to slaughter I cannot subdue, is a peregrine falcon, which never loses an opportunity of killing any duck or hen that may venture within his reach. Even the wild partridges and woodpigeons, which frequently feed with the poultry, are left unmolested by the dogs. The terrier, who is constantly at warfare with cats and rabbits in a state of nature, leaves those about the house in perfect peace; while the wildest of all wild fowl, the common mallards and sheldrakes, eat corn from the hand of the "hen-wife."

Though naturally all men are carnivorous, and therefore animals of prey, and inclined by nature to hunt and destroy other creatures, and although I share in this our natural instinct to a great extent, I have far more pleasure in seeing these different animals enjoying themselves about me, and in observing their different habits, than I have in hunting down and destroying them.

MY PETS

WOOD-PIGEONS

CHAPTER XV

Increase of Wood-Pigeons and other Birds—Service to the farmer of these Birds—Tame Wood-Pigeons: Food of—The Turtle-Dove—Blue Rock-Pigeons: Caves where they breed—Shooting at the Rocks near Cromarty.

OWING to the decrease of vermin, that is, of all the carnivorous birds and beasts of the country, there is a proportionate increase in the numbers of the different living creatures on which they preyed. I do not here allude to game only, but to all the other *feræ naturæ* of the district. Wood-pigeons, blackbirds, thrushes, and all the smaller birds increase yearly in consequence of the destruction of their natural enemies. The wood-pigeon [1] in particular has multiplied to a great extent. The farmers complain constantly to me of the mischief done by these birds, whom I cannot defend by giving them the credit of atoning for their consumption of corn by an equal or greater consumption of grubs and other noxious insects, as they feed wholly on seeds and vegetables. An agricultural friend of mine near this place, who had yielded with a tolerably good grace to my arguments in favour of the rook, pointed out to me the other day (March 6th) an immense flock of wood-pigeons busily at work on a field of young clover which had been under barley the last season. "There," he said, "you constantly say that every bird does more good than harm; what good are those birds doing to my young clover?" On this, in furtherance of my favourite axiom, that *every wild animal is of some service to us*, I determined to shoot some of the wood-pigeons, that I might see what they actually were feeding on; for I did not at all fall into my friend's idea that they were grazing on his clover. By watching in their line of flight from the field to the woods, and sending a man round to drive them off the clover, I managed to kill eight of the birds as they flew over my head. I took them to his house, and we opened their crops to see what they contained. Every pigeon's crop was as full as it could possibly be of the seeds of two of the worst weeds in the country, the wild mustard and the ragweed, which they had found remaining on the surface of the ground, these plants ripening and dropping their seeds before the corn is cut. Now no amount of human labour and search could have collected on the same ground, at that time of the year, as much of these seeds as was consumed by each of these five or six hundred wood-pigeons daily, for two or three weeks together. Indeed, during the whole of the summer and spring, and a considerable part of the winter, all pigeons must feed entirely on the seeds of different wild plants, as no grain is to be obtained by these soft-billed birds excepting immediately

---

[1] *C. palumbus* (wood-pigeon or ring-dove) feeds on small potatoes.—C. St. J.
Very abundant in cultivated districts, yet "its first appearance is an event actually within the recollection of old people now living in the county (East Lothian) in which the species is most abundant. About eighty years ago it was quite unknown there. The introduction of the clovers and turnip effected this increase." From December 1862 to 6th June 1870, 130,440 of these birds were killed under the auspices of the United East Lothian Agricultural Society, yet no perceptible diminution of the nuisance has taken place. Of course the native birds are largely reinforced by migratory flocks every winter. It is very injurious to the farmer from the amount of grain which it eats (Gray, p. 213).

after the sowing-time, and when the corn is nearly ripe, or for a short time after it is cut. Certainly I can enter into the feelings of a farmer who sees a flock of hundreds of these birds alighting on a field of standing wheat or devouring the newly-sown oats. Seeing them so employed must for the moment make him forget the utility they are of at other times. For my own part, I never shoot at a wood-pigeon near my house, nor do I ever kill one without a feeling of regret, so much do I like to hear their note in the spring and summer mornings. The first decisive symptom of the approach of spring and fine weather is the cooing of the wood-pigeon. Where not molested, they are very fond of building their nest in the immediate vicinity of a house. Shy as they are at all other times of the year, no bird sits closer on her eggs or breeds nearer to the abode of man than the wood-pigeon. There are always several nests close to my windows, and frequently immediately over some walk, where the birds sit in conscious security, within five or six feet of the passer-by; and there are generally a pair or two that feed with the chickens, knowing the call of the woman who takes care of the poultry as well as the tame birds do.

I have frequently attempted to tame young wood-pigeons, taking them at a very early age from the nest. They generally become tolerably familiar till the first moult; but as soon as they acquire strength of plumage and wing, they have invariably left me, except in one instance which occurred two years ago. I put some wood-pigeons' eggs under a tame pigeon of my children's, taking away the eggs on which she was sitting at the time. Only one of the young birds grew up, and it became perfectly tame. It remained with its foster parents, flying in and out of their house, and coming with them to be fed at the windows. After it had grown up, and the cares of a new nest made the old birds drive it out of their company, the wood-pigeon became still tamer, always coming at breakfast-time or whenever he was called to the window-sill, where he would remain as long as he was noticed, cooing and strutting up and down as if to challenge attention to his beautiful plumage.

However, like all pets, this poor bird came to an untimely end, being struck down and killed by a hen-harrier. I never on any other occasion saw a wood-pigeon remain perfectly tame, if left at liberty; and if they are entirely confined, they seldom acquire their full beauty of feather. The bird seems to have a natural shyness and wildness which prevent its ever becoming domesticated like the common blue rock-pigeon.

It is very difficult to approach wood-pigeons when feeding in the fields. They keep in the most open and exposed places, and allow no enemy to come near them. It is amusing to watch a large flock of these birds while searching the ground for grain. They walk in a compact body, and in order that all may fare alike, the hindmost rank every now and then fly over the heads of their companions to the front, where they keep the best place for a minute or two, till those now in the rear take their place in the same manner. They keep up this kind of fair play during the whole time of feeding. Almost every kind of seed is eaten by them, and the farmers accuse them of destroying their turnips in severe snow and frost. They feed also on fruit of all kinds, both the wild berries, such as mountain-ash, ivy, etc., and also upon almost all garden fruits that are not too large to be swallowed. Numbers of them come every evening to my cherry-trees, where they fearlessly swallow as many cherries as they can hold, although the gardener may be at work close at hand. Strawberries also are occasionally laid waste by them; and in the winter and early spring they devour the young cabbage and lettuce-plants. Where acorns are plentiful, the wood-pigeons seem to prefer them to anything else; and the quantity they manage to stow away in their crop is perfectly astonishing.

There are many months of the year, however, during which they are compelled, *nolentes volentes*, to feed wholly on the seeds of wild plants, thereby saving the farmers an infinity of trouble in weeding and cleaning their lands. The wood-pigeons breed here in great numbers, the large fir-woods and ivy-covered banks of the river affording them plenty of shelter. Their greatest enemy in the breeding-season is the hooded crow, which is constantly searching for their eggs, and from their white colour, and the simplicity of the nest, he can distinguish them at a great distance off. The sparrowhawk, too, frequently carries off the young birds, when nearly ready to fly, taking them out of the nest. It is a curious fact, but one I have very often observed, that this hawk, though I have seen him in the vicinity of the wood-pigeon's nest, and have no doubt that he has known of the young birds in it, never carries them off till they have attained to a good size, watching their daily growth till he thinks them fit to be killed.

In game-preserves wood-pigeons are certainly of some use, both in affording to vermin a more conspicuous and more favourite food than even partridge or pheasant, and in taking the attention of the larger hawks from the game. But he also does good service in giving notice of the approach of any danger, loudly flapping his wings as he flies off the trees on the first alarm. And at night no bird is so watchful. I have frequently attempted to approach the trees where the wood-pigeons were roosting; but even in the darkest nights these birds would take the alarm, affording in this respect a great contrast to the pheasant. The poor wood-pigeon has no defence against its enemies excepting its watchful and never-sleeping timidity, not being able to do battle against even the smallest of its numerous persecutors.

Though the turtle-dove never breeds here, and is supposed never to visit this part of the country, I have twice seen a pair about my house, both times towards the end of autumn. Last year a pair remained for about three weeks here, from the middle of October to the beginning of November, when they disappeared; probably returning southwards, not being nearly so hardy a bird as the wood-pigeon. Besides the wood-pigeon, we have considerable numbers of the little blue rock-pigeon, breeding along the caves and rocks of the coast, and feeding inland in large flocks. On the opposite coast of Ross-shire and Cromarty, very great numbers are found during the whole year. The caves there are much more extensive, and the rocks less easy of access, than they are along our coast by Burghead, Gordonston, etc.; the rock-pigeons therefore make those rocks their headquarters.

Being at Cromarty early in last June, I made an excursion along the rocks, for the double purpose of seeing the coast, which is peculiarly bold and magnificent on the Ross-shire side of the Cromarty Ferry, and also of shooting some pigeons[1] and other birds which bred in the caves and cliffs.

---

[1] The rock-pigeon (*C. livia*) is very abundant over the coast-line of the west of Scotland, especially in the numerous caverns, such as those at the Haskan Rocks, Mull, Staffa, etc. They lay two eggs, and have several broods in the year (Gray, p. 220).

Having hired a boat and crew, we started from Cromarty at the first of the ebb on a bright calm day, with the little wind that there was coming from the west. If the slightest east wind comes on, the roll of the sea from the German Ocean is so heavy on these rocks that it is impossible to approach them. This is also the case for some days after an east wind has been blowing, as there still remains a considerable swell. On nearing the west end of the rocks, which are several hundred feet high, we disturbed a good many cormorants, who were resting on some points of the cliff, and basking with open wings in the morning sun. Some parts of the rocks were quite white with the dung of these birds. In the ivy-covered recesses, far up, were every here and there a pair of small hawks, and rabbits hopping about high over our heads, along narrow paths on the face of the rock. I shot a rabbit at a great height with a rifle, and he came tumbling over and over, till he finally fell right into a hawk's nest, to the great astonishment of the young birds. Innumerable jackdaws breed in every crevice. As we rowed farther on, we came opposite a large cave, which the boatmen told me was a great place of resort for the pigeons. So, stopping our course, the men shouted, and out came a large flock of these birds, flying directly over our heads. I killed two or three, and the rest flew on, winding round the angles and headlands of the coast with inconceivable rapidity. Having picked up the birds, I landed with great difficulty on the rocks, and making my way over the slippery seaweed, got into the cave, which extended some distance under the cliffs. There were several pigeons' nests, though none that I could get at; but I shot a couple of young ones that had left the nest. The reverberation that succeeded the report of the gun in the arched cave nearly deafened me.

Soon afterwards we landed at another point; and here, following the example of one of my crew, I crept through a small aperture on my hands and knees, which led into a large and nearly dark cave, said to be the abode of otters. Before I could set fire to some dry fir-roots, which we brought with us, my dog was barking furiously, some distance within the cave. We got our light and went to examine what he had. By the tracks, he had evidently come on an otter, which had made his escape into a small hole that seemed to go into the very heart of the rocks, and from which we had no chance of extracting him. This cave was too damp for the birds, but was much marked with the footprints of otters. Though the entry was so small, the cave itself was both lofty and extensive.

As we floated along the coast, stopping at the mouths of several caves, and occasionally landing, we put up several large flocks of pigeons, and here and there cormorants and other sea-birds. On one shelf of the rocks, far up above the sea, was the nest of the raven. It was once inhabited by a pair of eagles, but is now quietly tenanted by the raven. These birds had flown; but both young and old were flying about the tops of the cliff, croaking and playing fantastic antics, as if in great astonishment at our appearance; for I fancy that they have very few visitants here. I tried a shot at one with a rifle-ball, but only splintered the rock at his feet.

Some of the caves were of great extent, and very full of pigeons, old and young, several of which I killed. The birds were nearly all blue; here and there a sandy-coloured one, but no other variety. Having made our way a considerable distance along the coast, and the tide being now quite out, we landed on a green spot of grass that stretched down between the rocks to the water's edge. Above our heads, and in every direction, were heron-nests; some built in the clusters of ivy, and others on the bare shelves of rocks. The young ones were full grown, but still in the nests, standing upright and looking gravely at us. Though I thought it a shame to make any of them orphans, I took the opportunity of killing three fine old male herons, whose black feathers I coveted much for my salmon-flies; sitting quietly at the foot of the rocks, I could distinctly see which birds were well supplied with these feathers, as they flew in to feed their young over my head. The feathers that are so useful in fly-dressing are the black drooping feathers on the breast of the cock heron: neither the young bird nor the hen bird has them. While resting my men here, I sent rifle-balls through three of the herons, each of whom afforded me a goodly supply of feathers.

Looking with my glass to the opposite coast of the firth, I could distinctly see the long range of sandhills between Nairn and the Bay of Findhorn, and could distinguish many familiar points and nooks. While resting here, too, a large seal appeared not above a hundred and fifty yards out at sea, watching us with great attention, but would not come within sure range of my rifle. As we returned homewards, the pigeons were in great numbers flying into the caves to feed their young. A pair of peregrine falcons also passed along, on their way to a rock where they breed, farther eastwards than we had been.

We saw too a flock of goats winding along the most inaccessible-looking parts of the cliff; and now and then the old patriarchal-looking leader would stop to peer at us as we passed below him, and when he saw that we had no hostile intention towards his flock, he led them on again, stopping here and there to nibble at the scanty herbage that was to be found in the clefts of the rocks. In one place where we landed, my dog started an old goat and a pair of kids, who dashed immediately at what appeared to be a perpendicular face of rock, but on which they contrived to keep their footing in a way that quite puzzled me. The old goat at one time alighted on a point of the rock where she had to stand with her four feet on a spot not bigger than my hand, where she stood for a minute or two seemingly quite at a loss which way to go, till her eye caught some (to me invisible) projections of the stone, up which she bounded, looking anxiously at her young, who, however, seemed quite capable of following her footsteps wherever she chose to lead them. We caught sight also of a badger, as he scuffled along a shelf of rock and hurried into his hole.

As the evening advanced, the cormorants kept coming in to their roosting-places in great numbers, and I shot several of them. We saw a good many seals as we approached the stake-nets near the ferry, but did not get any shots at them; and at one place two otters were playing about in the water near the rocks, but they also took good care to disappear before we came within reach of them; and as I wished to get back to Cromarty before it was late, I would not stop to wait for their reappearance. I was much pleased on the whole with my day's excursion—the beautiful scenery of the rocks, with the harbour of Cromarty, and the distant hills of Ross-shire and Inverness-shire, forming altogether as magnificent and varied a view as I have ever seen.

On an excursion along these same rocks I was once nearly drowned. I had just killed a pigeon that had dropped in the water in a recess between the rocks. We rowed in after it and just as I was leaning over the bow of the boat to pick it up, a rolling swell of the sea lifted the boat nearly upright, grating her keel on the edge of the rock. I was hoisted with the bow of the boat into the air, and holding on looked round to see what had happened, the day being perfectly calm; the boatmen were pale with fright as we appeared for a moment balanced between life and death, the chances rather in favour of the latter. The same wave, however, as it receded, took us twenty or thirty yards out to sea, and the men immediately rowed as hard as they could to get a good offing. The wave that had nearly upset us was the forerunner of a heavy swell and wind from the east, which was coming on unobserved by us, for we had been wholly intent on our sport. I never could understand how our boat could have righted again after the position she was in for a few moments. The face of the rocks was too perpendicular at the place to admit of our making good a landing had we been upset. Once away from the rocks we were safe enough, and rigging out a couple of strong lines with large white flies, we caught as many fish of different kinds as we could pull in during our way over to Cromarty. A large gull made two swoops at one of the flies, and had not a fish forestalled him, we should probably have hooked him also.[1] I do not know a day's sport more amusing than one along these rocks on a fine summer day, what with the variety of birds and the beauty and grandeur of the scenery, taking good care, however, to avoid the rocks when there is the least wind or swell from the east or north.

[1] My friend the late E. R. Alston, while fly-fishing for trout in Loch Assynt in 1877, did actually hook a large gull. One of the same pair which was nesting on a rock in that loch pestered me the following year on drawing near its rock, and, had I wished, I could probably have taken it with my artificial flies.

ACROSS CROMARTY BAY

WILD DUCK

CHAPTER XVI

Wild Ducks: Edible kinds of—Breeding-places of Mallards—Change of Plumage—Shooting—Feeding-places—Half-bred Wild Ducks—*Anas glacialis*—*Anas clangula*: Habits of—Teeth of Goosander—Cormorants—Anecdotes.

A FEW years ago I used to see a great many scaup ducks in the pools and burns near the coast, but now it is very seldom that I meet with a single bird of this kind; the last which I killed here was in the month of July. This is one of the few ducks frequenting the shore which has not a rank or fishy flavour:[1] out of the numerous varieties of birds of the duck kind, I can only enumerate four that are really good eating, namely, the common mallard, the widgeon, the teal, and the scaup duck.

[1] This opinion differs from that generally entertained, for the scaup is regarded by most persons as unfit for the table.

The best of these is the mallard: with us, they breed principally about the most lonely lochs and pools in the hills; sometimes I have seen these birds during the breeding-season very far up among the hills: a few hatch and rear their young about the rough ground and mosses near the sea, but these get fewer and fewer every year, in consequence of the increase of draining and clearing which goes on in all the swamps and wild grounds.

Some few breed in furze-bushes and quiet corners near the mouth of the river, and may be seen in some rushy pool, accompanied by a brood of young ones. Though so wild a bird, they sit close, allowing people to pass very near to them without moving. When they leave their nest, the eggs are always carefully concealed, so that a careless observer would never suppose that the heap of dried leaves and grass that he sees under a bush covers twelve or thirteen duck's eggs.

Occasionally a wild duck fixes on a most unlikely place to build her nest in; for instance, in a cleft of a rock, where you would rather expect to find a pigeon or jackdaw building, and I once, when fishing in a quiet brook in England, saw a wild duck fly out of an old pollard oak-tree. My curiosity being excited by seeing the bird in so unusual a place, I examined the tree, and found that she had a nest built of sticks and grass, containing six eggs, placed at the junction of the branches and the main stem. I do not know how she would have managed to get her young ones safely out of it when hatched, for on carefully measuring the height, I found that the nest was exactly fifteen feet from the ground.

As soon as hatched, the young ones take to the water, and it is very amusing to see the activity and quickness which the little fellows display in catching insects and flies as they skim along the surface of the water, led on by the parent bird, who takes the greatest care of them, bustling about with all the hurry and importance of a barn-yard hen. Presently she gives a low warning quack, as a hawk or carrion crow passes in a suspicious manner over them. One cry is enough, away all the little ones dart into the rushes, screaming and fluttering, while the old bird, with head flat on the water and upturned eye, slowly follows them, but not until she sees them all out of danger. After a short time, if the enemy has disappeared, the old bird peers cautiously from her covert, and if she makes up her mind that all is safe, she calls forth her offspring again, to feed and sport in the open water.

The young birds do not fly till they are quite full grown. I have observed that, as soon as ever the inner side of the wing is fully clothed, they take to flying; their bones, which before this time were more like gristle than anything else, quickly hardening, and giving the bird full power and use of its pinions. The old bird then leads them forth at night to the most distant feeding-places, either to the grass meadows where they search for snails or worms, or to the splashy swamps, where they dabble about all night, collecting the different insects and young frogs that abound in these places. As the corn ripens, they fly to the oat-fields in the dusk of the evening, preferring this grain and peas to any other. They are now in good order and easily shot, as they come regularly to the same fields every night. As soon as they have satisfied their hunger, they go to some favourite pool, where they drink and wash themselves. After this, they repair, before dawn, to their resting-place for the day, generally some large piece of water, where they can float quietly out of reach of all danger. In October, the drakes have acquired their splendid plumage, which they cast off in the spring, at that time changing their gay feathers for a more sombre brown, resembling the plumage of the female bird, but darker. During the time that they are clothed in this grave dress, the drakes keep in flocks together, and show themselves but little, appearing to keep as much out of observation as possible. During the actual time of their spring moulting, the drakes are for some days so helpless that I have frequently seen a dog catch them. The same thing occurs with the few wild geese that breed in the north of Scotland. With regard to shooting wild ducks, I am no advocate or follower of the punt and swivel system. I can see little amusement in taking a long shot at *the sound* of feeding water-fowl, killing and maiming you know not what; nor am I addicted to punting myself in a flat boat over half-frozen mud, and waiting for hours together for the chance of a sweeping shot. There may be great sport in this kind of proceeding, but I cannot discover it. I much prefer the more active and independent amusement of taking my chance with a common gun, meeting the birds on their way to and from their feeding or resting places, and observing and taking note of their different habits and ways of getting their living.

No rule can be laid down for wild-fowl shooting; what succeeds in one place fails in another. The best plan, in whatever district the sportsman is located, is to take note where the birds feed, where they rest in the daytime, and where they take shelter in heavy winds. By observing these different things, it is always easy enough to procure a few wild ducks. On the coast, the birds change their locality with the ebb and flow of the tide, generally feeding with the ebb, and resting with the flow. I believe that about the best wild-fowl shooting in the kingdom is in the Cromarty Firth, where thousands of birds of every variety pass the winter, feeding on the long sea-grass, and passing backwards and forwards constantly at every turn of the tide. I have here often killed wild ducks by moonlight. It is an interesting walk in the bright clear winter nights, to go round by the shore, listening to the various calls of the birds, the constant quack of the mallard, the shrill whistle of the widgeon, the low croaking note of the teal, and the fine bugle voice of the wild swan, varied every now and then by the loud whistling of a startled curlew, or oyster-catcher. The mallard and teal are the only exclusively night-feeding birds; the others feed at any time of the night or day, being dependent on the state of the tide to get at the banks of grass and weed, or the sands where they find shell-fish. All ducks are quite as wary in the bright moonlight as in the daytime, but at night are more likely to be found near the shore. Between the sea and the land near my abode is a long stretch of green embankment, which was made some years back in order to reclaim from the sea a great extent of land, which then consisted of swampy grass and herbage, overflowed at every high tide, but which now repays the expense of erecting the embankments, by affording as fine a district of corn-land as there is in the kingdom. By keeping the landward side of this grass-wall, and looking over it with great care, at different spots, I can frequently kill several brace of ducks and widgeon in an evening; though, without a clever retriever, the winged birds must invariably escape. Guided by their quacking, I have also often killed wild ducks at springs and running streams on frosty nights. It is perfectly easy to distinguish the birds as they swim about on a calm moonlight night, particularly if you can get the birds between you and the moon. It is a great assistance in night shooting to paste a piece of white paper along your gun-barrel, half-way down from the muzzle. In the stillness of the night the birds are peculiarly alive to sound, and the slightest noise sends them immediately out of shot. Their sense of smelling being also very acute, you must always keep to leeward of them. The mallard duck is more wary than any other kind in these respects, rising immediately with loud cries of warning, and putting all the other birds within hearing on the alert. I have seen the wild swans at night swim with a low cheeping note close by me; their white colour, however, makes them more difficult to distinguish than any other bird. It is quite easy to shoot ducks flying by moonlight, as long as you can get them between you and the clear sky. Practice, however, is required to enable the shooter to judge of distance at night-time.

I have frequently caught and brought home young wild ducks. If confined in a yard, or elsewhere, for a week or two with tame birds, they strike up a companionship which keeps them from wandering when set at liberty. Some few years back I brought home three young wild ducks: two of them turned out to be drakes. I sent away my tame drakes, and, in consequence, the next season had a large family of half-bred and whole wild ducks, as the tame and wild breed together quite freely. The wild ducks which have been caught are the tamest of all; throwing off all their natural shyness, they follow their feeder, and will eat corn out of the hand of any person with whom they are acquainted. The half-bred birds are sometimes pinioned, as they are inclined to fly away for the purpose of making their nests at a distance: at other times they never attempt to leave the field in front of the house. A pair or two always breed in the flower-garden. They appear to have a great *penchant* for forming their nests in certain flower-beds, and they are allowed to have their own way in this respect, as their elegant and high-bred appearance interests even the gardener, enemy as he is to all intruders on his favourite flowers.

These birds conceal their eggs with great care, and I have often been amused at the trouble the poor duck is put to in collecting dead leaves and straw to cover her eggs, when they are laid in a well-kept flower-bed. I often have a handful of straw laid on the grass at a convenient distance from the nest, which the old bird soon carries off, and makes use of. The drakes, though they take no portion of the nesting labours, appear to keep a careful watch near at hand during the time the duck is sitting. The half-bred birds have a peculiarity in common with the wild duck—which is, that they always pair, each drake taking charge of only one duck—not, as is the case with the tame ducks, taking to himself half a dozen wives. The young, too, when first hatched, have a great deal of the shyness of wild ducks, showing itself in a propensity to run off and hide in any hole or corner that is at hand. When in full plumage my drakes also have the beautifully-mottled feathers above the wing which are so much used in fly-dressing. With regard to the larder, the half-wild ducks are an improvement on both the tame and wild, being superior to either in delicacy and flavour. Their active and neat appearance, too, makes them a much more ornamental object (as they walk about in search of worms on the lawn or field) than a waddling, corpulent barn-yard duck.

There is a very pretty and elegant little duck, which is common on our coast—the long-tailed duck,[1] *Anas glacialis*. Its movements and actions are peculiarly graceful and amusing, while its musical cry is quite unlike that of any other bird, unless a slight resemblance to the trumpeting of the wild swan may be traced in it. Lying concealed on the shore, I have often watched these birds, as they swim along in small companies within twenty yards of me; the drake, with his gay plumage, playing quaint antics round the more sad-coloured female—sometimes jerking himself half out of the water, at others diving under her, and coming up on the other side. Sometimes, by a common impulse, they all set off swimming in a circle after each other with great rapidity, and uttering their curious cry, which is peculiarly wild and pleasing. When feeding, these birds dive constantly, remaining under water for a considerable time. Turning up their tails, they dip under with a curious kind of motion, one after the other, till the whole flock is under water. They are not nearly so wild or shy as many other kinds of wild-fowl, and are easily shot, though if only winged it is almost impossible to catch them, even with the best retriever, so quickly

---

[1] Known in some places as the "Calloo," from the cry they utter.

do they dive. They swim in with the flowing tide, frequently following the course of the water to some little distance from the mouth of the river. When I see them in the heavy surf on the main shore, they seem quite at their ease, floating high in the water, and diving into the midst of the wildest waves. When put up, they seldom fly far, keeping low, and suddenly dropping into the water again, where they seem more at their ease than in the air. When I have shot one of these birds, its mate (whether the duck or the drake is the survivor) returns frequently to the spot, flying round and round, and uttering a plaintive call.

On the open part of the coast they are often seen in company with the velvet duck. The latter very seldom comes into the bay, but keeps without the bar, quite regardless of storm or wind. It is a fine handsome bird, though of a rather heavy make. When flying, they have very much the appearance of a blackcock, having the same white mark on the wing, and being black in all other parts of their plumage. It is not difficult to approach these birds in a boat, but as they are not fit to eat, they are not much sought after. They are excellent divers, and must be shot dead, or they generally escape.

The golden-eye, *Anas clangula*, and the morillon are common about the mouth of the river and burns. I have often heard it argued that these two birds are merely the same species in different degrees of maturity; but I do not consider that there is the least doubt as to their being quite distinct. I have frequently shot what I suppose to be the young golden-eye not arrived at its full plumage; but in these the white spot at the corner of the mouth is more or less visible. The birds are larger than the morillon, besides which the golden-eye, in whatever stage of maturity it is found, always makes that peculiar noise with its wings, when flying, which is not heard in the flight of the morillon, or of any other kind of duck. I remember, too, once watching a pair of morillons in a Highland loch, late in the spring; they had evidently paired, and were come to the age of maturity, and ready for breeding.

The golden-eye dives well, remaining a considerable time under water seeking its food, which consists of the small shell-fish which it finds at the bottom. The morillon frequents the same places as the golden-eye, but always remains singly or in pairs, whereas the latter birds frequently unite in small flocks, particularly when they take to the inland lochs, which they do at the commencement of the spring. The golden-eye is frequently very fat and heavy, but is of a rank, coarse flavour.

The goosander [1] and merganser [2] fish constantly in the river: they remain late in the spring and return early in the autumn. Quick-sighted, they perceive an enemy at a great distance and keep a watch on all his movements. As long as he remains in full view and at a safe distance the birds do not move; but the moment the sportsman conceals himself, or approaches too near, they rise and go out to sea. They are easily killed by sending a person above them, and concealing oneself some way down the course of the stream, as when put up, although they may at first fly a short way up the water, they invariably turn downwards and repair to the open sea, following the windings of the river during their whole flight. If winged, they instantly dive, and rise at a considerable distance, keeping only their heads above the water, and making for the sea as fast as they can.

They feed on small trout and eels, which they fish for at the tails of the streams or in comparatively shallow water, unlike the cormorant, who, feeding on good-sized fish, is always seen diving in the large deep pools, where they are more likely to find trout big enough to satisfy their voracious appetite. The throat of the cormorant stretches to a very great extent, and its mouth opens wide enough to swallow a good-sized sea-trout. I saw a cormorant a few days ago engaged with a large white trout which he had caught in a quiet pool, and which he seemed to have some difficulty in swallowing. The bird was swimming with the fish across his bill, and endeavouring to get it in the right position, that is, with the head downwards. At last, by a dexterous jerk, he contrived to toss the trout up, and, catching it in his open mouth, managed to gulp it down, though apparently the fish was very much larger in circumference than the throat of the bird. The expanding power of a heron's

---

[1] *Mergus castor* is very destructive to fish in rivers and fresh-water lakes. Macgillivray mentions that eighteen trout were found in the gullet of one killed on the Tweed in 1838 (Gray, 403).

[2] The merganser (*Mergus serrator*), often called the red-breasted merganser, to distinguish it from an American visitor, the hooded merganser (*M. cucullatus*). The nest is generally placed on heath in unfrequented islands (Gray, 400). It breeds throughout the Arctic regions, and is frequently met in winter in most parts of England (Seebohm, *Siberia in Europe*, p. 188).

throat is also wonderfully great, and I have seen it severely tested when the bird was engaged in swallowing a flounder something wider than my hand. As the flounder went down, the bird's throat was stretched out into a fan-like shape, as he strained, apparently half-choked, to swallow it. These fish-eating birds having no crop, all they gulp down, however large it may be, goes at once into their stomach, where it is quickly digested. Like the heron, the cormorant swallows young water-fowl, rats, or anything that comes in its way.

There is a peculiarity in the bills of most birds which live on worms or fish: they are all more or less provided with a kind of teeth, which, sloping inwards, admit easily of the ingress of their prey, but make it impossible for anything to escape after it has once entered. In the goosander and merganser this is particularly conspicuous, as their teeth are so placed that they hold their slippery prey with the greatest facility. The common wild duck has it also, though the teeth are not nearly so projecting or sharp; feeding as it does on worms and insects, it does not require to be so strongly armed in this respect as those birds that live on fish.

I wonder that it has never occurred to any one in this country to follow the example of the Chinese in teaching the cormorant to fish.[1] The bold and voracious disposition of this bird makes it easy enough to tame, and many of our lochs and river-mouths would be well adapted for a trial of its abilities in fishing; and it would be an amusing variety in sporting to watch the bird as he dived and pursued the fish in clear water. We might take a hint from our brethren of the Celestial Empire with some advantage in this respect.

A curious anecdote of a brood of young wild ducks was told me by my keeper to-day. He found in some very rough, marshy ground, which was formerly a peat-moss, eight young ducks nearly full grown, prisoners, as it were, in one of the old peat-holes. They had evidently tumbled in some time before, and had managed to subsist on the insects, etc., that it contained or that fell into it. From the manner in which they had under-mined the banks of their watery prison, the birds must have been in it for some weeks. The sides were perpendicular, but

---

[1] Since the author's time several have practised this mode of fishing with success in England.

there were small resting-places under the bank which prevented their being drowned. The size of the place they were in was about eight feet square, and in this small space they had not only grown up, but thrived, being fully as large and heavy as any other young ducks of the same age.

In shooting water-fowl I have often been struck by the fact that as soon as ever life is extinct in a bird which falls in the sea or river, the plumage begins to get wet and to be penetrated by the water, although as long as the bird lives it remains dry and the wet runs off it. I can only account for this by supposing that the bird, as long as life remains, keeps his feathers in a position to throw off and prevent the water from entering between them. This power is of course lost to the dead bird, and the water penetrating through the outer part of the feathers wets them all. This appears to be more likely than that the feathers should be only kept dry by the oil supplied by the bird, as the effect of this oil could not be so instantaneously lost as to admit of wet as soon as the bird drops dead, while if the bird be only wounded they remain dry.

THE SYMPATHETIC MATE.

OYSTER-CATCHERS AT HOME

CHAPTER XVII

Birds that come in Spring—The Pewit: Pugnacity; Nests of; Cunning—Ring-Dotterel—Redshank—Oyster-Catcher: Food; Swimming of; Nest—Curlew—Redstart—Swallows, etc.

THE pewit is the first bird that visits us for the purpose of nidification. About the middle of February a solitary pewit appears, or perhaps a pair, and I hear them in the evening flying from the shore in order to search for worms in the field. Towards the end of the month, great flocks arrive and collect on the sands, always, however, feeding inland; it is altogether a nocturnal bird as far as regards feeding: at any hour of the night, and however dark it is, if I happen to pass through the grass-fields, I hear the pewits rising near me. Excepting to feed, they do not take much to the land till the end of March, when, if the weather is mild, I see them all day long flying about in their eccentric circles—generally in pairs; immediately after they appear in this manner, they commence laying their eggs, almost always on the barest fields, where they scratch a small hole just large enough to contain four eggs—the usual number laid by all waders; it is very difficult to distinguish these eggs from the ground, their colour being a brownish-green mottled with dark spots. I often see the hooded crows hunting the fields frequented by the pewits, as regularly as a pointer, flying a few yards above the ground, and searching for the eggs. The cunning crow always selects the time when the old birds are away on the shore; as soon as he is perceived, however, the pewits all combine in chasing him away: indeed, they attack fearlessly any bird of prey that ventures near their breeding-ground; and I have often detected the *locale* of a stoat or weasel by the swoops of these birds: also when they have laid their eggs they fight most fiercely with any other bird of their own species which happens to alight too near them. I saw a cock pewit one day attack a wounded male bird which came near his nest; the pugnacious little fellow ran up to the intruder, and taking advantage of his weakness, jumped on him, trampling upon him and pecking at his head, and then dragging him along the ground as fiercely as a game-cock.

The hen pewit has a peculiar instinct in misleading people as to the whereabouts of her nest; as soon as any one appears in the field where the nest is, the bird runs quietly and rapidly in a stooping posture to some distance from it, and then rises with loud cries and appearance of alarm, as if her nest was immediately below the spot she rose from. When the young ones are hatched too, the place to look for them is, *not* where the parent birds are screaming and fluttering about, but at some little distance from it; as soon as you actually come to the spot where their young are, the old birds alight on the ground a hundred yards or so from you, watching your movements. If, however, you pick up one of the young ones, both male and female immediately throw off all disguise, and come wheeling and screaming round your head, as if about to fly in your face. The young birds, when approached, squat flat and motionless on the ground, often amongst the weeds and grass in a shallow pool or ditch, where, owing to their colour, it is very difficult to distinguish them from the surrounding objects.

Towards the end of March, the ring-dotterel,[1] the redshank, the curlew, the oyster-catcher, and some other birds of the same kind begin to frequent their breeding-places. On those parts of the sandhills which are covered with small pebbles, the ring-dotterels take up their station, uttering their plaintive and not unmusical whistle for hours together, sometimes flitting about after each other with a flight resembling that of a swallow, and sometimes running rapidly along the ground, every now and then jerking up their wings till they meet above their back. Both the bird and its eggs are exactly similar in colour to the ground on which they breed; this is a provision of nature, to preserve the eggs of birds that breed on the ground from the prying eyes of their numerous enemies, and is observable in many different kinds; the colour of the young birds is equally favourable to their concealment.

The redshank does not breed on the stones or bare ground, but in some spot of rough grass; their motions are very curious at this time of year, as they run along with great swiftness, clapping their wings together audibly above their heads, and flying about round and round any intruder with rapid jerks, or hovering in the air like a hawk, all the time uttering a loud and peculiar whistle. They lead their young to the banks of any pool or ditch at hand, and they conceal themselves in the holes and corners close to the water's edge.

The oyster-catchers[2] sit quietly in pairs the chief part of the day on the banks or islands of shingle about the river or on the shore, but resort in the evenings to the sands in large flocks. I have often been puzzled to understand why, during the whole of the breeding-season, the oyster-catchers remain in large flocks along the coast, notwithstanding their duties of hatching and rearing their young. When all the other birds are paired off, they still every now and then collect in the same numbers as they do in winter.

---

[1] It is not found east of the Himalayas. In the British Isles it is principally a spring and autumn migrant, a few only remaining to breed on the Cumberland and Scotch mountains. Its great breeding-grounds are on the grassy hills on the tundras of Siberia, beyond the limits of forest growth (Seebohm, *Siberia in Europe*, p. 199).

[2] Eggs very large. Breed commonly many miles inland on the gravelly banks of most northern rivers. No nest.—C. St. J.

They lay very large eggs, of a greenish-brown colour mottled with black; both these birds and pewits soon become tame and familiar if kept in a garden or elsewhere, watching boldly for the worms turned up by the gardener when digging. The oyster-catcher's natural food appears to be shell-fish only; I see them digging up the cockles with their powerful bill, or detaching the small mussels from the scarps, and swallowing them whole, when not too large; if, however, one of these birds finds a cockle too large to swallow at once, he digs away at it with the hard point of his bill till he opens it, and then eats the fish, leaving the shell.

It is a curious fact with regard to this bird, that if it drops winged on the sea, it not only swims with great ease, but dives, remaining under water for so long a time, and rising again at such a distance, that I have known one escape out to sea in spite of my retriever, and I have watched the bird swim gallantly and with apparent ease across the bay, or to some bank at a considerable distance off. The feet of the oyster-catcher seem particularly ill adapted for swimming, as the toes are very short and stiff in proportion to the size of the bird. Most of the waders, when shot above the water and winged, will swim for a short distance, but generally with difficulty; none of them, however, excepting this bird, attempt to dive.

When in captivity the oyster-catcher eats almost anything that is offered to it. From its brilliant black and white plumage and red bill, as well as from its utility in destroying slugs and snails in the garden, where it searches for them with unceasing activity, it is both ornamental and useful, and worthy of being oftener kept for this purpose where a garden is surrounded by walls; it will, if taken young, remain with great contentment with poultry without being confined. I have found its nest in different localities, sometimes on the stones and sometimes on the sand close to high-water mark—very often on the small islands and points of land about the river, at a considerable distance from the sea; its favourite place here is on the carse land between the two branches of the Findhorn near the sea, where it selects some little elevation of the ground just above the reach of the tide, but where at spring-tides the nest must be very often entirely surrounded by the water—I never knew either this or any bird make the mistake of building within reach of the high tides, though, from the great difference there is in the height of the spring-tides, one might suppose that the birds would be often led into such a scrape.

Unlike most birds of similar kind, the sandpiper[1] builds a substantial, comfortable nest, in some tuft of grass near the river-side, well concealed by the surrounding herbage, instead of leaving its eggs on the bare stones or sand. It is a lively little bird, and is always associated in my mind with summer and genial weather as it runs jerking along the water's edge, looking for insects or flies, and uttering its clear, pipe-like whistle. The young of the sand-piper are neatly and elegantly mottled, and are very difficult to be perceived. The eggs are brown and yellow, nearly the colour of the withered grass and leaves with which the bird forms its nest.

Towards the end of March the curlew[2] begins to leave the shore, taking to the higher hills, where it breeds, near the edge of some loch or marsh. During the season of breeding this bird (though so shy and suspicious at all other times) flies boldly round the head of any passer-by, with a loud, screaming whistle. The eggs are very large. When first hatched, the young have none of the length of bill which is so distinguishing a feature in the old bird. On the shore the curlews feed mostly on cockles and other shell-fish, which they extract from the sand with ease, and swallow whole, voiding the shells broken into small pieces. During open weather they frequent the turnip and grass fields, where they appear to be busily seeking for snails and worms.

There is no bird more difficult to get within shot of than the curlew. Their sense of smelling is so acute that it is impossible to get near them excepting by going against the wind, and they keep too good a look-out to leeward to admit of this being always done. I have frequently killed them when feeding in fields surrounded by stone walls, by showing my hand or some small part of my dress above the wall, when they have come wheeling round to discover what the object was.

[1] The sandpiper (*Totanus hypoleucus*) is everywhere in Scotland a common bird. It "is a well-known object as it skims the surface of the quiet lochs with arched and almost motionless wings, or stands on some isolated stone, vibrating its body as it salutes the rambling intruder on its haunts." Its cry resembles "killi leepie," and itself is so called in some districts (Gray, p. 296).

[2] Lays four eggs (C. St. J.) During the breeding season, like most wild birds at such times, it becomes much tamer, and even approaches habitations.

Besides the sea-birds that come into this country to breed, such as sand-pipers, pewits, terns, etc., there are some few of our smaller birds that arrive in the spring to pass the summer here. Amongst these I may name the redstart, the spotted flycatcher, the whitethroat, the wheatear, etc.

The redstart is not very common: it breeds in several places, however, up the Findhorn; at Logie, for instance, where year after year it builds in an old ivy-covered wall. The young, when able to fly, appear often in my garden, for a few weeks, actively employed in doing good service, killing numbers of insects; and every spring a pair or two of flycatchers breed in one of the fruit-trees on the wall, building, as it were, only half a nest, the wall supplying the other half. They cover the nest most carefully with cobwebs, to make it appear like a lump of this kind of substance left on the wall; indeed, I do not know any nest more difficult to distinguish. It is amusing to see the birds as they dash off from the top of the wall in pursuit of some fly or insect, which they catch in the air and carry to their young. The number of insects which they take to their nest in the course of half an hour is perfectly astonishing.

Another bird that comes every spring to the same bush to breed is the pretty little whitethroat. On the lawn close to my house a pair come to the same evergreen, at the foot of which, on the ground, they build their nest, carrying to it an immense quantity of feathers, wool, etc. The bird sits fearlessly, and with full confidence that she will not be disturbed, although the grass is mown close up to her abode; and she is visited at all hours by the children, who take a lively interest in her proceedings. She appears quite acquainted with them all, sitting snugly in her warmly-feathered nest, with nothing visible but her bright black eyes and sharp-pointed bill. As soon as her eggs are hatched, she and her mate are in a great bustle, bringing food to their very tiny offspring—flying backwards and forwards all day with caterpillars and grubs.

Both this and the larger kind of whitethroat which visits us have a lively and pleasing song. They frequently make their nest on the ground in the orchard, amongst the long grass, arching it over in the most cunning manner, and completely concealing it. When they leave their eggs to feed, a leaf is laid over the entrance of the nest to hide it; in fact, nothing but the eyes of children (who in nest-finding would beat Argus himself) could ever discover the abode of the little whitethroat. Before they leave this country, these birds collect together, and are seen searching the hedges for insects in considerable but scattered flocks. They frequently fly in at the open windows in pursuit of flies, and chase them round the room quite fearlessly. The gardener accuses them of destroying quantities of cherries, by piercing them with their bills: they certainly do so, but I am always inclined to suppose that it is only the diseased fruit that they attack in this way, or that which has already been taken possession of by small insects.

The wheatear[1] does not arrive till the first week of April, when they appear in considerable numbers on the sand-hills, flying in and out of the rabbit-holes and broken banks, in concealed corners of which they hatch. Their eggs are peculiarly beautiful, being of a pale blue delicately shaded with a darker colour at one end. Though of such repute in the south of England, it is not ever sought after here. As a boy, on the Wiltshire downs, I used to be an adept at catching them in horsehair nooses, as we used to consider them particularly good eating. The shepherds there, as well as on the South downs, make a considerable addition to their income by catching wheatears and sending them to the London and Brighton markets.

The swallows and swifts arrive also about the middle of April. It is a curious thing to observe how a pair of swallows season after season build their nest in the same angle of a window, or corner of a wall, coming immediately to the same spot, after their long absence and weary flight, and either repairing their old residence or building a new one.

Great numbers of sand-martins build in the banks of the river, returning to the same places every year, and after clearing out their holes, they carry in a great quantity of feathers and dried grass, which they lay loosely at the end of their subterranean habitation.

The swifts appear always to take up their abode about the highest buildings in the towns and villages, flying and screaming

[1] The wheatear (*Saxicola œnanthe*), an abundant summer visitor, arrives by a few pairs at a time on the west coast, but on the eastern side of Scotland in flocks of thousands at a time. In hilly districts the nest is generally placed in the holes of dry-stone walls, but on the coast mostly in deserted rabbit-holes (Gray, p. 87; Saxby, p. 69).

like restless spirits round and round the church steeple for hours together, sometimes dashing in at a small hole under the eaves of the roof, or clinging with their hard and powerful claws to the perpendicular walls; at other times they seem to be occupied the whole day in darting like arrows along the course of the burn in pursuit of the small gnats, of which they catch great numbers in their rapid flight. I have found in the throat of both swift and martin a number of small flies, sticking together in a lump as large as a marble, and though quite alive, unable to escape. It is probably with these that they feed their young, for the food of all swallows consisting of the smaller gnats and flies, they cannot carry them singly to their nests, but must wait till they have caught a good quantity.

We are visited too by that very curious little bird the tree-creeper, *Certhia familiaris*, whose rapid manner of running round the trunk of a tree in search of insects is most amusing. Though not exactly a bird of passage, as it is seen at all seasons, it appears occasionally to vanish from a district for some months, and then to return, without reference to the time of year. I found one of their nests built within an outbuilding, which the bird entered by a small opening at the top of the door.

LOGIE HOUSE.

WATER-HEN

CHAPTER XVIII

Sheldrake: Nest; Food—Teal: Breeding-places; Anecdotes—Landrail: Arrival of —Cuckoo—Nightjar: Habits of—Quail—Grebe: Arrival; Account of Nest and Young—Bald Coot—Water-Hen—Water-Rail.

BESIDES the birds mentioned in the last chapter there are several others which come here to breed, such as the sheldrake, the corncrake, the cuckoo, etc.

I should certainly call the sheldrake the most beautiful bird of the duck tribe that visits this country. Its clear black and white plumage, the beautiful bronze on the wing, and the bright red bill, give it a particularly gay and at the same time neat appearance. They arrive here in March or the end of February. They float in large flocks in the sheltered creeks and bays, swimming high in the water and making a great show. When the tide recedes, they take to the sands in search of their food, which consists of shell-fish, the sea-worms, etc. Their manner of catching the latter is curious. When the sheldrake perceives that he is above the hole of one of these insects, which he knows by the worm-casts similar to those of a common earth-worm, he begins patting the ground with his feet, dancing as it were over the hole. This motion on the sands generally brings the worm out of his abode. My tame sheldrakes, when they come to ask for food, pat the ground in an impatient and rapid manner, their natural instinct evidently suggesting this as the usual way of procuring food. Though among the most wary of birds when wild, their sharp eye detecting the least movement, yet they become extremely fearless and bold when once domesticated, and certainly no bird is more ornamental. They breed freely in a tame state, if allowed a certain degree of liberty, and I have no doubt would be quite as good eating as a common duck when fed on corn and clean food. In their wild state they have a rank, fishy flavour, but so would any duck that lived on the same food as they do. My tame birds eat anything, and will take their food out of my hand without the least hesitation. They are pugnacious creatures, and the drakes are always the masters of the poultry-yard, pursuing the other birds with a peculiar croaking quack. The sheldrakes breed in old rabbit-holes, laying their eggs several feet under ground. When I am on the sandhills in May, early in the morning, I frequently see their tracks in and out of the holes. It is curious to watch the male bird standing and strutting in the sun on some hillock waiting for the female, who is employed in her domestic duties under ground. When she appears, the drake goes to her, and after a short flirtation they fly away together to the sea-shore. When the hen is sitting, she leaves the nest during the time of low water, appearing to have an instinctive knowledge of when that time arrives, as it is the part of the day in which she can most quickly procure her food. This done, she returns to her nest, and after wheeling several times over it to see that nothing is amiss, she alights and walks to her hole. The sheldrake has a quick, smart step, quite unlike the waddling gait of most ducks. When hatched, the young take at once to the sea, and never seem to leave it or the sand-banks till their plumage is complete. I have occasionally found a large flock of young birds nearly full grown on the sands, but never could manage to catch one, as they run with great rapidity and dash into the sea before I can get up to them.

The flight of the sheldrake is not so rapid or easy as that of other ducks, rather resembling the heavy flapping of a goose than the quick flight of a wild duck. I cannot understand why this beautiful bird is not oftener kept on ornamental pieces of water, as his fine plumage, his boldness, and familiarity render him peculiarly interesting and amusing.

The teal[1] can scarcely be called a winter bird with us, although occasionally a pair or two appear; but in the spring they come in numbers to breed and rear their tiny young in the swamps and lochs. Nothing can exceed the beauty and neatness of this miniature duck. They fly with great swiftness, rising suddenly into the air when disturbed, and dropping as quickly after a short flight, much in the same manner as a snipe. In the spring the drake has a peculiar whistle, at other times their note is a low quack. A pair of teal, if undisturbed, will return year after year to the same pool for the purpose of breeding. Like the wild duck, they sometimes hatch their young a considerable distance from the water, and lead the young brood immediately to it. I once, when riding in Ross-shire, saw an old teal with eight newly-hatched young ones cross the road. The youngsters could not climb up the opposite bank, and young and old all squatted flat down to allow me to pass. I got off my horse and lifted all the little birds up and carried them a little distance down the road to a ditch, for which I concluded they were making, the old bird all the time fluttering about me and frequently coming within reach of my riding-whip. The part of the road where I first found them passed through thick fir-wood with rank heather, and it was quite a puzzle to me how such small animals, scarcely bigger than a half-grown mouse could have got along through it. The next day I saw them all enjoying themselves in a small pond at some little distance off, where a brood of teal appeared every year. In some of the mountain lakes the teal breed in great numbers. When shooting in August I have seen a perfect cloud of these birds occasionally rise from some grassy loch. The widgeon[2] never breeds with us, but leaves this country at the end of April.

[1] Nest, composed of dry grass (C. St. J.), is generally placed on the higher tufts of heather. [2] Moray. Breeds in Sutherland, Loch Naver, etc.—C. St. J.

We have great numbers of landrails here in their breeding-season. I have for several years first heard them on the 1st of May. Hoarse and discordant as their voice is, I always hear it with pleasure, for it brings the idea of summer and fine weather with it. Oftentimes have I opened my window during the fine dewy nights of June to listen to these birds as they utter their harsh cry in every direction, some close to the very window, and answered by others at different distances. I like too to see this bird, as at the earliest dawn she crosses a road followed by her train of quaint-looking, long-legged young ones, all walking in the same stooping position; or to see them earlier in the year lift up their snake-like heads above the young corn, and croak in defiance of some other bird of the same kind, whose head appears now and then at a short distance. At other times, one hears the landrail's cry apparently almost under one's feet in the thick clover, and he seems to shake the very ground, making as much noise as a bull. How strange it is that a bird with apparently so soft and tender a throat can utter so hard and loud a cry, which sounds as if it was produced by some brazen instrument. I never could ascertain whether this cry is made by the male or female bird, or by both in common: I am inclined to suppose the latter is the case, as in endeavouring to make this out I have watched carefully a small piece of grass and shot four landrails in it in as many minutes, every bird in the act of croaking. Two of them were larger and of a redder plumage than the others, and were apparently cock birds: this inclines me to think that the croaking cry is common to both sexes. Their manner of leaving the country is a mystery. Having hatched their young, they take to the high corn-fields, and we never see them again, excepting by chance one comes across a brood at dawn of day, hunting along a path or ditch side for snails, worms, and flies, which are their only food, this bird being entirely insectivorous, never eating corn or seeds. By the time the corn is cut they are all gone; how they go, or whither, I know not, but with the exception of a stray one or two I never see them in the shooting-season, although the fields are literally alive with them in the breeding-time. You can seldom flush a landrail twice; having alighted he runs off at a quick pace, and turning and doubling round a dog, will not rise. I have caught them more than once when they have pitched by chance in an open wood, and run into a hole or elsewhere at the root of a tree; they sometimes hide their head, like the story of the ostrich, and allow themselves to be lifted up. Unlike most other migrating birds, the landrail is in good order on his first arrival, and being then very fat and delicate in flavour, is very good eating. Their nest is of a very artless description, a mere hollow scratched in the middle of a grass-field, in which they lay about eight eggs. The young ones at first are quite black, curious-looking little birds, with the same attitudes and manner of running as their parents, stooping their heads and looking more like mice or rats than a long-legged bird.

Besides those already mentioned, I can only call to mind two other birds that visit us for the breeding-season—the cuckoo and the nightjar.

The cuckoo, like the landrail, is connected in all my ideas with spring and sunshine, though frequenting such a different description of country; the landrail always inhabiting the most open country, while the cuckoo frequents the wooded glades and banks of the rivers and burns; flitting from tree to tree, alighting generally on some small branch close to the trunk, or chasing each other, uttering their singular call. So much has been written respecting their habit of laying their egg in the nest of some other bird, that I can add nothing to what is already known. In this country they seem to delight in the woods on the hill-sides by the edge of loch or river, where I constantly hear their note of good omen. When the young ones are fledged, they remain for a week or two about the gardens or houses, perching on the railings, and darting off, like the flycatcher, in pursuit of passing insects.

The nightjar[1] is a summer resident here, building its nest—or rather laying its eggs, for nest it has none—in some bare spot of ground, near the edge of a wood, and seldom quite within it. The eggs are of a peculiarly oval shape. The nightjar, during the daytime, will lie flat and motionless for hours together on some horizontal branch of a tree near the ground, or on some part of the ground itself which exactly resembles its

---

[1] This bird sits or rather lies on a branch of a tree, *longways*, not perching across it like all other birds. It is common quite to the north of the island wherever there is any wood, as at Tongue, etc., in Sutherland. The goatsucker makes no nest whatever; not even does it scratch a hollow in the ground, but lays its two oval eggs without the least preparation.—C. St. J.

own plumage in colour. In this manner the bird will allow a person to approach nearly close to it before it moves, although watching intently with its dark eye to see if it is observed. If it fancies that you are looking at it, up it rises straight into the air, and drops again perpendicularly in some quiet spot, with a flight like that of an insect more than of a bird. With the shades of evening comes its time of activity. With rapid and noiseless flight the nightjar flits and wheels round and round as you take your evening walk, catching the large moths and beetles that you put into motion. Sometimes the bird alights in the path near you, crouching close to the ground, or sits on a railing or gate motionless, with its tail even with its head. Frequently, too, these birds pitch on a house-top, and utter their singular jarring noise, like the rapid revolving of a wheel or the rush of water, and the house itself appears to be trembling, so powerful is their note. It is a perfectly harmless, indeed a useful bird; and I would as soon wantonly shoot a swallow as a nightjar. I admire its curiously-mottled plumage, and manner of feeding and flying about in the summer and autumn evenings, which make it more interesting when alive than it can possibly be when dead. Often, when I have been fishing late in the evening, has the nightjar flitted round, or pitched on a rock or bank close to me, as if inclined to take an interest in what I was at—confident, too, of not being molested. Its retreat in the daytime is usually in some lonely wild place. Though feeding wholly at night, I do not think that it is annoyed by sunshine, as it frequently basks in an open spot, appearing to derive enjoyment from the light and glare which are shining full upon it; unlike the owl, whose perch in the daytime is in some dark and shady corner, where the rays of the sun never penetrate.

The quail[1] is sometimes killed here, but very rarely. I once shot a couple on the Ross-shire side of the Moray Firth, but never happened to meet with one on this side, though I have heard of their being killed, and also of their having been seen in the spring-time, as if they came occasionally to breed.

Another singular bird visits this country regularly in the

---

[1] The quail is frequently killed in Morayshire, though in very small numbers. Every autumn a few are seen, and during the spring I constantly hear them calling in the fields, so that in all probability some few breed in this county.—C. St. J.

spring, the lesser grebe[1] (in England commonly called the dabchick). It is difficult to understand how this bird makes out its journey from the region, wherever it may be, where they pass the winter. No bird is less adapted for a long flight, yet they suddenly appear in some rushy loch. Generally a pair take possession of some small pool, where they build their singular nest and rear their young, till the returning autumn warns them that it is time to return to some country less liable than this to have its pools and lochs frozen. In a small rushy pond in Inverness-shire I had frequent opportunities of observing their domestic economy, and the manner in which they build their nest and rear their young. Though there was no stream connecting this pool with any other larger piece of water, a pair, and only a pair, of these little grebes came to it every spring. After two or three days spent in recruiting their strength and making love to each other, the little birds set about making their nest in a tuft of rushes, at a shallow part of the water, a few yards from the shore. They first collected a considerable quantity of dead rushes, which they found in plenty floating about the edges of the water. Both male and female were busily employed in building, swimming to and fro with the greatest activity. After laying a good foundation of this material, they commenced diving for the weeds which grew at the bottom of the water, bringing up small bunches of it, and clambering up the sides of their nest (the bottom of which was in the water), they made a layer of this, hollowed out in the middle. They worked only in the morning and very late in the evening. Their eggs were six in number, and when first laid, quite white, and nearly oval. During the time of sitting, whenever the old bird left her nest she covered her eggs most carefully. The singular part of this proceeding was, that she always dived for a quantity of green weed, which grew at the bottom of the pond, and used this, wet as it was, to cover her eggs. By the time that they had been laid for a few days they became green and dirty-looking, having quite the appearance of being addled—and no wonder, as the nest was constantly wet from below, the water coming up through the rushes

---

[1] I never saw the nest floating, but well fixed in a tuft of rushes. The old birds cover the eggs with wet weeds, etc., when they leave them. Six eggs.— C. St. J.

The dabchick (*Podiceps minor*). St. John's account of this bird's nest is an admirable example of his skill and powers of observation.

and weeds of which it was composed; and she gave them a fresh wet covering every time that she left them, arranging it around the eggs, so that the edges of the nest gradually became higher and higher. The bird appeared to be very frequently off during the daytime, remaining away for hours together, playing about on the water with her mate. After a fortnight of this kind of sitting, I one day saw her followed by six little dabchicks, scarcely bigger than large beetles, but as active and as much at home on the water as their parents. A very windy day came on, and the young birds collected in a group behind a floating rail, which being half grounded at an angle of the pool, made a kind of breakwater for them. The old birds swam out of this harbour when I came, but the little ones crept close up to the railing, uttering a feeble squeak like a young chicken. Huddled up in a group, they certainly were the smallest and quaintest-looking little divers that I ever saw. I have heard it argued that it was impossible that eggs could be hatched in a situation constantly exposed to so much wet and damp, but those of this kind of grebe are certainly an exception, as they were continually wet below, and frequently covered with wet green weed. I do not know why the bird should always bring the covering from below the water, but she invariably did so, and the pool being in a convenient place for my watching them closely, I took some trouble to be sure that my observations were correct. It is a pretty, amusing little bird, and quite harmless: I have always much pleasure in watching their lively actions in the water. Where undisturbed, they soon become bold and confident. These little fellows used to swim close to me, and after looking up in my face with an arch cock of their tiny head, turn up their round sterns and dip under the water. They often remained so long under water, that the circles made in the calm pool from their last dive were quite obliterated from the surface before the saucy-looking little fellows would rise again, often in exactly the same spot, when they would look at me again, as if to be sure of who I was; then, turning half over in the water, they would scratch their neck with their curiously-formed foot, shake their apology of a wing, and dip under again.

One day my dog jumped into the water for a swim, and the motions of the birds were then very different. They dived rapidly to the other end of the pool, where they rose, showing only the very tip of their bill, which I could distinguish by the small wave in the water made when it first came up. After remaining in this position for a short time, they gradually lifted up more and more of their head, till, seeing that all danger was over and that the dog had left their pool, they rose entirely to the surface, and shaking their feathers resumed their usual attitudes, keeping, however, at a respectful distance and watching the dog. After the young ones were hatched and full grown they again disappeared, leaving us for the winter. *How or where they went it is difficult to imagine.*

If the weather is tolerably open, the bald coot[1] arrives here early in the spring. It is very difficult to make this bird fly, unless it happens to be surprised in the open part of the lake, when it darts off immediately to the rushes, where, diving and wading with great quickness, it remains so completely concealed that neither dog nor man can put it up again. Its young ones are like a ball of black down, but swim about and dive as cleverly as their parents. They build a very large nest amongst the rushes growing in the water, and sit very close. The coot has an ornamental appearance on a sheet of water, from their constant activity in swimming about, and their loud, wild cry adds an interest to the solitude of the Highland lake.

The water-hen[2] is another bird which deserves encouragement and protection, as they repay it by becoming tame and familiar, leaving the water to feed with the poultry, and walking about all day on the grass, with an air of the greatest confidence and sociability. I know nothing prettier than the young ones, as they follow their parents in their active search for flies and insects. When first hatched they are perfectly black, with a small spot of bright red skin on the top of their beaks.

These birds remain with us all the winter, only changing their location from the pools to the open ditches in severe frosts.

The water-rail[3] I only see in the winter, and even then rarely. I do not think that it is a regular visitor to us, for

---

[1] Lays eight eggs.—C. St. J.
[2] *Gallinula chloropus*, a bird always inclined to be tame and familiar, and to associate with common fowls, etc.—C. St. J.
[3] *Rallus aquaticus*, breeds in Spynie. Took the nest 17th May 1851, eight eggs.— C. St. J.

were it so, notwithstanding its habits of concealment, my dogs would, when looking through the wet places and ditches for snipes, certainly find it oftener than they do. I sometimes see it in frosty weather, feeding at all hours of the day in a running stream or ditch, busily searching amongst the weeds for its food.

LOCH INDORWI

SHOOTING WILD GEESE

CHAPTER XIX

Wild Geese: Arrival of; Different kinds of; Anecdotes of—Shooting Wild Geese—Feeding - places—Wariness — Habits — Breeding - places—Black-headed Gull – Birds that breed on the River-banks.

ON the 2nd of March a flock of twelve wild geese passed over my house, flying eastwards towards the Loch of Spynie: these are the first birds of the kind I have seen this spring. On the 6th I hear of the same flock being seen feeding on a clover-field to the eastward, in the flat country between this place and Loch Spynie. This flock of geese are said to have been occasionally seen during the whole winter about the peat-mosses beyond Brodie, there having been no severe frost or snow to drive them southward.

The first wild geese that we see here are not the common grey goose, but the white-fronted or laughing goose,[1] *Anas albifrons*, called by Buffon *l'Oye rieuse*. This bird has a peculiarly harsh and wild cry, whence its name. It differs in another respect also from the common grey goose, in preferring clover and green wheat to corn for its food. Indeed this bird appears to me to be wholly graminiferous. Unlike the grey goose too, it roosts, when undisturbed, in any grass-field where it may have

[1] Moray. Not so numerous as the bean-goose.—C. St. J.

been feeding in the afternoon, instead of taking to the bay every night for its sleeping-quarters. The laughing goose also never appears here in large flocks, but in small companies of from eight or nine to twenty birds.

Though very watchful at all times, they are more easily approached than the grey goose, and often feed on ground that admits of stalking them. I see them occasionally feeding in small swamps and patches of grass surrounded by high banks, furze, or trees. The grey goose appears to select the most open and extensive fields in the country to feed in, always avoiding any bank or hedge that may conceal a foe.

On the 10th of March last year, when out rabbit-shooting in a small furze cover, I saw a flock of some fifteen or sixteen white-fronted geese hovering over a small clover-field not far from where I was. My attendant, who has a most violent liking for a "wild-goose-chase," immediately caught up the dogs, and made me sit down to watch the birds, who presently pitched, as we expected, on the clover-field. I was for immediately commencing the campaign against them, but this he would not admit of, and pointing out a part of the field sheltered by a bank overgrown with furze, where the clover was greener than elsewhere, he told me that in ten minutes the birds would be there. Knowing his experience and cunning in these matters, I put myself entirely under his orders, and waited patiently. The geese, after sitting quietly for a few minutes, and surveying the country around, began to plume their feathers, and this done, commenced feeding in a straight line for the green spot of grass, keeping, however, a constant watch in all directions. "They will be in that hollow in a minute, Sir," said Simon; "and then, Sir, you must just run for it till you get behind the bank, and then you can easily crawl to within thirty yards of where they will pass." Accordingly, the moment they disappeared in the hollow, I started literally *ventre à terre*. One of the wary birds, however, evidently not liking that the whole flock should be in the hollow at once, ran back and took up her station on the rising ground which they had just passed over, where she stood with her neck erect and looking in all directions. I was in full view of her, and at the moment was crossing a wet rushy spot of ground; nothing was left for it but to lie flat on the ground, notwithstanding the humid nature of my *locale*; the bird appeared rather puzzled by my appearance, and my grey clothes not making much show in the rushy ground and withered herbage which I was lying in, she contented herself with giving some private signal to the rest, which brought them all at a quick run up to her side, where they stood looking about them, undecided whether to fly or not. I was about two hundred yards from the birds; we remained in this manner for, I daresay, five minutes, the birds appearing on the point of taking wing during the whole time: suddenly I heard a shout beyond the birds, and they instantly rose in confusion and flew directly towards me. As soon as they were over my head I stood up: the effect of my sudden appearance was to make them break their line and fly straight away from me in all directions, thus giving me what I wanted, shots at them when flying away from me, in which case they are easy to kill. My cartridges told with good effect, and I killed a brace, one dropping perfectly dead and the other extending her wings and gradually sinking, till she fell on the top of a furze-bush three or four hundred yards off, where I found her lying quite dead. It appeared that Simon, seeing that the birds had observed me, ran round them, and then setting up a shout, had luckily driven them *nolentes volentes* over my head. They were the white-fronted goose, with pure white spots on their foreheads. About three weeks after this time, at the end of March, large flights of grey geese appear here, feeding on the fresh-sown oats, barley, and peas during the day, and passing the night on the sands of the bay, whither they always repair soon after sunset.

I had passed a great part of several days in endeavouring to get at these wary birds, and had occasionally killed a stray one or two, but some ill luck or error on my part (Simon would never admit that his own tactics were wrong) had always prevented my getting a good shot at the flocks. As for Simon, he protested that "his heart was quite broken with the beasts." One morning, however, I got up at daylight and went to the shore; a heavy mist was rolling over the bay, and I could see nothing, but heard the wild and continued cry of hundreds of geese answering each other, and apparently consulting as to what direction they should seek their morning's repast in. Presently I knew from their altered cry that the birds were on wing, and were coming directly towards where I was: I sat down, and very soon a long line of geese came cackling and chattering within fifteen yards of me, and I killed a brace with no trouble. In the afternoon, while walking on the shore, I saw a large flock of geese rise off the sea and fly inland, in a long undulating line, evidently looking for a place to feed on. I watched them with my glass, and saw the field in which they alighted, at the distance of at least two miles from me. I sent for Simon, and started in pursuit. We came within two fields of the birds, and could advance no nearer without risk of putting them up. On two sides of the field "in which they were feeding," was a deep open drain; and once in this we were nearly sure of a shot. Luckily a farmer was ploughing in an adjoining field, and though at every turn he approached the ditch of the oatfield where the geese were, the birds, according to their usual custom, took no notice of him. We joined the ploughman, and keeping behind the horses, slipped unperceived by the geese into the ditch, which, by the by, had in it about a foot of the coldest water that I ever felt. It was deep enough, however, to conceal us entirely, and following Simon I went about three hundred yards down the drain, till we came to another which ran at right angles to the first; we turned along this ditch, which, not being cut so deep as the other, obliged us to stoop in a manner that made my back ache most unmercifully. Simon appeared to understand exactly what he was at, and to have a perfect knowledge of the geography of all the drains in the country. Putting on a nondescript kind of cap, made of dirty canvas, exactly the colour of a ploughed field, he peered cautiously through a bunch of rushes which grew on the edge of the ditch; then looking at me with a most satisfied grin, floundered on again till he came to another ditch that crossed us at right angles; up this he went, and of course I had nothing to do but to follow, though as I occasionally sank above my knees into cold spring water, I began to wish all the wild geese were consigned to his black majesty: we went about a hundred yards up this last drain, till we came to a part where a few rushes grew on the banks; looking through these we saw about fifty geese coming straight towards us, feeding; we got our guns cautiously on the top of the bank and waited till the birds were within twenty-five yards of us, they then began to turn to cross the field back again. Some were within shot, however, and on our giving a low whistle they ran together, preparatory to rising; this was our moment: only one of my barrels went off, the other having got wet through, copper cap and everything, during our progress in the ditch. We, however, bagged three birds, and another flew wounded away, and at last fell close to the sea-shore, where we afterwards found her. Having collected our game, I was not sorry to walk off home in double-quick time to put a little caloric into my limbs, as I felt perfectly benumbed after wading for such a distance in a cold March wind.

On our way home we saw an immense flock of geese alight to feed on a small field of newly-sown peas. Simon was delighted, and promised me a good shot in the morning, if I left him at the nearest farm-house to take his own steps towards ensuring me the chance.

Accordingly the next morning, at daylight, I went with him to the spot: the geese were still resting on the sands, not having yet made their morning meal. In the very centre of the pea-field Simon had constructed what he called an "ambush"; this was a kind of hut, or rather hole in the ground, just large enough to contain one person, whose chin would be on a level with the field. The ground was rather rough, and he had so disposed the clods of earth that I was quite invisible till the geese came within a yard or two of me. Into this hole he made me worm myself, while he went to a hedge at some distance, for the chance of the birds coming over his head after I had fired. The sun was not yet up when I heard the cackle of the geese, and soon afterwards the whole flock came soaring over my head; round and round they flew, getting lower every circle. I could several times have fired at single birds as they flew close by me, and so well concealed was I with clods of earth, dried grass, etc., that they never suspected my presence in the midst of their breakfast-table. Presently they all alighted at the farthest end of the field from me, and commenced shovelling up the peas in the most wholesale manner. Though the field was small, they managed to feed from one end to the other without coming within sixty yards of me; having got to the end of the field, they turned round, and this time I saw that they would pass within shot. Suddenly they all halted, and I saw that something had alarmed them; I looked cautiously out, and saw, in the direction in which their heads were turned, a large fox sitting upright and looking wistfully at the geese, but seeming quite aware that he had no chance of getting at them. The morning sun, however, which was just rising, and which, shining on his coat, made it appear perfectly red, warned him that it was time to be off to the woods, and he trotted quietly away, passing my ambuscade within forty yards, but always keeping his head turned towards the geese, as if unwilling to give up all hope of getting one of them. The distant bark of a dog, however, again warned him, and he quickened his pace and was soon out of sight. The geese seemed quite relieved at his departure, and recommenced feeding. I cocked my gun and arranged my ambuscade, so as to be ready for them when they came opposite to me; presently one or two stragglers passed within ten yards; I pulled the dead grass in front of my face, so that they could not see me, and waited for the main flock, who soon came by, feeding hurriedly as they passed; when they were opposite to me, I threw down part of the clods and grass that concealed me, and fired both barrels at the thickest part of the flock: three fell dead, and two others dropped before the flock had flown many hundred yards. Simon ran from his hiding-place to secure them; one was dead, the other rose again, but was stopped by a charge from his gun. Our five geese were no light load to carry home, as they had been feeding on the corn for a fortnight or three weeks, and had become very fat and heavy.

The common grey goose, after having fed for some time in the fresh-sown corn-fields, is by no means a bad bird for the larder. But before they can procure grain to feed on, their flesh is neither so firm nor so well flavoured. In this country there are three kinds of geese, all called by the common name of "wild geese," namely, the white-fronted goose, already mentioned (p. 172 note); the common grey-leg goose, *Anas Anser*;[1] and the bean-goose.[2] The latter kind differs from the grey goose

---

[1] In Moray rare. Breeds in Sutherland, and will breed freely with tame goose. Lays from five to seven eggs (C. St. J.) "To my surprise I found this species of goose breeding in considerable numbers in the islands and about the shores of some of the Sutherland lakes. They place their nests, which are exactly similar, though of course on a larger scale, to that of a wild duck, either in the rank heather, or in any other long herbage; some that I found were imbedded in the wild garlic which often clothes the small islands of the lakes with its bright and beautiful green. They breed early in the year" (*Natural History and Sport in Moray*, p. 120).

[2] Moray. Not uncommon in March and April.—C. St. J.

in having a small black mark at the end of their bill, about the size and colour of a horse-bean. This bird, too, differs in being rather smaller and more dark in its general colour than the grey goose. It is a great libel to accuse a goose of being a silly bird. Even a tame goose shows much instinct and attachment ; and were its habits more closely observed, the tame goose would be found to be by no means wanting in general cleverness. Its watchfulness at night-time is, and always has been, proverbial ; and it certainly is endowed with a strong organ of self-preservation. You may drive over dog, cat, hen, or pig ; but I defy you to drive over a tame goose. As for wild geese, I know of no animal, biped or quadruped, that is so difficult to deceive or approach. Their senses of hearing, seeing, and smelling are all extremely acute ; independently of which, they appear to act in so organised and cautious a manner when feeding or roosting, as to defy all danger. Many a time has my utmost caution been of no avail in attempting to approach these birds ; either a careless step or a piece of gravel, or an eddy of wind, however light, or letting them perceive the smallest portion of my person, has rendered useless whole hours of manœuvring. When a flock of geese have fixed on a field of new-sown grain to feed on, before alighting they make numerous circling flights round and round it, and the least suspicious object prevents their pitching. Supposing that all is right, and they do alight, the whole flock for the space of a minute or two remain motionless, with erect head and neck reconnoitring the country round. They then, at a given signal from one of the largest birds, disperse into open order, and commence feeding in a tolerably regular line. They now appear to have made up their minds that all is safe, and are contented with leaving one sentry, who either stands on some elevated part of the field, or walks slowly with the rest—never, however, venturing to pick up a single grain of corn, his whole energies being employed in watching. The flock feed across the field ; not waddling, like tame geese, but walking quickly, with a firm, active, light-infantry step. They seldom venture near any ditch or hedge that might conceal a foe. When the sentry thinks that he has performed a fair share of duty, he gives the nearest bird to him a sharp peck. I have seen him sometimes pull out a handful of feathers, if the first hint is not immediately attended to, at the same time uttering a querulous kind of cry. This bird then takes up the watch, with neck perfectly upright, and in due time makes some other bird relieve guard. On the least appearance of an enemy, the sentinel gives an alarm, and the whole flock invariably run up to him, and for a moment or two stand still in a crowd, and then take flight; at first in a confused mass, but this is soon changed into a beautiful wedge-like rank, which they keep till about to alight again. Towards evening, I observe the geese coming from the interior, in numerous small flocks, to the bay; in calm weather, flying at a great height; and their peculiar cry is heard some time before the birds are in sight. As soon as they are above the sands, where every object is plainly visible, and no enemy can well be concealed, flock after flock wheel rapidly downwards, and alight at the edge of the water, where they immediately begin splashing and washing themselves, keeping up an almost incessant clamour. In the morning they again take to the fields. Those flocks that feed at a distance start before sunrise; but those that feed nearer to the bay do not leave their roosting-place so soon. During stormy and misty weather, the geese frequently fly quite low over the heads of the work-people in the fields, but even then have a kind of instinctive dread of any person in the garb of a sportsman. I have also frequently got shots at wild geese, by finding out the pools where they drink during the daytime. They generally alight at the distance of two or three hundred yards from the pool; and after watching motionless for a few minutes, all start off in a hurry to get their drink. This done, they return to the open fields or the sea-shore.

In some parts of Sutherland—for instance on Loch Shin, and other lonely and unfrequented pieces of water—the wild goose breeds on the small islands that dot these waters. If their eggs are taken and hatched under tame geese, the young are easily domesticated; but, unless pinioned or confined, they always take to flight with the first flock of wild geese that pass over the place during the migrating season. Even when unable to fly, they evince a great desire to take wing at this season, and are very restless for a few weeks in spring and autumn. In a lonely and little-frequented spot on the banks of Loch Shin, where the remains of walls and short green herbage point out the site of some former shealing or residence of cattle-herds, long since gone to ruin, I have frequently found the wild goose with her brood feeding on the fine grass that grows on what was once the dwelling of man. The young birds do not fly till after they are full grown, but are very active in the water, swimming and diving with great quickness.

March is a month full of interest to the observer of the habits of birds, particularly of those that are migratory. During the last week of February and the first week in March thousands of pewits appear here: first a few stragglers arrive, but in the course of some days the shores of the bay are literally alive with them.

The black-headed gulls also arrive in great numbers. This bird loses the black feathers on the head during the winter, and at this season begins to resume them. I see the birds with their heads of every degree of black and white just now; in a fortnight their black cowl is complete. In the evenings and at night-time thousands of these birds collect on the bay, and every one of them appears to be chattering at once, so that the whole flock together make a noise that drowns every other sound or cry for a considerable distance round them.

March 6th.—I observe that the herons in the heronry on the Findhorn [1] are now busily employed in sitting on their eggs, the heron being one of the first birds to commence breeding in this country. A more curious and interesting sight than the Findhorn heronry I do not know: from the top of the high rocks on the east side of the river you look down into every nest, the herons breeding on the opposite side of the river, which is here very narrow. The cliffs and rocks are studded with splendid pines and larch, and fringed with all the more lowly but not less beautiful underwood which abounds in this country. Conspicuous amongst these are the bird-cherry and mountain-ash, the holly and the wild rose; while the golden blossoms of furze and broom enliven every crevice and corner in the rock. Opposite to you is a wood of larch and oak, on the latter of which trees are crowded a vast number of the nests of the heron. The foliage and small branches of the oaks that they breed on

[1] For a full account of this far-famed heronry at Darnaway, and the manner of the birds deserting it owing to the persecution of crows and jackdaws, see *Natural History and Sport in Moray,* p. 55 and notes.

seem entirely destroyed, leaving nothing but the naked arms and branches of the trees on which the nests are placed. The same nests, slightly repaired, are used year after year. Looking down at them from the high banks of the Altyre side of the river, you can see directly into their nests, and can become acquainted with the whole of their domestic economy. You can plainly see the green eggs, and also the young herons, who fearlessly, and conscious of the security they are left in, are constantly passing backwards and forwards and alighting on the topmost branches of the larch or oak trees, whilst the still younger birds sit bolt upright in the nest, snapping their beaks together with a curious sound. Occasionally a grave-looking heron is seen balancing himself by some incomprehensible feat of gymnastics on the very topmost twig of a larch-tree, where he swings about in an unsteady manner, quite unbecoming so sage-looking a bird. Occasionally a thievish jackdaw dashes out from the cliffs opposite the heronry and flies straight into some unguarded nest, seizes one of the large green eggs, and flies back to his own side of the river, the rightful owner of the eggs pursuing the active little robber with loud cries and the most awkward attempts at catching him.

The heron is a noble and picturesque-looking bird, as she sails quietly through the air with outstretched wings and slow flight; but nothing is more ridiculous and undignified than her appearance as she vainly chases the jackdaw or hooded crow which is carrying off her egg and darting rapidly round the angles and corners of the rocks. Now and then every heron raises its head and looks on the alert as the peregrine falcon, with rapid and direct flight, passes their crowded dominion; but, intent on his own nest, built on the rock some little way farther on, the hawk takes no notice of his long-legged neighbours, who soon settle down again into their attitudes of rest. The kestrel-hawk frequents the same part of the river, and lives in amity with the wood-pigeons that breed in every cluster of ivy which clings to the rocks. Even that bold and fearless enemy of all the pigeon race, the sparrowhawk, frequently has her nest within a few yards of the wood-pigeon, and you see these birds (at all other seasons such deadly enemies) passing each other in their way to and fro from their respective nests in perfect peace and amity. It has seemed to me that the sparrowhawk and wood-pigeon during the breeding-season frequently enter into a mutual compact against the crows and jackdaws, which are constantly on the look-out for the eggs of all other birds. The hawk appears to depend on the vigilance of the wood-pigeon to warn him of the approach of these marauders; and then the brave little warrior sallies out, and is not satisfied till he has driven the crow to a safe distance from the nests of himself and his more peaceable ally. At least in no other way can I account for these two birds so very frequently breeding not only in the same range of rock, but within two or three yards of each other.

SITE OF HERONRY ON THE FINDHORN

SANDHILLS OF MORAY

CHAPTER XX

The Sandhills of Morayshire: Description of; Origin of—Foxes: Destructiveness and Cunning of; Anecdote of—Roe-hunting in the Sandhills—Anecdotes

BETWEEN the fertile plains of Moray and the shores of the Moray Firth there lies one of the most peculiarly barren and strange districts of country in Scotland, consisting of a stretch of sandhills,[1] in most parts formed of pure and very fine

---

[1] Compare the account of these sandhills given by the author in his *Natural History and Sport in Moray*, p. 271.
"The lands of Godowine, near the mouth of the Thames, and likewise the land of Moray on the east coast of Scotland, together with many villages, castles, towns, and extensive woods both in England and Scotland, were overwhelmed by the sea, and the labours of men laid waste by the discharge of sand from the sea" at the close of the eleventh century (Boethius).
In the Hebrides the sandy sea-tracts known as *machars* are bound together by a wiry bent grass. If sheep nibble this too closely and tear the protecting surface, the winds soon enlarge it, and produce wild drifts of sand which do much damage. "This is said to have been the cause of that overwhelming sand-drift which converted the fertile lands of Culbyn, in Morayshire, into that vast chain of sandhills which now extends along the coast. Seven disastrous years of famine had reduced the people to such extremity of poverty, that they were driven to collect fuel where and how they could. Thus the broom and bent grass which had hitherto bound the shore were all torn up, and the wind catching the sand, blew it in thick clouds upwards of twenty-five miles along the coast, burying

yellowish sand, without a blade of vegetation of any description, and constantly shifting and changing their shape and appearance on the recurrence of continued dry winds. Looking from the hills more inland, this range of sand, in the evening sun, has the appearance of a golden boundary line to the beautiful picture of the firth. With the magnificent rocks of Cromarty, and the snow-capped mountains of Ross-shire and Sutherland in the distance, I know no more striking picture than the *coup d'œil* of this landscape, with the smiling plains and groves of Morayshire as a foreground.

In other parts of these sandhills are tracts covered with a dry and rough kind of bent, the long roots of which, stretching along the surface of the sand, and throwing out innumerable fibres and holders, serve in some measure to prevent the drifting of the sand. It is a matter of surprise how this bent can find enough sustenance and moisture in the sand, which is always moving and always dry. At the extremity, opposite Findhorn, is a peninsula, with a solitary farm-house, and a tolerably-sized arable farm, with tracts of broom and furze around it. The furze-bushes are all eaten by the rabbits into peculiar shapes, as the old yew and box trees in a Dutch garden are cut into figures to humour the quaint fancies of their heavy-sterned proprietors. The rabbits ought, by the bye, to be well clothed, as they nibble the furze into regular cushions and ottomans, on which they sit and look out in the fine summer evenings, without fear or dread of the sharpness of the thorns, which in this arid district appear to me sharper and more penetrating than anywhere else.

Westwards, towards Nairn, the sandhills are interrupted by an extent of broken hillocks, covered with the deepest heather that I ever met with, which conceals innumerable pits and holes,[1] many of the latter not above a foot in diameter, three or four feet deep, and so completely concealed by the growth of moss and heather as to form the most perfect traps for the unwary passer-by. I never could find out what these holes were originally made for, as they evidently are not the work of

thousands of acres beneath this deep, ever-shifting sand desert" (Miss C. F. Gordon Cumming, *In the Hebrides*, pp. 134, 292: Chatto and Windus, London, 1883).

Many specimens, chiefly of prehistoric objects in stone and bronze, have been collected upon Culbyn Sands, and may be seen in the Antiquarian Museum, Edinburgh.

[1] In the heathery hill-side under Ben More, and over Loch Assynt in Sutherland, similar curious holes and pits are to be found.

nature. A large part of the ground is here well wooded; the trees do not, however, appear likely ever to come to a large size, well as they flourish when young. This district of wood and heath is here and there intersected by nearly impassable swamps, the abode of mallards and teal, and occasionally of geese. In the wooded parts are plenty of roe, who feed about the swamps, and in the warm weather lie like hares on the hillocks covered with long heath, and under the stunted fir-trees in the midst of the wet places. Throughout the whole tract of this wild ground there are great numbers of foxes, who live undisturbed, and grow to a very great size; feeding during the season on young roe, wild ducks, and black game; and when these fail, they make great havoc amongst the game, poultry, and rabbits in the adjoining country. I have frequently started and shot a fox here out of the rough heather, when I have been looking for wild ducks, or passing through the place on my way to the sea-shore. Farther westward, the sandhills are bounded by a large extent of marsh and water, terminating at last in an extensive lake, dreary and cold-looking, the resort of wild-fowl of every kind, from the swan to the teal, but said to contain no fish excepting eels.

I never yet could get a good account of the origin of these sandhills; I say origin, because they are evidently of a more recent formation than any of the surrounding land. In several places, where the sand is blown off, you see the remains of cultivated ground, the land below the sand being laid out in regular furrows and ridges, made by the plough; and, from their regularity and evenness, one would suppose that agriculture must have been well advanced when these lands were in cultivation. Did the covering that now conceals these fields consist wholly of sand, one would agree with the popular story of their having been overwhelmed with it by the wind; but in some parts the ground is covered to a good depth by shingle and water-worn stones of a size to preclude the possibility of their having been brought there by the action of the wind. In certain places, too, there are curious regularly-formed pyramids of shingle, about sixteen feet high, and of the same diameter at the base. These, and long banks of shingle, having exactly the appearance of the sea-beach, make me suppose that the destruction of what was once a fertile country was brought about by some sudden and unaccountable inroad of the sea. Indeed, the appearance of the whole of this barren district would lead one to the same conclusion. At any rate, amongst the numerous traditions regarding the origin of the sandhills, I never heard one that quite satisfied my mind. Whatever it once was, it is now a mere barren waste, or, as a friend of mine named it, a kind of Arabia Infelix, inhabited only by wild animals; and it seems a wonder that even these have not long ago been starved out of it. Whatever the rabbits and hares feed on, they are larger there than in the more cultivated and fertile parts of the country; and the foxes are like wolves in size and strength. Owing to the solitude and quietness of the place, I have seen the foxes at all hours of the day prowling about, or basking in the sun, or sometimes coolly seated on the top of a sandhill watching my movements. I have occasionally fallen in with their earth or breeding-place. The quantity of remains of different animals, which they have brought to these places to feed their young, proves the fox to be a most universal depredator. Turkeys which have been caught at several miles' distance, tame geese from the farms, and wild geese from the sea-shore; fowls, ducks, pheasants, and game of every kind, including old roe that have been wounded, and young roe too weak to resist their attacks, all appear to form part of this wily robber's larder.[1] He also takes home to his young any fish that he finds on the shore, or that he can catch in the shallow pools of the streams during the night-time. No animal is cunning enough to escape the fox; wild duck or wood-pigeon (the most wary of all birds) fall to his share. Patient and cunning, the fox finds out the pool where the mallard and his mate resort to in the evenings, and lying in wait to the leeward of the place, in some tuft of rushes, catches the bird before it can take wing. One night, seven of my domesticated wild ducks were taken from the poultry-yard, close to the house. After some search, we found some of the birds concealed in different places in the adjoining fields, where the fox had buried them, not having time to carry them all to his earth that night. He fell a victim to his greediness, however, being caught in a trap a few nights afterwards.

[1] Even small birds are not disdained, yellow-hammers and hedge-sparrows, as we have seen. Moles too are a favourite food.

A fox, after he has lost one of his feet in a trap, is still able to get his own living, and to keep himself in as good plight as if he had his whole complement of legs effective. One, which had left a foot in a trap, and escaped on the other three, lived for two years afterwards about the same ground. We knew his track in the sand by the impression of his stump. This winter, while shooting in the sandhills, we saw a fox sneak quietly into a small thicket of trees. I immediately placed the two sportsmen who were with me at different points of the thicket, and then took my retriever on the track. The dog, who, from his former battles with fox and otter, is very eager in his enmity against all animals of the kind, almost immediately started the fox, and, after a short chase, turned him out within shot of a very sure gun. The consequence was the instant death of Mr. Reynard. On examining, he turned out to be the very fox whose foot had been nailed up two years before. He was an immense old dog-fox, in perfect condition, although he had only three legs to hunt on. The fox is a constant attendant on the rabbit-trapper, robbing him of most of the rabbits that are caught in his traps or snares. He sometimes, however, pays dearly, by getting caught in the wires; and although he generally breaks the snare and escapes, does not do so without most severe punishment. I shot a fox this season who had the remains of a rabbit-wire round his hind-leg, which was cut to the bone by his struggles to escape.

When living in Ross-shire, I went one morning in July before daybreak to endeavour to shoot a stag, which had been complained of very much by an adjoining farmer as having done great damage to his crops. Just after it was daylight, I saw a large fox come very quietly along the edge of the plantation in which I was concealed; he looked with great care over the turf wall into the field, and seemed to long very much to get hold of some hares that were feeding in it—but apparently knew that he had no chance of catching one by dint of running; after considering a short time, he seemed to have formed his plans, and having examined the different gaps in the wall by which the hares might be supposed to go in and out, he fixed upon the one that seemed the most frequented, and laid himself down close to it in an attitude like a cat watching a mouse-hole. Cunning as he was, he was too intent on his own hunting to be aware that I was within twenty yards of him with a loaded rifle, and able to watch every movement he made; I was much amazed to see the fellow so completely outwitted, and kept my rifle ready to shoot him if he found me out and attempted to escape. In the meantime I watched all his plans: he first with great silence and care scraped a small hollow in the ground, throwing up the sand as a kind of screen between his hiding-place and the hares' meuse—every now and then, however, he stopped to listen, and sometimes to take a most cautious peep into the field; when he had done this, he laid himself down in a convenient posture for springing upon his prey, and remained perfectly motionless, with the exception of an occasional reconnoitre of the feeding hares. When the sun began to rise, they came one by one from the field to the cover of the plantation; three had already come in without passing by his ambush, one of them came within twenty yards of him, but he made no movement beyond crouching still more flatly to the ground—presently two came directly towards him; though he did not venture to look up, I saw by an involuntary motion of his ears that those quick organs had already warned him of their approach; the two hares came through the gap together, and the fox springing with the quickness of lightning caught one and killed her immediately; he then lifted up his booty and was carrying it off like a retriever, when my rifle-ball stopped his course by passing through his backbone, and I went up and despatched him. After seeing this I never wondered again as to how a fox could make prey of animals much quicker than himself, and apparently quite as cunning.

One day this winter, we attempted to beat the thickets and rough ground in the sandhill district for foxes. Having appointed a place of meeting, I went with a friend and four couple of beagles well entered to fox and roe, to meet the owner of part of the ground and an adjoining proprietor. We were only four guns. Having placed the other three in passes along the edge of the swamps, through which the roe and foxes would have to make their way on going from one wood to the other, I went into the thickets with the keepers and hounds. We had hardly entered when up got a fine buck, and the beagles were immediately laid on, and away they went; I ran to a small height from which I had a good view of the country—away went the buck at a rattling pace, and the gallant little pack hard on his track, making the woods echo with their enlivening cry. The buck first took a line into the roughest part of the ground, expecting no doubt to throw off the dogs at once, as he probably had often done with sheep-dogs or curs that had chased him; but finding that his persevering little enemies were not to be so outwitted, after standing still for a short time to deliberate, he turned back and went straight for the swamp where the guns were, but seeing the hat of one of the gentlemen posted there, and not liking to cross the water directly in his face, he turned along the edge of it, half inclined to go back. But just at this instant the little pack came full cry out of the wood—their deep notes sounding in full chorus as they came upon the open ground; they were rather at a loss for a moment or two, and I ran up to put them on the scent. The buck, who had been watching us as he went quietly along, was decided as to his course by seeing this, and the moment the dogs' cry gave notice that they had found the scent again, he dashed into the water at a place where there was no pass—it was not above a hundred yards in width, and excepting two or three yards in the middle where he had to swim, not deeper than a few inches. The beagles came full cry on his track, and just viewed him as he was cantering up a steep ascent on the other side of the water; they at once dashed in, and, encouraged by a view holloa, swam through the water and took up the scent immediately— away they went, till we lost all sound of them; presently we heard their notes borne down on the wind from a great distance —the sound came nearer and nearer, and soon the buck appeared on the top of the brae, near the water's edge, directly above two of the guns, who had got together tired of waiting, and were discussing the price of railway-sleepers, etc. The deer stood watching them for some minutes, till the hounds came within fifty yards of him in the thicket behind him; the gentlemen, hearing the dogs, ran to their respective posts, and the roe came down the brae, passed between them unobserved, and crossed the water again; the dogs full cry and all together immediately behind them. Hark away! hark away! was the cry, and away they *did* go, in a straight line towards the seashore. The buck (whom I constantly saw) appeared quite bewildered and was evidently getting distressed; after a twenty minutes' burst along the shore and the open part of the cover, he turned back and passed me within a hundred yards at a slow canter—the hounds had got well warmed to their work, and never lost the scent for a moment. The buck, after a great many turns and windings, was fairly driven to the swamp again, which he crossed this time quite slowly, stopping in the water every now and then, as if to cool himself; but the dogs did not leave him much time, and were soon at the edge of the water. The buck crouched down in the middle of a small heath-covered island in the water, which was here of a considerable width: the hounds, however, went right across the water, and began trying for the scent along the opposite edge. I had seen the roe stop where he was, and ran down to call the hounds back, but before I could do so, one of the pack, a very excellent young bitch, whom I had got from the New Forest in Hampshire, gave a cast and got the wind of the roe, giving a quiet cheep, sufficient however to warn the rest of the pack, who all joined her; she trotted through the water straight up to the island, and very soon the whole of them in full cry were at the roe's heels, and driving him directly in the face of one of the guns, who finished the hunt with a cartridge, killing him not twenty yards ahead of the dogs. When the roe was opened afterwards, the whole cartridge, wire and all, was found embedded in his heart, a proof of the great efficacy of this kind of charge, and the superiority of its strength over that of loose shot.

After resting the dogs and talking over the chase, I left my friends at their passes again, and went back to draw the cover for another roe. The dogs were very soon in full cry again, and as luck would have it, out of four roe that had started they had got on the track of a fine buck; this roe was run for some time in as good style as the last, and after he had narrowly escaped being shot two or three times, I shot him dead about fifty yards before the hounds. During the run I saw two foxes start; one of them waded quietly through the swamp towards my English friend, who, however, did not shoot at him, because he was afraid, he said, of losing a chance at the roe; but I rather suspect that, having been bred a fox-hunter in his own country, he had a kind of holy horror against killing a fox in any but the orthodox manner to which he had been accustomed.

After having opened one of the bucks and rewarded the beagles with the entrails, liver, etc., we repaired to a cottage at hand, where our host for the day had provided a capital luncheon.

Frequently when passing these swamps and rugged ground, I have seen roe start up from the rough heather, or feeding, knee-deep in the water, on the rank weeds and herbage. The best part of this ground for wild-fowl is gradually getting drained, and what was (a few years since) a dreary waste of marsh and swamp has now become a range of smiling corn-land. I shall not easily forget my old keeper's exclamation, on his first seeing one of his favourite spots for stalking wild-fowl turned into an oat-field. We had walked far, with little success, but he had depended on our finding the ducks in a particular spot, not being aware that it had been drained since his last visit to it. Having taken a long and sonorous pinch of snuff, according to his usual custom when in any dilemma, he turned to me, muttering, "Well, well, the whole country is spoilt with their improvements, as they ca' them. It will no be fit for a Christian man to live in much longer." He thought that oats and wheat were a bad exchange for his favourite ducks and geese.

A CAUTIOUS PEEP

DEATH OF MY FIRST STAG

CHAPTER XXI

Death of my first Stag

WHERE is the man who does not remember and look back with feelings of energy and delight to the day, the hour, and the wild scene, when he killed unaided his first stag? Of course, I refer only to those who have the same love of wild sport, and the same enjoyment in the romantic solitude and scenery of the mountain and glen that I have myself: shooting tame partridges and hares from the back of a well-trained shooting-pony in a stubble field does not, in my eyes, constitute a sportsman; though there is a certain interest attached even to this kind of pursuit, arising more from observing the cleverness and instinct of the dogs employed, than in killing the birds. But far different is the enjoyment derived from stalking the red-deer [1] in his native mountain, where every energy of the sportsman must be called into active use before he can command success.

Well do I remember the mountain-side where I shot my first stag, and though many years have since passed by, I could now, were I to pass through that wild and lovely glen, lay my hand on the very rock under which he fell.

Though a good rifle-shot, indeed few were much better, there seemed a charm against my killing a deer. On two occasions, eagerness and fear of missing shook my hand when I ought to have killed a fine stag. The second that I ever shot at came in my way in a very singular manner.

I had been looking during the chief part of the day for deer, and had, according to appointment, met an attendant with my gun and pointers at a particular spring in the hills, meaning to shoot my way home. This spring was situated in the midst of a small green spot, like an oasis in the desert, surrounded on all sides by a long stretch of broken black ground. The well itself was in a little round hollow, surrounded by high banks.

I was resting here, having met my gillie, and was consoling myself for my want of success by smoking a cigar, when, at the same moment, a kind of shadow came across me, and the pointers who were coupled at my feet pricked up their ears and growled, with their eyes fixed on some object behind me. My keeper, who had been out with me all day, was stretched on his back, in a half slumber, and the gillie was kneeling down taking a long draught at the cool well, with the enjoyment of one who had had a long toiling walk on a hot August day. Turning my head lazily to see what had roused the dogs, and had cast its shadow across me, instead of a shepherd, as I expected—could I believe my eyes!—there stood a magnificent stag, with the fine-shaped horns peculiar to those of the Sutherland forests. He was standing on the bank immediately behind

---

[1] In the forests or grounds cleared of sheep the red-deer has increased considerably of late years.—C. St. J.

me, and not above fifty yards off, looking with astonishment at the group before him, who had taken possession of the very spot where he had intended to slake his thirst. The deer seemed too much astonished to move, and for a moment I was in the same dilemma. The rifle was on the ground just behind the slumbering Donald. I was afraid the deer would be off out of sight, if I got up to take it, or if I called loud enough to awake Donald. So I was driven to the necessity of giving him a pretty severe kick, which had the effect of making him turn on his side, and open his eyes with a grunt. "The rifle, Donald, the rifle," I whispered, holding out my hand. Scarcely knowing what he was at, he instinctively stretched out his hand to feel for it, and held it out to me. All this takes some time to describe, but did not occupy a quarter of a minute. At the same instant that I got the rifle, the gillie lifted up his head from the water, and half turning, saw the stag, and also saw that I was about to shoot at him. With a presence of mind worthy of being better seconded, he did not raise himself from his knees, but remained motionless with his eyes fixed on the deer. As I said before, I had never killed a deer, and my hand shook, and my heart beat. I fired, however, with, as I thought, a good aim at his shoulder. The deer at the instant turned round. After firing my shot, we all (including Donald, who by this time comprehended what was going on) ran to the top of the bank to see what had happened, as the deer disappeared the instant I fired. I had, I believe, missed him altogether, though he looked as large as an ox, and we saw him going at a steady gallop over the wide flat. Donald had out the glass immediately, and took a steady sight at him, but having watched the noble animal, as he galloped up the opposite slope and stood for two or three minutes on the summit, looking back intently at us, he shut up the telescope with a jerk that threatened to break every glass in it, and giving a grunt, vastly expressive of disgust, returned to the well, where he took a long draught. His only remark at the time was, "There's no the like of that stag in the country ; weel do I mind seeing him last year when shooting ptarmigan up yonder, and not a bullet had I. The deil's in the rifle, that she did na kill him ; and he'll cross the river before he stops." It required some time, and some whisky also, to restore Donald to his usual equanimity.

This was on a Saturday. On the Monday following, at a very early hour, Donald appeared, and after his morning salute of "It's a fine day, Sir," he added, "There will be some deer about the west shoulder of the hill above Alt-na-cahr. Whenever the wind is in the airt it now is, they feed about the burn there." We agreed to walk across to that part of the ground, and were soon *en route*. Bran galloped round us, baying joyously, as if he expected we should have good luck. We had not gone half a mile from the house, when we met one of the prettiest girls in the country, tripping along the narrow path, humming a Gaelic air, and looking bright and fresh as the morning. "How are you all at home, Nanny, and how is your father getting on? does he see any deer on the hill?" said I; her father was a shepherd not far from the house, and she was then going down on some errand to my servants. "We are all no' that bad, thank you, Sir, except mother, who still has the trouble on her. Father says that he saw some hinds and a fine *stag* yesterday as he crossed the hill to the kirk; they were feeding on the top of Alt-na-cahr, and didna mind him a bit."

Donald looked at me, with a look full of importance, at this confirmation of his prophecy. "'Deed, Sir, that's a bonny lass, and as gude as she is bonny. It's just gude luck our meeting her; if we had met that auld witch, her mother, not a beast would we have seen the day." I have heard of Donald turning home again if he met an old woman when starting on any deer-stalking excursion. The pretty young girl, however, was a good omen in his eyes. We passed through the woods, seeing here and there a roebuck standing gazing at us as we crossed some grassy glade where he was feeding. On the rocks near the top of the woods, Donald took me to look at a trap he had set, and in it we found a beautiful marten cat, which we killed, and hid amongst the stones—another good omen in Donald's eyes.

On we went, taking a careful survey of the ground here and there. At a loch whose Gaelic name I do not remember, we saw a vast number of wild ducks, and at the farther extremity of it a hind and calf feeding. We waited here for some time, and I amused myself with watching the two deer as they fed, unconscious of our neighbourhood, and from time to time drank at the burn which supplied the loch. We then passed over a long dreary tract of brown and broken ground, till we came to the picturesque-looking place where we expected to find the deer—a high conical hill, rising out of rather flat ground, which gave it an appearance of being of a greater height than it really was. We took a most careful survey of the slope on which Donald expected to see the deer. Below was an extensive level piece of heather with a burn running through it in an endless variety of windings, and fringed with green rushes and grass, which formed a strong contrast to the dark-coloured moor through which it made its way, till it emptied itself into a long narrow loch, beyond which rose Ben Cleebrich and some more of the highest mountains in Scotland. In vain we looked and looked, and Donald at last shut up his telescope in despair: "They are no' here the day," was his remark. "But what is that, Donald?" said I, pointing to some bluish-looking object I saw at some distance from us, rising out of the heather. The glass was turned towards it, and after having been kept motionless for some time, he pronounced it to be the head and neck of a hind. I took the glass, and while I was looking at it, I saw a fine stag rise suddenly from some small hollow near her, stretch himself, and lie down again. Presently six more hinds and a two-year-old stag got up, and after walking about for a few minutes, they, one by one, lay down again, but every one seemed to take up a position commanding a view of the whole country. We crept back a few paces, and then getting into the course of the burn, got within three hundred yards of the deer, but by no means whatever could we get nearer. The stag was a splendid fellow, with ten points, and regular, fine-shaped horns. Bran winded them, and watched us most earnestly, as if to ask why we did not try to get at them. The sensible dog, however, kept quite quiet, as if aware of the importance of not being seen or heard. Donald asked me what o'clock it was; I told him that it was just two. "Well, well, Sir, we must just wait here till three o'clock, when the deer will get up to feed, and most likely the brutes will travel towards the burn. The Lord save us, but yon's a muckle beast." Trusting to his experience, I waited patiently, employing myself in attempting to dry my hose by wringing them, and placing them in the sun. Donald took snuff and watched the deer, and Bran laid his head on his paws as if asleep, but his sharp eye, and ear pricked up on the slightest movement, showed that he was ready for action at a moment's warning. As nearly as possible at three o'clock they did get up to feed: first the hinds rose and cropped a few mouthfuls of the coarse grass near them; looking at and waiting for their lord and master, who, however, seemed lazily inclined and would not move; the young stag fed steadily on towards us.

Frequently the hinds stopped and turned back to their leader, who remained quite motionless, excepting that now and then he scratched a fly off his flank with his horn or turned his head towards the hill-side when a grouse crowed or a plover whistled. The young stag was feeding quietly within a hundred and fifty yards of us, and we had to lie flat on the ground now and then to escape his observation. The evening air already began to feel chill, when suddenly the object of our pursuit jumped up, stretched himself, and began feeding. Not liking the pasture close to him, he trotted at once down into the flat ground right away from us. Donald uttered a Gaelic oath, and I fear I added an English one. The stag that had been feeding so near us stood still for a minute to watch the others, who were all now several hundred yards away, grazing steadily. I aimed at him, but just as I was about to fire he turned away, leaving nothing but his haunch in view, and went after the rest. Donald applauded me for not shooting at him, but told me that our case was hopeless, and that we had better make our way home and attempt no more, as they were feeding in so open a place that it was impossible to get at them: even Bran yawned and rose, as if he too had given up all hope. "I will have one try, Donald; so hold the dog." "You need na fash yoursel', Sir; they are clean out of all hope and reason." I determined to make an effort before it became dusk; so leaving Donald, I set off down the burn, looking for some hollow place that might favour my getting up to them, but I could find none: at last it struck me that I might by chance get up within a long shot by keeping a small hillock, which was in the middle of the plain, between me and the deer. The hillock was not two feet high, and all depended on the animals keeping together and not outflanking me.

On I went, not on my hands and knees, but crawling like a snake, and never rising even to my knee. I could see their hind-quarters as they walked away, feeding, however, most eagerly, and when they looked up I lay still flatter on the ground with my face buried in the heather. They appeared, however, not to suspect danger in the open plain, but often looked anxiously towards the burn or the rocky side of the mountain. One old long-legged hind kept me in a constant state of alarm, as she frequently looked in my direction, turning her ears as if to catch some suspicious sound. As for the stag, he never looked about him once, leaving that to the hinds. I at last got within about a hundred yards of the whole of them : as they fed in a group turned away from me, I could not get a shot at anything but their hind-quarters, and I did not wish to shoot unless I could get a fair broadside towards me. While waiting for an opportunity, still flat on the ground, a grouse cock walked out of the heather close to me, and strutted on with head erect and his bright eye fixed on me till he came to a little hillock, where he stopped and began to utter a note of alarm. Instantly every deer left off eating. I saw that no time was to be lost and raised myself on my elbow, and with cocked rifle waited for the hinds to move, that I might get at the stag, who was in the midst of them. The hinds soon saw me and began to trot away, but their leader seemed determined to see what the danger was, and before he started turned round to look towards the spot where the grouse was, giving me a good slanting shot at his shoulder. I immediately touched the trigger, feeling at the same time sure of my aim. The ball went true and down he fell. I began reloading, but before I had half done the stag was up again and making play after the hinds, who were galloping up a gentle slope of the hill. The poor beast was evidently moving with the greatest difficulty and pain ; sometimes coming to his knees, and then recovering himself with a strong effort, he still managed to keep not far behind them. I sat down in utter despair : looking round too for Donald and Bran I could see nothing of them. Between anxiety and vexation I did not know what to do. All at once I saw the hinds dash away in different directions, and the next moment my gallant Bran appeared in the midst of them. I shouted with joy. On came the dog, taking no notice of the hinds, but making straight for the stag, who stood still for one instant, and then rushed with apparently full vigour down the hill. Down they came towards the burn, the dog not five yards behind the stag, but unable to reach his shoulder (the place where he always struck his game). In a few moments deer and hound went headlong and seemingly both together into the burn. Donald appeared running like a lunatic: with good judgment he had, when I left him, gone to cut off the deer in case I wounded one and it took up the hill. As good luck would have it, the hinds had led off the stag right up to where Donald and Bran were, notwithstanding his inclination to go the other way. I ran to see what had become of them in the burn, expecting to find the stag at bay. When I got there, however, it was all over. The deer had probably tumbled from weakness, and Bran had got his fangs well into the throat of the poor brute before he could rise again. The gallant dog, when I was up with him, lay down panting with his fore-paws on the deer, and wagging his tail, seemed to congratulate me on my victory and to expect to be caressed for his share in it. A fine stag he was, in perfect order, with noble antlers. Donald added to my satisfaction by applauding my manner of getting up to him, adding that he never would have thought it possible to kill a stag on such bare and flat ground. Little did I feel the fatigue of our three hours' walk, two of them in the dark and hard rain. We did not go home, but went to a shepherd's house, whose inhabitants were at evening prayer when we arrived; we did not interrupt them, but afterwards the wife prepared us a capital supper of eggs and fresh trout, which we devoured with vast relish before the bright peat-fire, our wet clothes steaming all the time like a boiler. Such was the death of my first stag.

FINDHORN BAY

THE FINDHORN RIVER

CHAPTER XXII

The Findhorn River—Excursion to Source—Deer-stalking—Shepherds—Hind and Calf—Heavy Rain—Floods—Walk to Lodge—Fine Morning—Highland Sheep—Banks of River—Cottages.

I DO not know a stream that more completely realises all one's ideas of the beauty of Highland scenery than the Findhorn, taking it from the spot where it is no more than a small rivulet bubbling and sparkling along a narrow gorge in the far-off recesses of the Monaghliahd mountains, down to the Bay of Findhorn, where its accumulated waters are poured into the Moray Firth. From source to mouth, this river is full of beauty and interest.

On a bright August day, the 6th of the month, I joined a friend in a deer-stalking expedition, near the source of the Findhorn, in the Monaghliahd. We went from near Inverness to our quarters. For the greatest part of our way our road was over a flat though elevated range of dreary moor, more interesting to the eye of a grouse-shooter than to any one else. When within a few miles of the end of our journey, the Findhorn came in sight, passing like a silver stripe, edged with bright green, through the brown mountains, and sparkling brightly in the evening sun. The sides of the hills immediately overhanging the river are clothed with patches of weeping-birch and juniper, with here and there a black hut perched on a green knoll, dotted with groves of the rugged and ancient-looking birch-trees. About these solitary abodes, too, were small patches of oats and potatoes. The mavis with its joyous note, and the blackbird's occasional full and rich song, greeted us as we passed through these wooded tracts. Sometimes a wood-pigeon would crash through the branches close to us as we wound round some corner of the wood.

Having arrived at our destination, we made ourselves as comfortable as we could, and retired to rest.

In the morning we started in different directions. I, accompanied by a shepherd, went westward towards the sources of the river. I cannot say that I had much hope of finding deer, as the whole line of my march was full of sheep; and red-deer will very seldom remain quiet when this is the case, either from a dislike to the sheep themselves, or from knowing that where there are sheep there are also shepherds and shepherds' dogs. With black cattle, on the contrary, deer live in tolerable amity; and I have frequently seen cattle and deer feeding together in the same glen.

I went some miles westward, keeping up the course of the river, or rather parallel to it, sometimes along its very edge, and at other times at some distance from the water. The highest building on the river, if building it can be termed, is a small shealing, or summer residence of the shepherds, called, I believe, Dahlvaik. Seeing some smoke coming from this hut, we went to it. When at some few hundred yards off, we were greeted with a most noisy salute from some half-dozen sheep-dogs, who seemed bent on eating up my bloodhound. But having tried her patience to the uttermost, till she rolled over two or three of them rather roughly (not condescending, however, to use her teeth), the colleys retreated to the door of the shealing, where they redoubled, if possible, their noise, keeping up a concert of howling and barking enough to startle every deer in the country. My companion, whose knowledge of the English tongue was not very deep, told me that the owners of the dogs would be some "lads from Strath Errick," who were to hold a conference with him about some sheep.

A black-headed, unshaven Highlander having come out, and kicked the dogs into some kind of quiet, we entered the hut, and found two more "lads" in it, one stretched out on a very rough bench, and the other busy stirring up some oatmeal and hot water for their breakfast. The smoke for a few moments prevented my making out what or who were in the place. I held a short (very short) conversation with the three shepherds, they understanding not one word of English, and I understanding very few of Gaelic. But, by the help of the man who accompanied me, I found out that a stag or two were still in the glen, besides a few hinds. The meal and water having been mixed sufficiently, it was emptied out into a large earthen dish, and placed smoking on the lid of a chest. Each man then produced from some recess of his plaid a long wooden spoon; whilst my companion assisted in the ceremony by fetching some water from the river in a bottle. They all three, then, having doffed their bonnets, and raising their hands, muttered over a long Gaelic grace. Then, without saying a word, they set to with good will at the scalding mess before them, each attacking the corner of the dish nearest him, shovelling immense spoonfuls down their throats; and when more than usually scalded—their throats must have been as fire-proof as that of the Fire King himself—taking a mouthful of the water in the bottle, which was passed from one to the other for that purpose. Having eaten a most extraordinary quantity of the pottage, each man wiped his spoon on the sleeve of his coat, and again said a grace. The small remainder was then mixed with more water and given to the dogs, who had been patiently waiting for their share. After they had licked the dish clean, it was put away into the meal-chest, the key of which was then concealed in a hole of the turf wall. I divided most of my cigars with the men to smoke in their pipes, and handed round my whisky-flask, reserving a small modicum for my own use during the day.

From this place to its source the river is very narrow, and

THE VALLEY OF THE FINDHORN

confined between steep and rocky hills that come down to the edge of the water; varied here and there by less abrupt ascents, covered with spreading juniper-bushes and green herbage. On one of these bright spots we saw a hind and her calf, the former standing to watch us as we passed up the opposite side of the river, while her young one was playing about her like a lamb. They did not seem to care much for our coming there; and having watched us for some time, and seeing that we had no evil intention towards them, the hind recommenced feeding, only occasionally stopping to see that we did not turn. The ring-ouzel, that near cousin of the blackbird, frequently flitted across the glen, and, perching on a juniper-bush, saluted us with its wild and sweet song.

The morning was bright, and the river sparkled and danced over its stony bed; while every little pool was dimpled by the rising of the trout, which jumped without dread of hook and line at the small black gnats that were playing about the surface of the water. A solitary heron was standing on a stone in the middle of the stream, seemingly quite regardless of us. But while I was looking at his shadowy figure, which was perfectly reflected in the water beneath him, the bird suddenly flew off with a cry of alarm, occasioned by the appearance of a peregrine falcon, who passed with even and rapid flight at no great height along the course of the river, without taking the least notice of the heron.

Beautiful in its grand and wild solitude is the glen where the Findhorn takes its rise; seldom does the foot of man pass by it. It is too remote even for the sportsman; and the grouse cock crows in peace, and struts without fear of pointer or gun, when he comes down from the hill-slopes at noonday to sip the clear waters of the springs that give birth to this beautiful river. The red-deer fearlessly quenches his thirst in them, as he passes from the hills of Killen to the pine-woods in Strathspey. Seldom is he annoyed by the presence of mankind, unless a chance shepherd or poacher from Badenoch happens to wander in that direction. Having rested for a short time, and satisfied my curiosity respecting the source of the river, we struck off over some very dreary slopes of high ground on the north-east, interspersed with green stripes, through which small burns make their way to swell the main stream of the river. Not a deer did we see, but great quantities of grouse, which, when flushed, flew to short distances, and alighting on some hillock, crowed as it were in defiance. A cold chill that passed over me made me turn and look down the course of the stream, and the first thing that I saw was a dense shower or cloud of rain working its way up the valley, and gradually spreading over the face of the country, shutting out hill after hill from our view as it crept towards us. In the other direction all was blue and bright.

CROSSING THE BURN

"We must turn home, or we shall never get across the streams and burns," was my ejaculation to the shepherd. "'Deed, ay, Sir," was his answer; and, tightening our plaids, we turned our faces towards the east. As the rain approached, the ring-ouzel sang more loudly, as if to take leave of the sunshine; and the grouse flew to the dry and bare heights, where they crowed incessantly.

The rain gradually came on, accompanied by a cold cutting wind. I never saw such rain in my life; it was a perfect deluge; and in five minutes I was as wet as if I had been swimming through the river. We saw the burns we had to cross on our way home tumbling in foaming torrents down the hill-sides. In the morning we had stepped across them without wetting our feet. The first one that we came to I looked at with wonder. Instead of a mere thread of crystal water, creeping rather than flowing through the stones which filled its bed, we had to wade through a roaring torrent, which was carrying in its course pieces of turf, heather, and even large stones. We crossed with some difficulty, holding by each other's collar. Two or three burns we passed in this manner, the rain still continuing, and if possible increasing. I looked round at my companion, and was only prevented from laughing at his limp and rueful countenance by thinking that he probably had just as much cause for merriment in my appearance. The poor hound was perfectly miserable, as she followed me with the rain running in streams down her long ears.

After some time we came opposite the shealing where we had been with the shepherds in the morning. And here my companion said that he must leave me, having particular business with the other men, who had come on purpose to meet him there. He warned me to be very careful in crossing the burns, as, if I once lost my footing in any of them, I should probably never get up again.

Off I tramped through the sodden ground. I managed the first burn pretty well. But the next one was wider, and, if possible, more rapid. I had no stick to sound its depth, but saw that it was too strong to venture into; so I turned up its course, hoping it would get narrower and shallower higher up. Its banks were steep and rocky, and covered in some parts with hazel and birch. On a withered branch of one of the latter was a large buzzard,[1] sitting mournfully in the rain, and uttering its shrill, wild cry, a kind of note between a whistle and a scream. The bird sat so tamely, that in a pet I determined to try if I could not stop his ominous-sounding voice with a rifle-ball. But, after taking a most deliberate aim at him, the copper cap snapped. I tried another with equally bad success. So I had to continue my way, leaving the bird where he was. I could find no place in the burn that was fordable for some

---

[1] The buzzard (*Buteo vulgaris*) is regarded by Gray as a useful bird in game-preserves (Gray, p. 46). Having kept one in confinement for nearly five years, we can quite confirm Gray's view. Our bird, though kept in a large cage with old and young rabbits and guinea-pigs, never injured any of them, even when itself pressed for food. It lived solely on carrion, thus rendering it a strong probability that the buzzard does not kill young rabbits or poults.

distance; and I said to myself, "If I had but a stick to sound the water with!" The next moment almost I saw one about six feet in length standing upright in the ground. I could scarcely believe my eyes. The stick must have been left by mere chance by some shepherd. It came most opportunely for me, however. The first place I tried in the water with it (a spot where I thought I could wade), it went in to the depth of at least five feet. This would never do; so on I went up the hill, splashing through the wet bog and heather. At last I came to a place in the burn, where, by leaping from one stone to the other, at no small risk to myself, I managed to get across. My poor hound had to swim, and was very nearly carried off by the stream. Instead of turning down again towards the river, I still kept the high ground, remembering that I had to pass through two or three other burns, one of them, at least, much larger than any I had already crossed. I had now to make my way over a long flat, covered with coarse grass, and full of holes of water and rotten bog. I never walked a more weary mile in my life, sinking, as I did, up to my knees at nearly every step. When in the middle of this, I saw three hinds and a calf walk deliberately along a ridge not three hundred yards from me. I had to lead the hound for some distance, as she lost all her fatigue on coming on their scent, which she did as we passed their track. I made no attempt on them, knowing the useless state of my rifle. We kept on, and at last got across all the burns excepting the largest, which was still between me and my dry clothes and dinner. I had now got quite high up on the barren hill, leaving everything but rock and heather far below me, the birch-woods not extending above half a mile from the river. I came here to another long flat piece of ground; and having to make many windings and turnings to cross different small streams, I suddenly discovered that I had entirely lost my points of the compass. So, sitting down, I tried to make out which way the wind blew, as my only guide. This soon set me right; and after another hour or two of weary walking, I found myself on the hill-top almost immediately overhanging the Lodge, the smoke from whose chimneys was a most welcome sight. On getting to it, I found the river raging and pouring down between its narrow banks in a manner that no one who has not seen a Highland river in full flood can imagine, carrying with it every kind of debris that its course could produce.

At eleven o'clock at night, when looking at it by the light of a brilliant northern moon (every cloud having long disappeared), we found that the water had already begun to subside, though it still roared on with great fury. On the opposite rocks we could see many a mountain burn as they glanced in the moonlight. Every bird and animal was at rest, excepting a couple of owls answering each other with loud hootings, which were plainly heard above the noise of the waters.

The friend I was with being obliged to go home the next day, I determined also to wend my way to the low country, and to follow the river till I reached my own house.

We started on horseback very early. Nothing could exceed the beauty of the morning, and everything, animate and inanimate, seemed to smile rejoicingly. The Findhorn had returned to its usual size, and danced merrily in the sunshine. The streams on the opposite cliffs were again like silver threads, and the sheep were winding along the narrow paths on the face of the rocks, the animals looking to us as if they were walking, like flies, on the very face of the perpendicular cliffs. We saw a flock of some thirty or so making their way in single file along these paths: while we watched them they came to a place where their road was broken up by the yesterday's torrents. We could not understand what they would do. The path was evidently too narrow to turn; and, as well as we could see with our glasses, to proceed was impossible. However, after a short halt the leader sprang over the obstacle, whatever it was, and alighted safely on the opposite side. The least false step would have sent him down many hundred feet. However, they all got over in safety, and having filed away for some little distance slowly along the face of the precipice, they came to a small green shelf, apparently only a few yards square, the object of all their risk and labour. As fast as they got on this they dispersed, and commenced feeding quickly about it. We did not wait to see them return, as we had a long day's journey before us. Behind the house the hill seemed alive with grouse, crowing in the morning sun. My hound came out baying joyously to see me, and we started on our day's journey. Our road took us through birch-woods, fragrant from the yesterday's rain, and in which the birds sang right merrily. As we descended the river we passed the plantations at Dalnigaric and considerable tracts of corn-ground—the corn in this high country being still perfectly green. Here and there was a small farm-house on a green mound, with a peat-stack larger than the house itself. As we passed these, a bare-headed and bare-legged urchin would look at us round a corner of the building, and then running in, would bring out the rest of the household to stare at us. If we entered one of the houses, we were always greeted with hospitable smiles, and the goodwife, wiping a chair with her apron, would produce a bowl of excellent milk (such milk as you only can get in the Highlands) and a plate of cheese and oat-cake, the latter apparently consisting of chopped straw, and seasoned with gravel, though made palatable by the kind welcome with which it was given. Frequently, too, a bottle of whisky would be produced, and a glass of it urged on us, or we were pressed to stop to take an egg or something warm. At Freeburn we parted—my friend to go by coach to Inverness, and I to keep my course down the river, which is surrounded by dreary grey hills. As I got on, however, the banks grew more rocky and picturesque, enlivened here and there by the usual green patches of corn, and the small farm-houses, with their large peat-stack but diminutive corn-stack. Near Freeburn I talked to an old Highlander, who was flogging the water with a primitive-looking rod and line and a coarse-looking fly, catching, however, a goodly number of trout. He was the first angler I had as yet passed, with the exception of a kilted boy, belonging to the shepherd at our place of rest, who was already out when we left home, catching trout for his own breakfast and that of a young peregrine falcon which he had caught in the rocks opposite the house, and was keeping wholly on a fish diet—and a more beautiful and finer bird I never saw, although she had fed for many weeks on nothing but small trout, a food not so congenial to her as rabbits and pigeons and the other products of the low country. I bought the hawk of him, and have kept her ever since. Below Freeburn I had to wade the river, in order to avoid a very difficult and somewhat dangerous pass on the rocks. Frequently I met with fresh tracks of the otter. In some places, where the water fell over rocks of any height, so as to prevent the animal from keeping the bed of the river, there were regularly hard beaten paths by which they passed in going from one pool to the other. The water-ouzel, too, enlivened the scene by its curious rapid flight and shrill cry, as it flew from one shallow to another, or passed back over my head to return to its favourite resting-stone from which I had disturbed it.

The kestrel seems to abound in the rocks through which the river runs, as I saw this bird very frequently either sitting on some projecting angle of stone or hovering high above me.

The country here appears as good for grouse as the hills near the sources would be for red-deer, were they free from sheep. I do not know a district in Scotland that would make a better deer-forest than that immediately round and to the westward of Coignafern, where the Monaghliahd mountains afford every variety of ground suited to these animals, with most excellent feeding for them along the burns and straths which intersect the high grounds in every direction, and the most perfect solitude. It is almost a pity that the Mac Intosh does not turn this district into a forest.

VALLEY OF THE FINDHORN

DULSIE BRIDGE

CHAPTER XXIII

Findhorn River—Bridge of Dulsie—Beauty of Scenery—Falls of River—Old Salmon-fisher—Anglers—Heronry—Distant View—Sudden Rise of River—Mouth of River.

NOTHING can exceed the beauty of the river and the surrounding scenery when it suddenly leaves the open and barren ground and plunges at once into the wild and extensive woods of Duncarn and Fairness. The woods at Duncarn are particularly picturesque, in consequence of the fir-trees (at least those near the river) having been left rather farther apart than is usual; and no tree adds more to the beauty of scenery than the Scotch fir, when it has room to spread out into its natural shape. The purple heather, too, in these woods forms a rich and soft groundwork to the picture. What spot in the world can excel in beauty the landscape comprising the old Bridge of Dulsie, spanning with its lofty arch the deep black pool, shut in by grey and fantastic rocks, surmounted with the greenest of grass swards, with clumps of the ancient weeping-birches with their gnarled and twisted stems, backed again by the dark pine-trees? The river here forms a succession of very black and deep pools, connected with each other by foaming and whirling falls and currents, up which in the fine pure evenings you may see the salmon making curious leaps. I shall never forget the impression this scenery made on me when I first saw it. The bridge of the Dulsie, the dark-coloured river, and the lovely woodlands, as I viewed them while stretched on the short green sward above the rocks, formed a picture which will never be effaced from my memory. I cannot conceive a more striking *coup d'œil*, or one more worthy of the pencil of an artist. On these rocks are small flocks of long-horned, half-wild goats, whose appearance, with their shaggy hair and long venerable beards, adds much to the wildness of the scene.

The blackcock and the roebuck now succeed the grouse and red-deer. The former is frequently to be seen either sitting on the trunk of a fallen birch-tree or feeding on the juniper-berries, while the beautiful roebuck (the most perfect in its symmetry of all deer) is seen either grazing on some grassy spot at the water's edge, or wading through a shallow part of the river, looking round when half-way through as timid and coy as a bathing nymph. When disturbed by the appearance of a passer-by, he bounds lightly and easily up the steep bank of the river, and after standing on the summit for a moment or two to make out the extent of the danger, plunges into the dark solitudes of the forest.

On the left side of the river, as it proceeds towards the sea, is a succession of most beautiful banks and heights, fringed with the elegant fern and crowned with juniper, which grows to a very great size, twisting its branches and fantastic roots in the quaintest forms and shapes imaginable over the surface of the rocks. The lovely weeping-birch is everywhere, and about Coulmony are groves of magnificent beech and other forest-trees. On the opposite side are the wooded hills and heights of Relugas, a spot combining every description of beauty. The Findhorn here receives the tributary waters of the Divie, a burn, or rather river, not much inferior in size and beauty to the main river. Hemmed in by the same kind of birch-grown banks and precipitous rocks, every angle of the Findhorn river presents a new view and new beauty, and at last one cannot restrain the exclamation of " Surely there is no other river in the world so beautiful." At Logie the view of the course of the river, and the distance seen far up the glen till it is gradually lost in a succession of purple mountains, is worth a halt of some time to enjoy. The steep banks opposite Logie, clothed with every variety of wood, are lovely, and give a new variety to the scene as we enter on the forests of Darnaway and Altyre. The wood-pigeon cooes and breeds in every nook and corner of the woods, and towards evening the groves seem alive with the song of blackbirds and thrushes, varied now by the crow of the cock pheasant, as he suns himself in all his glittering beauty on the dry and sheltered banks of the river.

Still for many miles is the river shut in by extensive woods and overhung by splendid fir, larch, and other trees, while the nearly perpendicular rocks are clothed with the birch and the ladylike bird-cherry, the holly and bright-berried mountain-ash growing out of every niche and cleft, and clinging by their serpent-like roots to the bare face of the rock; while in the dark, damp recesses of the stone grow several most lovely varieties of pale green ferns and other plants. In the more sunny places you meet with the wild strawberry and purple foxglove, the latter shooting up in graceful pyramids of flower. Between Logie and Sluie are some of the highest rocks on the river, and from several hundred feet above it you can look straight down into the deep pools and foaming eddies below you. At a particular gorge, where the river rushes through a passage of very few feet in width, you will invariably see an old salmon-fisher perched on a point of rock, with his eye intent on the rushing cataract below him, and armed with a staff of some sixteen feet in length ending in a sharp hook, with which he strikes the salmon as they stop for a moment to rest in some eddy of the boiling torrent before taking their final leap up the fall. Watch for a few moments, and you will see the old man make a peculiar plunge and jerk with his long clip into the rushing water, and then hoisting it into the air he displays a struggling salmon impaled on the end of the staff, glancing like a piece of silver as it endeavours to escape. Perhaps it tumbles off the hook, and dropping into the water, floats wounded away, to fall a prey to the otter or fox in some shallow below. If, however, the fish is securely hooked, there ensues a struggle between it and the old man, who, by a twist of his stick, turns himself and the fish towards the dry rock, and having shaken the salmon off the hook, and despatched it with a blow from a short cudgel which he keeps for the purpose, covers it carefully up with wet grass, and lowering the peak of his cap over his eyes, resumes his somewhat ticklish seat on the rock to wait for the next fish. On some days, when the water is of the right height, and the fish are numerous and inclined to run up the river, the old man catches a considerable number; though the capture of every fish is only attained by a struggle of life and death between man and salmon, for the least slip would send the former into the river, whence he could never come out alive. I never see him catch one without feeling fully convinced that he will follow the example of his predecessor in the place, who was washed away one fine day from the rock, and not found for some days, when his body was taken out of the river several miles below. In these pools (every one of which has a name) you will see some sportsman angling, not like the *sans-culotte* shepherd's boy at Coignafern, with his hazel-wand and line made by himself, but here you have a well-equipped and well-accoutred follower of the gentle craft in waterproof overalls, and armed with London rod and Dublin fly, tempting the salmon from their element with a bright but indefinable mixture of feathers, pigs'-wool, and gold thread; while his attendant, stretched at his ease, wonders at the labour his master undertakes, and watches quietly the salmon as he rises from some dark abyss of the water, poises himself for a moment steadily opposite the glittering hook, makes a dash rapid as thought at it, and then swims slowly back to his ambuscade in the depth of the water, not aware, till he feels the jerk of the line, that he is carrying with him, not a painted dragon-fly, but a carefully-prepared and strong weapon of death, which he will only get quit of with his life. The nets are at work too, sweeping a deep and quiet pool, but seldom with much success, owing to the inequalities of the bottom of the river. Making a wide turn here, the river passes by an object of great interest, the Findhorn heronry,[1] a collection of these birds quite unique in their way. They have taken possession of a number of old trees growing on the Darnaway side of the river, and here, year after year, they repair their old nests and bring up their young, not frightened away by the frequenters

THE HILLS OF SUTHERLAND FROM THE MOORS ABOVE THE FINDHORN

of a walk which passes immediately under their nests. Numbers of the old birds may be seen sitting motionless on the dead branches, or perched on the very topmost twig of a larch or birch-tree.

Sometimes the peregrine, on his way to Sluie, passes quickly through the midst of the community, while a constant chattering is kept up by the numberless jackdaws which breed in holes of the rock on the Altyre side, and keep flying in and out from far below the spot where you are standing. Far as you can see, and indeed still farther, are stretched the forests of Darnaway and Altyre. Following the river, or rather keeping the top of the bank above it, a new and most striking view meets your eye. Looking down the course of the water, you suddenly see beyond the woodland a wide extent of corn-land, interspersed with groves of timber and houses; beyond this

---

[1] Herons build at times on rocks.—C. St. J.

the golden line of the sand-hills of Culbin, dividing the plains of Morayshire from the Moray Firth, while beyond the line of blue sea-water are the splendid and lofty rocks on each side of the entrance of the Bay of Cromarty, backed by a succession of various-shaped peaks of the Sutherland and Caithness, the Ross-shire and the Inverness-shire mountains. Opposite you is the massive and square mountain of Ben Wyvis: to the west, on a clear day, you can see far into the peaked and sugar-loaf-shaped mountains of Strath Glass and Glen Strathfarrar, cutting the horizon with their curious outlines. The inland mountains of Sutherland on a clear day are also visible, and Ben Morven, in Caithness, in its solitary grandeur, always forms a conspicuous object; while the Moray Firth, gradually widening till it joins the German Ocean, and dotted here and there with the white sails of the passing ships, completes the scene. It is worth all the trouble of a voyage from London to see this view alone. Far and wide may you travel without finding such another combination of all that is lovely and grand in landscape scenery—wood and water, mountain and cultivated ground, all in their most beautiful forms, combine together to render it pre-eminent. The river has a wider and more open current as you leave the woods, and is little confined by cliff and rock. Many a destructive inroad has it made into the fertile plain below, carrying off sheep and cattle, corn and timber, to be deposited on the sand-banks near Findhorn harbour. Calm and peaceful as it looks when at its ordinary height, the angler, on a bright summer's evening, is sometimes startled by a sound like the rushing of a coming wind, yet wind there is none, and he continues his sport. Presently he is surprised to see the water near which he has been standing suddenly sweep against his feet; he looks up the stream and sees the river coming down in a perpendicular wall of water, or like a wave of the sea, with a roaring noise, and carrying with it trees with their branches and roots entire, large lumps of unbroken bank, and every kind of mountain debris. Some mountain storm of rain has suddenly filled its bed. Sometimes on the occasion of these rapid speats I have had to gather up my tackle and run for my life, which was in no small risk till I gained some bank or rock above the height of the flood. When this rush of water comes down between the rocks where the river has not room to spread, the danger is doubly great, owing to the irresistible force acquired by the pent-up water. The flood, when occasioned by a summer storm, soon subsides, and the next day no trace is left of it excepting the dark, coffee-coloured hue of the water. Passing the lime-quarries of Copthall, the river flows through a fertile country and under a beautiful suspension bridge, which was built after the great floods of 1829, when it was found that a bridge on no other construction would be large enough to admit of the floating masses of timber and the immense body of water during heavy floods. The net-fishing is in active operation from this point down to the sea, and the number of salmon and grilse sometimes caught is astonishing. Instead of rock and cliff, the river is banked in by heaps of shingle, which are constantly changing their shape and size. There seems to be a constant succession of stones swept down by the river: what in one season is a deep pool, is, after the winter floods, a bank of shingle. An endless supply seems to be washed off the mountains and rocks through which the river passes, and these stones, by the time they have been rolled down to the lower part of the river, are as rounded and water-worn in their appearance as the shingle on the sea-shore.

RELUGAS HOUSE.

THE SENTINEL.

CHAPTER XXIV

Migration of Birds in October—Wild Swans: Pursuit of; Manner of getting a Shot: Two killed—Habits of Wild Swan

October 1st.—There is no month more interesting, or productive of more amusement, both to the naturalist and the sportsman, than this—many new birds now appear, on their route from their more northern breeding-places, wending their weary way to the southern shores of the kingdom, where vast numbers fall victims to the guns which are brought to bear upon them—some for pleasure and some for profit.

Most migratory birds take advantage of the moonlight to help them on their journey; for example, woodcocks, snipes, field-fares, etc., generally arrive in this country during the lightest nights in October and November. The water-fowl seem more independent of the moon, and to be chiefly guided in their arrival by the weather.

October 6th.—To-day we saw in the bay as many as fifty or sixty wild swans,[1] evidently just arrived; we went home for swan-shot, Eley's cartridges, and other munitions of war, but by the time we had got all in readiness to open a campaign on the fleet of snow-white birds, they all took flight. After sailing two or three times round the bay, and after an amazing deal of trumpeting and noise, they divided into separate parties, and flew off, some to the east, and some to the west, towards their different winter-quarters.

October 7th.—My old *garde-chasse* insisted on my starting early this morning, *nolens volens*, to certain lochs six or seven miles off, in order, as he termed it, to take our "satisfaction" of the swans. I must say that it was a matter of very small satisfaction to me, the tramping off in a sleety, rainy morning, through a most forlorn and hopeless-looking country, for the chance, and that a bad one, of killing a wild swan or two. However, after a weary walk, we arrived at these desolate-looking lochs; they consist of three pieces of water, the largest about three miles in length and one in width; the other two, which communicate with the largest, are much smaller and narrower, indeed scarcely two gunshots in width; for miles around them the country is flat, and intersected with a mixture of swamp and sandy hillocks. In one direction the sea is only half a mile from the lochs, and in calm winter weather the wildfowl pass the daytime on the salt water, coming inland in the evenings to feed. As soon as we were within sight of the lochs we saw the swans on one of the smaller pieces of water, some standing high and dry on the grassy islands, trimming their feathers after their long journey, and others feeding on the grass and weeds at the bottom of the loch, which in some parts was shallow enough to allow of their pulling up the plants which they feed on as they swam about, while numbers of wild ducks of different kinds, particularly widgeons, swarmed round them and often snatched the pieces of grass from the swans as soon as they had brought them to the surface, to the great annoyance

---

[1] *Cygnus ferus*, Moray. *C. Bewickii* (Bewick's swan), killed in Morayshire, Spynie, Loch Lee, etc., is easily distinguished even at a distance from the *C. ferus*, being a shorter and rounder-looking bird. It is not so wild as the *C. ferus*, as far as my experience goes.—C. St. J.

of the noble birds, who endeavoured in vain to drive away these more active little depredators, which seemed determined to profit by their labours. Our next step was to drive the swans away from the loch they were on; it seemed a curious way of getting a shot, but as the old man seemed confident of the success of his plan, I very submissively acted according to his orders. As soon as we moved them, they all made straight for the sea. "This won't do," was my remark. "Yes, it will, though; they'll no' stop there long to-day with this great wind, but will all be back before the clock *chaps* two." "Faith, I should like to see any building that could contain a clock, and where we might take shelter," was my inward cogitation. The old man, however, having delivered this prophecy, set to work making a small ambuscade by the edge of the loch which the birds had just left, and pointed it out to me as my place of refuge from one o'clock to the hour when the birds would arrive.

In the meantime we moved about in order to keep ourselves warm, as a more wintry day never disgraced the month of October. In less than half an hour we heard the signal cries of the swans, and soon saw them in a long undulating line fly over the low sand-hills which divided the sea from the largest loch, where they all alighted. My commander for the time being then explained to me that the water in this loch was everywhere too deep for the swans to reach the bottom even with their long necks, in order to pull up the weeds on which they fed, and that at their feeding-time, that is about two o'clock, they would, without doubt, fly over to the smaller lochs, and probably to the same one from which we had originally disturbed them. I was accordingly placed in my ambuscade, leaving the keeper at some distance, to help me as opportunity offered—a cold, comfortless time of it we (*i.e.* my retriever and myself) had. About two o'clock, however, I heard the swans rise from the upper loch, and in a few moments they all passed high over my head, and after taking a short survey of our loch (luckily without seeing me), they alighted at the end of it farthest from the place where I was ensconced, and quite out of shot, and they seemed more inclined to move away from me than come towards me. It was very curious to watch these wild birds as they swam about, quite unconscious of danger and looking like so many domestic fowls. Now came the able generalship of my keeper, who, seeing that they were inclined to feed at the other end of the loch, began to drive them towards me, at the same time taking great care not to alarm them enough to make them take flight. This he did by appearing at a long distance off, and moving about without approaching the birds, but as if he was pulling grass or engaged in some other piece of labour. When the birds first saw him, they all collected in a cluster, and giving a general low cry of alarm, appeared ready to take flight: this was the ticklish moment, but, soon outwitted by his manœuvres, they dispersed again and busied themselves in feeding. I observed that frequently all their heads were under the water at once, excepting one—but invariably *one* bird kept his head and neck perfectly erect, and carefully watched on every side to prevent their being taken by surprise; when he wanted to feed, he touched any passer-by, who immediately relieved him in his guard, and he in his turn called on some other swan to take his place as sentinel.

After waiting some little time, and closely watching the birds in all their graceful movements, sometimes having a swan within half a shot of me, but never getting two or three together, I thought of some of my assistant's instruction which he had given me *en route* in the morning, and I imitated, as well as I could, the bark of a dog: immediately all the swans collected in a body, and looked round to see where the sound came from. I was not above forty yards from them, so gently raising myself on my elbow, I pulled the trigger, aiming at a forest of necks. To my dismay, the gun did not go off, the wet or something else having spoilt the cap. The birds were slow in rising, so without pulling the other trigger, I put on another cap, and standing up, fired right and left at two of the largest swans as they rose from the loch. The cartridge told well on one, who fell dead into the water; the other flew off after the rest of the flock, but presently turned back, and after making two or three graceful sweeps over the body of his companion, fell headlong, perfectly dead, almost upon her body. The rest of the birds, after flying a short distance away, also returned, and flew for a minute or two in a confused flock over the two dead swans, uttering their bugle-like and harmonious cries, but finding that they were not joined by their companions, presently fell into their usual single rank, and went undulating off towards the sea, where I heard them for a long time trumpeting and calling.

Handsome as he is, the wild swan is certainly not so graceful on the water as a tame one. He has not the same proud and elegant arch of the neck, nor does he put up his wings while swimming, like two snow-white sails. On the land a wild swan when winged makes such good way, that if he gets much start it requires good running to overtake him.

Their feathers are so strong and they have so much down beneath the breast-feathers, that when coming towards you over your head, no shot makes the least impression unless you aim at their head and neck.

If such constant warfare was not declared against these (now only occasional) visitors to this country, as well as against many others, our lakes and woods would have many more permanent winter and summer occupants than they have. I have no doubt that many birds which now only pass a few months here would domicile themselves entirely if left in peace; and swans, instead of returning to the deserts and swamps of Russia, Siberia, or Norway, would occasionally at least remain here to breed, and by degrees become perfectly domiciled during the whole year in some of the large marshes and lakes of Scotland or Ireland, where proper food and feeding-places could always be found by them. At present they visit us generally about the middle of October. On their first arrival in Findhorn Bay they are sometimes in immense flocks. Last year I saw a flock of between two and three hundred resting on the sands. After remaining quiet till towards evening, they broke off into different smaller companies, of from twenty to three or four birds in each, and dispersed in different directions, all of them, however, inclining southwards.

They probably return year after year to the same district of country, taking with them either their own broods of the season or any others that are inclined to join them. In the large flock that I mentioned having seen last year, I could not distinguish a single young bird. The cygnets of the wild swan, like those of the tame one, are during the first season of a greyish-white, and are easily distinguished amongst the dazzling white plumage of the old birds. When swans frequent any loch near the sea, or any chain of fresh-water lakes, if they are disturbed and fly either to the sea or to some adjoining piece of water, they keep always about the same line. When once you have taken notice of the exact line of their flight, it is easy to get shots by sending a person to put them up when seen feeding, having previously concealed yourself in the direction of their course.

It is useless shooting at them when coming towards you, and the best chance of killing them is either to allow them to pass before you fire, or, just as they are over your head, by jumping up and showing yourself, you may make them turn off to the right and left, in this way affording a fair chance to your shot, which easily penetrates them when flying straight away.

When in the water, a wild swan is not easy to kill, unless hit in the head or neck, as they swim very flat and low, and their feathers sit so close that shot will scarcely penetrate unless you can fire from above the birds.

I once winged a wild swan, which fell into a large and deep loch. The rest of the birds flew away towards another piece of water about a mile off. I had no retriever with me, but profiting by the advice of my keeper, instead of attempting to get at the bird in any way, I took a circuit, keeping myself concealed, towards the line of flight taken by the rest of the flock. The winged bird, after swimming about uneasily for a short time, seeing no enemy at hand, and finding that her companions did not return, went to the edge of the water, and having taken a careful survey of the country around, scrambled out, and commenced a journey after them on terra firma. I allowed her to walk to some distance from the loch, and then running up, cut her off from returning to it. As soon as she saw me she made over a hillock in their line of flight; I ran up, and not seeing her, tracked her a little way in the sand, and presently found her lying stretched out flat on the ground amongst some long grass, endeavouring to hide herself. When she found that I had discovered her she again made off, but was soon caught.

I mention this for the benefit of any one who may be in the predicament of having winged a swan on a lake, as this bird, if left alone and not seeing an enemy, will invariably make for the bank, and most probably leave the water to follow in the track of her companions if they have gone to any adjoining water.

Though, as I have said, not so graceful in the water as their tame relatives, nothing can be more splendid than the flight of a flock of wild swans, as they pass over your head with their transparently white pinions, and uttering their far-sounding and musical trumpeting, which is often heard before the birds come into sight.

I never ate a wild swan, but am told that their flesh, though dark-coloured, has not the least rank taste, like that of some water-fowl, but, on the contrary, is very palatable, and worthy of being cooked. From their food, which consists wholly of flavourless grasses, I can easily suppose that they may be as good if not better eating than the mallard or any other kind of wild duck, which all, more or less, feed on rank weeds, as well as on worms and a variety of other unclean food.

SWANS IN THE BAY.

THE WATER-OUZEL.

CHAPTER XXV

The Water-Ouzel: Nest; Singular Habits; Food; Song of—Kingfisher: Rare Visits of; Manner of Fishing—Terns: Quickness in Fishing; Nests of

FOR several years a pair of those singular little birds the water-ouzel[1] have built their nest and reared their young on a buttress of a bridge across what is called the Black burn, near Dalvey.

[1] Common in most Highland burns; in winter descending nearer the sea on the rivers and burns. Feeds on fish spawn and small aquatic beetles, etc., which it catches by turning over the pebbles under the water. It sings sweetly during the coldest days in the depth of winter, sometimes while floating on the surface of the water. It dives with great facility when in search of food.—C. St. J.

This year I am sorry to see that, owing to some repairs in the bridge, the birds have not returned to their former abode. The nest, when looked at from above, had exactly the appearance of a confused heap of rubbish, drifted by some flood to the place where it was built, and attached to the bridge just where the buttress joins the perpendicular part of the masonry. The old birds evidently took some trouble to deceive the eye of those who passed along the bridge, by giving the nest the look of a chance collection of material. I do not know, among our common birds, so amusing and interesting a little fellow as the water-ouzel, whether seen during the time of incubation, or during the winter months, when he generally betakes himself to some burn near the sea, less likely to be frozen over than those more inland. In the burn near this place there are certain stones, each of which is always occupied by one particular water-ouzel: there he sits all day, with his snow-white breast turned towards you, jerking his apology for a tail, and occasionally darting off for a hundred yards or so, with a quick, rapid, but straight-forward flight; then down he plumps into the water, remains under for perhaps a minute or two; and then flies back to his usual station. At other times the water-ouzel walks deliberately off his stone down into the water, and, despite Mr. Waterton's strong opinion of the impossibility of the feat, he walks and runs about on the gravel at the bottom of the water, scratching with his feet among the small stones, and picking away at all the small insects and animalcules which he can dislodge. On two or three occasions, I have witnessed this act of the water-ouzel, and have most distinctly seen the bird walking and feeding in this manner under the pellucid waters of a Highland burn. It is in this way that the water-ouzel is supposed to commit great havoc in the spawning beds of salmon and trout, uncovering the ova, and leaving what it does not eat[1] open to the attacks of eels and other fish, or

---

[1] Mr. St. John in another excellent account of this bird's habits (*Natural History and Sport in Moray*, p. 88) again repeats the charge that it feeds on trout spawn. Mr. Buckland (see note, same page) says "the water-ouzel is guiltless of eating trout or salmon spawn." At p. 283 Mr. St. John does not draw the bird's character in such dark shades: "I am inclined to think that it attacks the trout spawn more frequently than that of the salmon. If so, this bird also does fully as much good as harm; the most deadly enemy to salmon being the larger burn trout, whose favourite food is, undoubtedly, the ova of the salmon." On the other hand it is a great pleasure to refer the reader to Mr. Knox's admirable defence of the water-ouzel (*Autumns on the Spey*, pp. 150-154). He concludes: "Instead of being a destroyer of fish spawn, he really assists in its preservation, by

liable to be washed away by the current; and, notwithstanding my regard for this little bird, I am afraid I must admit that he is guilty of no small destruction amongst the spawn.

The water-ouzel has another very peculiar habit, which I have never heard mentioned. In the coldest days of winter I have seen him alight on a quiet pool, and with outstretched wings recline for a few moments on the water, uttering a most sweet and merry song—then rising into the air, he wheels round and round for a minute or two, repeating his song as he flies back to some accustomed stone. His notes are so pleasing, that he fully deserves a place in the list of our song-birds; though I never found but one other person, besides myself, who would own to having heard the water-ouzel sing. In the early spring, too, he courts his mate with the same harmony, and pursues her from bank to bank singing as loudly as he can—often have I stopped to listen to him as he flew to and fro along the burn, apparently full of business and importance; then pitching on a stone, he would look at me with such confidence, that, notwithstanding the bad name he has acquired with the fishermen, I never could make up my mind to shoot him. He frequents the rocky burns far up the mountains, building in the crevices of the rocks, and rearing his young in peace and security, amidst the most wild and magnificent scenery.

The nest is large, and built, like a wren's, with a roof—the eggs are a transparent white.

The people here have an idea that the water-ouzel preys on small fish, but this is an erroneous idea; the bird is not adapted in any way either for catching fish or for swallowing them.

During a severe frost last year, I watched for some time a common kingfisher, which, by some strange chance, and quite against its usual habits, had strayed into this northern latitude. He first caught my eye while darting like a living emerald along the course of a small unfrozen stream between my house and the river; he then suddenly alighted on a post, and remained a short time motionless in the peculiar strange attitude of his kind, as if intent on gazing at the sky. All at once a new idea

acting as a check on the increase of various predacious water-beetles and other aquatic insects whose ravenous grubs or *larvæ* furnish his favourite food. His persecutors are therefore, in my humble opinion, amenable to the double charge of injustice and ingratitude."

comes into his head, and he follows the course of the ditch, hovering here and there like a hawk, at the height of a yard or so above the water: suddenly down he drops into it, disappears for a moment, and then rises into the air with a trout about two inches long in his bill; this he carries quickly to the post where he had been resting before, and having beat it in an angry and vehement manner against the wood for a minute, he swallows it whole. I tried to get at him, coveting the bright blue feathers on his back, which are extremely useful in fly-dressing, but before I was within shot, he darted away, crossed the river, and sitting on a rail on the opposite side, seemed to wait as if expecting me to wade after him; this, however, I did not think it worth while doing, as the water was full of floating ice, so I left the kingfisher where he was, and never saw him again. Their visits to this country are very rare—I only have seen one other, and he was sitting on the bow of my boat watching the water below him for a passing trout small enough to be swallowed.

The kingfisher, the terns, and the solan geese are the only birds that fish in this way, hovering like a hawk in the air and dropping into the water to catch any passing fish that their sharp eyesight can detect. The rapidity with which a bird must move, to catch a fish in this manner, is one of the most extraordinary things that I know. A tern, for instance, is flying at about twenty yards high—suddenly he sees some small fish (generally a sand-eel, one of the most active little animals in the world),—down drops the bird, and before the slippery little fish (that glances about in the water like a silver arrow) can get out of reach, it is caught in the bill of the tern, and in a moment afterwards is either swallowed whole, or journeying rapidly through quite a new element to feed the young of its captor. Often in the summer have I watched flocks of terns fishing in this manner at a short distance from the shore, and never did I see one emerge after his plunge into the water without a sand-eel. When I have shot at the bird as he flew away with his prey, I have picked up the sand-eel, and there are always the marks of his bill in one place, just behind the head, where it seems to be invariably caught.

The terns which breed in the islands on a loch in the woods of Altyre, fully five miles in a straight line from where they fish, fly up to their young with every sand-eel they catch. I have seen them fly backwards and forwards in this way for hours together, apparently bringing the whole of their food from the sea, notwithstanding the distance; their light body and long swallow-like wings make this long flight to and fro less fatiguing to the tern than it would be to almost any other bird.

TERNS ON SALMON STAKES

Great numbers of terns [1] breed every year on the sandhills. Their eggs, three in number, are laid in a small hole scraped amongst the shingle, or on the bare sand. Generally, however, they choose a place abounding in small stones; and their eggs being very nearly of the same colour as the pebbles, it is very difficult to distinguish them. The nests being frequently at so considerable a distance from the water, it has often been a matter of surprise to me how the young birds can live till they

[1] Roseate Tern, Common Tern, Arctic Tern, and Lesser Tern (Moray).—C. St. J.

have strength to journey to the sea-shore. I never yet could find any of the newly-hatched terns near the nests, and am of opinion that the old birds in some way or other carry off their young, as soon as they are out of the egg, to some place more congenial to so essentially a water-bird than the arid ground on which they are hatched. During fine weather the terns never sit on their eggs in the daytime, but, uttering unceasing cries, hover and fly about over the spot where their nests are. All day long have I seen them hovering in this manner, with a flight more like that of a butterfly than of a bird. If a man approaches their eggs, they dash about his head with a loud angry clamour; and all the other terns which have eggs, for miles around, on hearing the cry of alarm, fly to see what it is all about, and having satisfied their curiosity, return to the neighbourhood of their own domicile, ready to attack any intruder. If a crow in search of eggs happens to wander near the terns' building-places, she is immediately attacked by the whole community, every bird joining in the chase, and striking furiously at their common enemy, who is glad to make off as quickly as she can. The terns, having pursued her to some distance, return seemingly well satisfied with their feat of arms. I have also detected the fox by the rapid swoops of the terns as they dash at him if he happens to pass near their nests.

There is one kind of tern that breeds on the sandhills, which is peculiarly beautiful, the Lesser Tern, or *Terna minuta*. This little bird, scarcely bigger than a swift, and of a pale blue in the upper part of her plumage, is of the most satin-like and dazzling whiteness in all the lower portions. It is a most delicate-looking creature, but has a stronger and more rapid flight than the larger kinds, and, when he joins in their clamorous attacks on any enemy, utters a louder and shriller cry than one could expect to hear from so small a body. Its eggs are similar in colour to those of the common tern, but much smaller.

The Roseate Tern also visits us. I do not know that I have ever found the eggs of this kind, but I have distinguished the bird by its pale bluish coloured breast, as it hovered over my head amongst the other terns.

A favourite position of the tern is on the stakes of the salmon-fishers' nets. Frequently every stake has a tern on it, where, if unmolested, they sit quietly watching the operations of the fishermen. Indeed, they are rather a tame and familiar bird, not much afraid of man, and seeming to trust (and, as far as I am concerned, *not* in vain) to their beauty and harmlessness as a safeguard against the wandering sportsman. Excepting when wanting a specimen for any particular purpose, I make a rule never to molest any bird that is of no use when dead, and which, like the tern, is both an interesting and beautiful object when living.

These birds make but a short sojourn with us, arriving in April in great numbers, and collecting in flocks on the sands of the bay for a few days. They then betake themselves to their breeding-places, and, having reared their young, leave us before the beginning of winter.

THE MORAY FIRTH FROM DAVA

"I DASHED MY PLAID OVER HIS HEAD"

CHAPTER XXVI

The Muckle Hart of Benmore

Sunday.—This evening, Malcolm, the shepherd of the shealing at the foot of Benmore, returning from church, reported his having crossed on the hill a track of a hart of extraordinary size; and he guessed it must be "the muckle stag of Benmore." This was an animal seldom seen, but which had long been the talk and marvel of the shepherds for its wonderful size and cunning. They love the marvellous, and in their report "the muckle stag" bore a charmed life; he was unapproachable and invulnerable. I had heard of him too, and, having got the necessary information, resolved to try to break the charm though it should cost me a day or two.

Monday.—This morning at sunrise, I with my rifle, Donald carrying my double-barrel, and Bran, took our way up the glen to the shealing at the foot of Benmore. Donald had no heart for this expedition. He is not addicted to superfluous conversation, but I heard him mutter something of a "feckless errand—as good deer nearer hame." Bran had already been the victor in many a bloody tussle with hart and fox. We held for the most part up the glen, but turning and crossing to seek every likely corrie and burn on both sides. I shot a wild cat stealing home to its cairn in the early morning; and we several times in the day came on deer, but they were hinds with their calves, and I was bent on higher game. As night fell, we turned down to the shealing rather disheartened; but the shepherd cheered me by assuring me the hart was still in that district, and describing his track, which he said was like that of a good-sized heifer. Our spirits were quite restored by a meal of fresh-caught trout, oatcake and milk, with a modicum of whisky, which certainly was of unusual flavour and potency.

Tuesday.—We were off again by daybreak. I will pass by several minor adventures, but one cannot be omitted. Malcolm went with us to show us where he had last seen the track. As we crossed a long reach of black and broken ground, the first ascent from the valley, two golden eagles rose out of a hollow at some distance. Their flight was lazy and heavy, as if gorged with food, and on examining the place we found the carcass of a sheep half eaten, one of Malcolm's flock. He vowed vengeance; and, merely pointing out to us our route, returned for a spade to dig a place of hiding near enough the carcass to enable him to have a shot at the eagles if they should return. We held on our way, and the greater part of the day without any luck to cheer us, my resolution "not to be beat" being, however, a good deal strengthened by the occasional grumbling of Donald. Towards the afternoon, when we had tired ourselves with looking with our glasses at every corrie in that side of the hill, at length, in crossing a bare and boggy piece of ground, Donald suddenly stopped, with a Gaelic exclamation, and pointed—and there, to be sure, was a full fresh footprint, the largest mark of a deer either of us had ever seen. There was no more grumbling. Both of us were instantly as much on the alert as when we started on our adventure. We traced the track as long as the ground would allow. Where we lost it, it seemed to point down the little burn, which soon lost itself to our view in a gorge of bare rocks. We proceeded now very cautiously, and taking up our station on a concealed ledge of one of the rocks, began to search the valley below with our telescopes. It was a large flat, strewed with huge slabs of stone, and surrounded on all sides but one with dark rocks. At the farther end were two black lochs, connected by a sluggish stream; beside the larger loch a bit of coarse grass and rushes, where we could distinguish a brood of wild ducks swimming in and out. It was difficult ground to see a deer in, if lying; and I had almost given up seeking, when Donald's glass became motionless, and he gave a sort of grunt as he changed his posture, but without taking the glass from his eye. "Ugh! I'm thinking yon's him, sir: I'm seeing his horns." I was at first incredulous. What he showed me close to the long grass I have mentioned looked for all the world like some withered sticks; but the doubt was short. While we gazed the stag rose and commenced feeding; and at last I saw the great hart of Benmore! He was a long way off, perhaps a mile and a half, but in excellent ground for getting at him. Our plan was soon arranged. I was to stalk him with the rifle, while Donald, with my gun and Bran, was to get round, out of sight, to the pass by which the deer was likely to leave the valley. My task was apparently very easy. After getting down behind the rock I had scarcely to stoop my head, but to walk up within shot, so favourable was the ground and the wind. I walked cautiously, however, and slowly, to give Donald time to reach the pass. I was now within three hundred yards of him, when, as I leant against a slab of stone, all hid below my eyes, I saw him give a sudden start, stop feeding, and look round suspiciously. What a noble beast! what a stretch of antler! with a mane like a lion! He stood for a minute or two, snuffing every breath. I could not guess the cause of his alarm; it was not myself—the light wind blew fair down from him upon me; and I knew Donald would give him no inkling of his whereabouts. He presently began to move, and came at a slow trot directly towards me. My pulse beat high. Another hundred yards forward and he is mine! But it was not so to be. He took the top of a steep bank which commanded my position, saw me in an instant, and was off, at the speed of twenty miles an hour, to a pass wide from that where Donald was hid. While clattering up the hill, scattering the loose stones behind him, two other stags joined him, which had evidently been put up by Donald, and had given the alarm to my quarry. It was then that his great size was conspicuous. I could see with my glass they were full-grown stags, and with good heads, but they looked like fallow-deer as they followed him up the crag. I sat down, disappointed for the moment, and Donald soon joined me, much crestfallen, and cursing the stag in a curious variety of Gaelic oaths. Still it was something to have seen "the muckle stag," and *nil desperandum* was my motto. We had a long and weary walk to Malcolm's shealing; and I was glad to get to my heather bed, after arranging that I should occupy the hiding-place Malcolm had prepared near the dead sheep next morning.

Wednesday.—We were up an hour before daylight; and in a very dark morning I sallied out with Malcolm to take my station for a shot at the eagles. Many a stumble and slip I made during our walk, but at last I was left alone fairly ensconced in the hiding-place, which gave me hardly room to stand, sit, or lie. My position was not very comfortable, and the air was nipping cold just before the break of day. It was still scarcely grey dawn when a bird, with a slow flapping flight, passed the opening of my hut, and lighted out of sight, but near, for I heard him strike the ground; and my heart beat faster. What was my disappointment when his low crowing croak announced the raven! and presently he came in sight, hopping and walking suspiciously round the sheep; till, supposing the coast clear, and little wotting of the double-barrel, he hopped upon the carcass, and began with his square cut-and-thrust beak to dig at the meat. Another raven soon joined him, and then two more; who, after a kind of parley, quite intelligible, though in an unknown tongue, were admitted to their share of the banquet. I was watching their voracious meal with some interest, when suddenly they set up a croak of alarm, stopped feeding, and all turned their knowing-looking eyes in one direction. At that moment I heard a sharp scream, but very distant. The black party heard it too; and instantly darted off, alighting again at a little distance. Next moment a rushing noise, and a large body passed close to me; and the monarch of the clouds alighted at once on the sheep, with his broad breast not fifteen yards from me. He quietly folded up his wings; and, throwing back his magnificent head, looked round at the ravens, as if wondering at their impudence in approaching his breakfast-table. They kept a respectful silence, and hopped a little farther off. The royal bird then turned his head in my direction, attracted by the alteration in the appearance of the ground which he had just noticed in the dim morning light. His bright eye that instant caught mine as it glanced along the barrel. He rose: as he did so I drew the trigger, and he fell quite dead half a dozen yards from the sheep. I followed Malcolm's directions, who had predicted that one eagle would be followed by a second, and remained quiet, in hopes that his mate was not within hearing of my shot. The morning was brightening, and I had not waited many minutes when I saw the other eagle skimming low over the brow of the hill towards me. She did not alight at once. Her eye caught the change in the ground or the dead body of her mate, and she wheeled up into the air. I thought her lost to me, when presently I heard her wings brush close over my head; and then she went wheeling round and round above the dead bird, and turning her head downwards to make out what had happened. At times she stooped so low that I could see the sparkle of her eye and hear her low complaining cry. I watched the time when she turned up her wing towards me, and fired, and dropped her actually on the body of the other. I now rushed out. The last bird immediately rose to her feet, and stood gazing at me with a reproachful, half-threatening look. She would have done battle, but death was busy with her; and as I was loading in haste, she reeled and fell perfectly dead. Eager as I had been to do the deed, I could not look on the royal birds without a pang. But such regrets were now too late. Passing over the shepherd's rejoicing, and my incredible breakfast, I must return to our great adventure. Our line of march to-day was over ground so high that we came repeatedly into the midst of ptarmigan. On the very summit, Bran had a rencontre with an old mountain fox, toothless, yet very fat, whom he made to bite the dust. We struck at one place the tracks of the three deer, but of the animals themselves we saw nothing. We kept exploring corrie after corrie till night fell; and as it was in vain to think of returning to the shealing, which yet was the nearest roof, we were content to find a sort of niche in the rock, tolerably screened from all winds; and having almost filled it with long heather, flower upwards, we wrapped our plaids round us, and slept pretty comfortably.

Thursday.—A dip in the burn below our bivouac renovated me. I did not observe that Donald followed my example in that; but he joined me in a hearty attack on the viands which still remained in our bag; and we started with renewed courage. About mid-day we came on a shealing beside a long narrow loch, fringed with beautiful weeping-birches, and there we found means to cook some grouse which I had shot to supply our exhausted larder. The shepherd, who had "no Sassenach," cheered us by his report of "the deer" being lately seen, and describing his usual haunts. Donald was plainly getting disgusted and home-sick. For myself, I looked upon it as my fate that I must have that hart; so on we trudged. Repeatedly, that afternoon, we came on the fresh tracks of our chase, but still he remained invisible. As it got dark, the weather suddenly changed, and I was glad enough to let Donald seek for the bearings of a "whisky bothie" which he had heard of at our last stopping-place. While he was seeking for it the rain began to fall heavily, and through the darkness we were just able to distinguish a dark object, which turned out to be a horse. "The lads with the still will no be far off," said Donald. And so it turned out. But the rain had increased the darkness so much, that we should have searched in vain if I had not distinguished at intervals, between the pelting of the rain and the heavy rushing of a black burn that ran beside us, what appeared to me to be the shrill treble of a fiddle. I could scarcely believe my ears. But when I communicated the intelligence to Donald, whose ears were less acute, he jumped with joy. "It's all right enough, sir; just follow the sound; it's that drunken deevil, Sandy Ross; ye'll never haud a fiddle frae him, nor him frae a whisky-still." It was clear the sound came from across the black stream, and it looked formidable in the dark. However, there was no remedy. So grasping each the other's collar, and holding our guns high over head, we dashed in, and staggered through in safety, though the water was up to my waist, running like a mill-race, and the bottom was of round slippery stones. Scrambling up the bank, and following the merry sound, we came to what seemed a mere hole in the bank, from which it proceeded. The hole was partially closed by a door woven of heather; and, looking through it, we saw a sight worthy of Teniers. On a barrel in the midst of the apartment—half hut, half cavern—stood aloft, fiddling with all his might, the identical Sandy Ross, while round him danced three unkempt savages; and another figure was stooping, employed over a fire in the corner, where the whisky-pot was in full operation. The fire, and a sliver or two of lighted bog-fir, gave light enough to see the whole, for the place was not above ten feet square. We made our approaches with becoming caution, and were, it is needless to say, hospitably received; for who ever heard of Highland smugglers refusing a welcome to sportsmen? We got rest, food, and fire—all that we required—and something more; for long after I had betaken me to the dry heather in the corner, I had disturbed visions of strange orgies in the bothie, and of my sober Donald exhibiting curious antics on the top of a tub. These might have been the productions of a disturbed brain; but there is no doubt that when daylight awoke me, the smugglers and Donald were all quiet and asleep, far past my efforts to rouse them, with the exception of one who was still able to tend the fire under the large black pot.

Friday.—From the state in which my trusty companion was, with his head in a heap of ashes, I saw it would serve no purpose to awake him, even if I were able to do so. It was quite clear that he could be good for nothing all day. I therefore secured some breakfast and provisions for the day (part of them oatcake, which I baked for myself), tied up Bran to wait Donald's restoration, and departed with my rifle alone. The morning was bright and beautiful, the mountain-streams overflowing with last night's rain. I was now thrown on my own resources, and my own knowledge of the country, which, to say the truth, was far from minute or exact. "Benna-skiach" was my object to-day, and the corries which lay beyond it, where at this season the large harts were said to resort. My way at first was dreary enough, over a long slope of boggy ground, enlivened, however, by a few traces of deer having crossed, though none of my "chase." I at length passed the slope, and soon topped the ridge, and was repaid for my labour by a view so beautiful, that I sat down to gaze at it, though anxious to get forward. Looking down into the valley before me, the foreground was a confusion of rocks of most fantastic shape, shelving rapidly to the edge of a small blue lake, the opposite shore of which was a beach of white pebbles, and beyond, a stretch of the greenest pasture, dotted with drooping white-stemmed birches. This little level was hemmed in on all sides by mountains, ridge above ridge, the lowest closely covered with purple heath, the next more green and broken by ravines, and the highest ending in sharp serrated peaks tipped with snow. Nothing moved within range of my vision, and nothing was to be seen that bespoke life but a solitary heron standing on one leg in the shallow water at the upper end of the lake. From hence I took in a good range, but could see no deer. While I lay above the lake, the day suddenly changed, and heavy wreaths of mist came down the mountain-sides in rapid succession. They reached me soon, and I was enclosed in an atmosphere through which I could not see twenty yards. It was very cold, too, and I was obliged to move, though scarcely well knowing whither. I followed the course of the lake, and afterwards of the stream which flowed from it, for some time. Now and then a grouse would rise close to me, and, flying a few yards, alight again on a hillock, crowing and croaking at the intruder. The heron, in the darkness, came flapping his great wings close past me ; I almost fancied I could feel the movement they caused in the air. Nothing could be done in such weather, and I was not sure that I might not be going away from my object. It was getting late too, and I made up my mind that my most prudent plan was to arrange a bivouac before it became quite dark. My wallet was empty, except a few crumbs, the remains of my morning's baking. It was necessary to provide food : and just as the necessity occurred to me, I heard, through the mist, the call of a cock grouse as he alighted close to me. I contrived to get his head between me and the sky as he was strutting and croaking on a hillock close at hand ; and aiming at where his body ought to be, I fired my rifle. On going up to the place, I found I had not only killed him, but also his mate, whom I had not seen. It was a commencement of good luck. Sitting down, I speedily skinned my birds, and took them down to the burn to wash them before cooking. In crossing a sandy spot beside the burn, I came upon—could I believe my eyes?—"the Track." Like Robinson Crusoe in the same circumstances, I started back; but was speedily at work taking my information. There were prints enough to show the hart had crossed at a walk leisurely. It must have been lately, for it was since the burn had returned to its natural size, after the last night's flood. But nothing could be done till morning, so I set about my cooking; and having after some time succeeded in lighting a fire, while my grouse were slowly broiling, I pulled a quantity of heather, which I spread in a corner a little protected by an overhanging rock: I spread my plaid upon it, and over the plaid built another layer of heather. My supper ended, which was not epicurean, I crawled into my nest under my plaid, and was soon sound asleep. I cannot say that my slumbers were unbroken. I dreamt of the great stag thundering up the hills with preternatural speed, and of noises like cannon (which I have since learnt to attribute to their true cause—the splitting of fragments of rock under a sudden change from wet to sharp frost), and above all, the constant recurrence of visions of weary struggles through fields of snow and ice kept me restless; and at length awoke me to the consciousness of a brilliant skylight and keen frost—a change that rejoiced me in spite of the cold.

Saturday.—Need I say my first object was to go down and examine the track anew. There was no mistake. It was impossible to doubt that "the muckle hart of Benmore" had actually walked through that burn a few hours before me, and in the same direction. I followed the track, and breasted the opposite hill. Looking round from its summit, it appeared to me a familiar scene, and on considering a moment, I found I overlooked from a different quarter the very same rocky plain and the two black lochs where I had seen my chase three days before. I had not gazed many minutes when I saw a deer lying on a black hillock which was quite open. I lay down immediately, and with my glass made out at once the object of all my wanderings. My joy was somewhat abated by his position, which was not easily approachable. My first object, however, was to withdraw myself out of his sight, which I did by crawling backwards down a little bank till only the tops of his horns were visible, and they served to show me that he continued still. As he lay looking towards me, he commanded with his eye three-fourths of the circle, and the other quarter, where one might have got in upon him under cover of the little hillock, was unsafe from the wind blowing in that direction. A burn ran between him and me, one turn of which seemed to come within two hundred yards of him. It was my only chance; so, retreating about half a mile, I got into the burn in hidden ground, and then crept up its channel with such caution that I never allowed myself a sight of more than the tips of his horns, till I had reached the nearest bend to him. There, looking through a tuft of rushes, I had a perfect view of the noble animal, lying on the open hillock, lazily stretched out at length, and only moving now and then to scratch his flank with his horn. I watched him for fully an hour, the water up to my knees all the time. At length he stirred, gathered his legs together, and rose; and arching his back, he stretched himself just as a bullock does when rising from his night's lair. My heart throbbed, as turning all round he seemed to try the wind for his security, and then walked straight to the burn, at a point about one hundred and fifty yards from me. I was much tempted, but had resolution to reserve my fire, reflecting that I had but one barrel. He went into the burn at a deep pool, and standing in it up to his knees, took a long drink. I stooped to put on a new copper cap and prick the nipple of my rifle; and —on looking up again, he was gone! I was in despair; and was on the point of moving rashly, when I saw his horns again appear a little farther off, but not more than fifty yards from the burn. By and by they lowered, and I judged he was lying down. "You are mine at last," I said; and I crept cautiously up the bed of the burn till I was opposite where he had lain down. I carefully and inch by inch placed my rifle over the bank, and then ventured to look along it. I could see only his horns, but within an easy shot. I was afraid to move higher up the bed of the burn, where I could have seen his body; the direction of the wind made that dangerous. I took breath for a moment, and screwed up my nerves; and then with my cocked rifle at my shoulder and my finger on the trigger, I kicked a stone, which splashed into the water. He started up

R

instantly; but exposed only his front towards me. Still he was very near, scarcely fifty yards, and I fired at his throat just where it joins the head. He dropped on his knees to my shot; but was up again in a moment, and went staggering up the hill. Oh, for one hour of Bran! Although he kept on at a mad pace, I saw he was becoming too weak for the hill. He swerved and turned back to the burn; and came headlong down within ten yards of me, tumbling into it apparently dead. Feeling confident, from the place where my ball had taken effect, that he was dead, I threw down my rifle, and went up to him with my hunting-knife. I found him stretched out, and as I thought dying; and I laid hold of his horns to raise his head to bleed him. I had scarcely touched him when he sprang up, flinging me backwards on the stones. It was an awkward position. I was stunned by the violent fall; behind me was a steep bank seven or eight feet high; before me the bleeding stag with his horns levelled at me, and cutting me off from my rifle. In desperation I moved; when he instantly charged, but fortunately tumbled ere he quite reached me. He drew back again like a ram about to butt, and then stood still with his head lowered, and his eyes bloody and swelled, glaring upon me. His mane and all his coat were dripping with water and blood; and as he now and then tossed his head with an angry snort, he looked like some savage beast of prey. We stood mutually at bay for some time, till recovering myself, I jumped out of the burn so suddenly, that he had not time to run at me, and from the bank above, I dashed my plaid over his head and eyes, and threw myself upon him. I cannot account for my folly, and it had nearly cost me dear. The poor beast struggled desperately, and his remaining strength foiled me in every attempt to stab him in front; and he at length made off, tumbling me down, but carrying with him a stab in the leg which lamed him. I ran and picked up my rifle, and then kept him in view as he rushed down the burn on three legs towards the loch. He took the water and stood at bay up to his chest in it. As soon as he halted, I commenced loading my rifle, when to my dismay I found that all the balls I had remaining were for my double-barrel, and were a size too large for my rifle. I sat down and commenced scraping one to the right size, an operation that seemed interminable. At last I succeeded ; and, having loaded, the poor stag remaining perfectly still, I went up within twenty yards of him, and shot him through the head. He turned over and floated, perfectly dead. I waded in and towed him ashore, and then had leisure to look at my wounds and bruises, which were not serious, except my shin-bone, which was scraped from ankle to knee by his horn. I soon had cleaned my quarry and stowed him away as safely as I could, and then turned down the glen at a gay pace. I found Donald with Bran reposing at Malcolm's shealing ; and for all reproaches on his misconduct, I was satisfied with sending him to bring home the " muckle hart of Benmore," a duty which he performed before nightfall.

BRINGING HOME THE "MUCKLE HART."

"THE WHOLE COMMUNITY ATTACKED HIM"

CHAPTER XXVII

Different kinds of Gulls: Large Collections of—Breeding-places—Islands on a Loch—Eggs of Gulls—Young Birds—Food and Voracity of Large Gulls: Salmon-fry killed by—Boatswain-Gull—Manner of procuring Food.

As great a variety of the gull tribe [1] frequents the Findhorn Bay and the Moray Firth as perhaps is to be seen in any one locality in Great Britain. To the uninterested passer-by a gull is a gull, and nothing more, whether the race is represented at the moment

---

[1] St. John here gives an excellent picture of a fresh-water loch in the North of Scotland. Black-headed gulls breed at Loch Lee and on Belivat Lake. The particular spot here meant is probably the "Pietarnies" Loch in Darnaway Forest.

by that splendid bird, the great black-backed gull, *Larus marinus*, or by the small but elegant black-headed gull, *Larus ridibundus* of Linnæus, or as Buffon, alluding also to its laugh-like cry, calls it, *la Mouette rieuse*. Yet, if closely observed, every kind of gull has its own peculiar ways and habits, all of which are worthy of note, and adapted to its own manner of feeding and providing for its wants. During March and April the black-headed gull, which has been absent during the winter, returns in innumerable flocks. After sunset they hold long consultations on the sands of the bay, and when the night is calm I can hear them from my windows at the distance of nearly two miles chattering and clamouring for hours together. In the daytime they frequent the fields, and wherever a plough is at work there are the black-headed gulls in thousands, hovering over the ploughman's head, and keeping up such a continual screaming, that I have seen both man and horses fairly bewildered by the noise. A man left his plough and came to me the other day, as I was passing in the next field, to beg me to fire a shot or two at these noisy and uninvited followers. As fast as a worm or grub is turned up by the plough, down drop two or three gulls to scramble for it. In this manner they soon get the necessary supply of food, and return to join the assembly on the sands, where, having drunk and bathed, they remain for the rest of the day. After passing a fortnight or more in this manner, they betake themselves to their breeding-place, which is generally either some rushy and quiet pool or island on some mountain lake, where they can breed and rear their young unmolested. There are several lochs in this neighbourhood where they breed. One they chiefly resort to is a small piece of water in the forest of Darnaway, where they are not allowed to be annoyed or disturbed during the time of incubation. In these places their nests are placed as close as possible to each other, and from the constant noise and flying backwards and forwards of the birds, one would suppose that the greatest confusion must prevail amongst their crowded commonwealth, but every bird knows and attends to her own nest, and though their cries sound angry and harsh, the greatest amity and the strictest peace are preserved. Though crossing and jostling each other in all directions, they never appear to quarrel or fight. On the contrary, the birds all unite and make common cause against any enemy, man or beast, that approaches them, or whose presence seems to threaten danger. I once took a boat to a mountain lake in Inverness-shire, where thousands of these birds bred on some small islands which dot the surface of the water.[1] The gulls, though not exactly attacking me, dashed unceasingly so close to my head that I felt the wind of their wings, and I sometimes really feared some one more venturous than the rest might drive his bill into my eyes. They had probably never had a visitor to their islands before. The shepherds, having a kind of superstitious dread of the place, from its being supposed to be haunted ground, never attempt to cross to the islands by swimming or wading. The greater part of the largest island was absolutely covered with eggs, laid in small hollows scraped by the birds, with little pretensions to any other kind of nest. I could scarcely walk without treading on them. Close to the edge of the water, indeed so near that the nest was always wet, was the domicile of a pair of black-throated divers, or loon, with a couple of long greenish-coloured eggs. The old birds swam out to a short distance, and watched me with great interest, uttering their strange hollow call. There were several smaller islands, or points of rock, appearing above the water, on each of which a pair of black-backed gulls had made their nest, constructed with more care and skill than those of their black-headed cousins. These large birds allowed none of the others to approach them, and each couple kept undisputed possession of their own particular kingdom, not joining in the same sociable kind of society as other gulls. When I approached the black-backed gulls' nest, they did not dash round me like the smaller kind, but flew in circles at some height, uttering a loud warlike kind of shout, much like the voice of a human being. The eggs of the black-headed gulls are exactly like those of the common lapwing, and are equally good eating; so I took home a great number, selecting them from the nests that had only one or two eggs, knowing that the owners of these would not have commenced sitting. I returned in a week, and found every nest with its full number in it. I was walking along the

---

[1] Mr. St. John mentions the following as being found in Moray: "The little gull (*Larus minutus*), shot in Spynie, Morayshire, early in May; *L. capistratus* (brown-headed gull); *L. ridibundus* (black-headed gull); *L. tridactylus* (kittiwake); *L. canus* (common gull); *L. argentatus* (herring gull); *L. fuscus* (lesser black-backed gull); *L. marinus* (great black-backed gull), nests inland."

shore of the lake some weeks afterwards, when the birds had hatched, and whole fleets of young gulls of a dark grey colour were swimming about. A young retriever I had with me swam into the water after them. He had scarcely got twenty yards from the shore when the whole community of gulls attacked him, and not content with harmless threats, struck down on the dog with right good will; and I am convinced that his life was only saved by my keeping up a constant fire on the large black-headed gulls, which, in defence of their young, made common cause with the others, and, from their great weight and strength, were most dangerous assailants. When lounging, gun in hand,

GULLS COMING INLAND

on the sea-shore here, or lying in wait for seals, I have frequent opportunities of watching unobserved the proceedings of the gulls of different kinds. The large black-backed gull soars slowly along the edge of the receding tide, with his sharp eye fixed on the beach, and turning his head and neck to observe every object that may be left by the tide. If anything is seen which his omnivorous appetite covets, down he pitches on it, and with his powerful bill soon tears up and swallows it. The sand-eel or small fish is swallowed whole. If a floating prize presents itself, such as the remains of a large fish or dead bird, it is soon discovered by one of the large gulls, who is not allowed, however, to enjoy his prize alone; for every one of his fellows within sight joins in tearing it to pieces. When I have winged a duck, and it has escaped and gone out to sea, I have frequently seen it attacked and devoured almost alive by these birds. If a dead fish is left on the shore they alight a few feet from it, and, having reconnoitred carefully, fall to and devour it. It is interesting to see these strong birds battling against a high wind, always working to windward, and taking advantage of every headland and cliff for a moment's shelter. When going to windward in their search for food (indeed, they never fly down wind if they can help it), and perceiving something edible, they keep on a short distance beyond it, and then drifting back with the wind, drop down upon it. I saw a seal last week (April) which had caught a salmon, and was eating it above the water. A number of large gulls had collected round him, and seemed inclined to dispute his prize, darting down at it with clamorous cries. The large grey gull, or wagel, hunts the shore in much the same manner; but is still more voracious than the black-backed gull. Nothing comes amiss to this greedy bird. I have seen a dozen of them feeding on a dead and putrid horse, digging it out with their powerful bills like so many ravens. I have no doubt a dead human being would be considered a fair and lawful prize also. While I am lying ensconced on the shore for seals, this bird frequently comes hovering over me, as if well inclined to pounce down. If wounded, he does good battle against my retriever, aiming (like a heron) at the eyes. When shot, he often disgorges a great quantity of food, generally small fish; and on one occasion a wounded wagel brought up, amongst a variety of undigested food, a well-sized young kitten, which he had somewhere made prize of. The grey gull, though frequently feeding in the fields, seems very seldom to take to fresh-water lakes. The next-sized gull which is common here is the blue-back, a beautiful clean-looking bird, though, as far as fish is concerned, as great a glutton as the two last-named kinds. This bird is particularly conspicuous in its attacks on the salmon-fry as they descend the river in May. Thousands of them fish in the shallow pools at low-water in the bay, and every bird seems to feed wholly on these silvery little creatures as long as they are to be had. The quantity that they disgorge when shot is perfectly astonishing, and they must be one of the most destructive enemies that the salmon has. Besides these larger kinds of gulls, there are several smaller species, who hover constantly about the shore and sand-banks, drifting to and fro, and beating against the wind in search of any prey, and darting fearlessly into the very foam of the breakers to obtain it, or floating as buoyantly as corks at a respectful distance from the larger gulls, who may be engaged in tearing to pieces any cast-up carcass, and being content to catch at the smaller morsels which are detached unperceived by the rightful owners of the prize.

I was much amused the other day by the proceedings of a pair of the black-toed gull, or boatswain.[1] These two birds were sitting quietly on an elevated ridge of sand, near which a number of other gulls of different kinds were fishing and hovering about in search of what the waves might cast up. Every bird, indeed, was busy and employed, excepting these two black robbers, who seemed to be quietly resting, quite unconcerned. When, however, a gull had picked up a prize, these birds seemed instinctively to know it, and darting off with the rapidity of a hawk (which bird they much resemble in their manner of flight), they attacked the unfortunate gull in the air, and, in spite of his screams and attempts to escape, they pursued and beat him till he disgorged the fish or whatever he had swallowed, when one of them darted down and caught the substance before it could reach the water. The two then returned quietly to their sand-bank, where they waited patiently to repeat the robbery, should an opportunity occur. As the flock of gulls moved on with the flow of the tide the boatswains moved on also, hovering on their flank like a pair of plundering freebooters. I observed that in chasing a gull they seemed perfectly to understand each other as to who should get the spoil; and in their attacks on the largest gulls (against whom they waged the most fearless warfare) they evidently acted so as to aid each other. If another pair of boatswains intruded on their hunting-ground, they immediately seemed to send them farther off, not so much by actual battle as by a noisy and screaming argument, which they continued most vigorously till the new-comers left the neighbourhood.

I never saw these birds hunt for their own living in any other way than by robbing the other gulls. Though not nearly so large as some of the birds which they attack, their hawk-like swoops and great courage seem to enable them to fight their

---

[1] Richardson's skua (*Lestris Richardsonii*), Moray.—C. St. J.

way most successfully. They are neatly and powerfully made; their colour, a kind of sooty dull black, with very little gloss or shining tints on their feathers. The boatswains seldom appear here excepting during April and May. All the gull tribe during their first year are of a dingy and mottled colour, very unlike the neat and elegant combination of colours they afterwards acquire.

THE FINDHORN FROM ALTYRE WOODS, LOOKING NORTH

WOODCOCKS TILTING

CHAPTER XXVIII

Woodcock's nest: Early Breeding of; Habits of, in Spring; First Arrival of; Anecdotes of; Manner of Carrying their Young—Habits of Snipe—Number of Jack-Snipes—Solitary Snipe.

March 9, 1846.—A woodcock's nest, with three eggs, was brought to me to-day. Two years ago, a boy brought me a young woodcock nearly full-grown, and fledged, in the second week of April—the exact day I do not remember. Reckoning from this, I should suppose that the woodcock is about the first bird to hatch in this country. A few years ago, it was supposed that none remained in Britain after the end of winter, except a few wounded birds, which were unable to cross the sea to their usual breeding-places.

However, since the great increase of fir plantations, great numbers remain to breed. In the woods of Altyre and Darnaway (as well as in all the other extensive plantations in the country), during the whole spring and summer, I see the woodcocks flying to and fro every evening in considerable numbers. As early as six or seven o'clock, they begin to fly, uttering their curious cry, which resembles more the croak of a frog than anything else; varied, however, by a short shrill chirp. Down the shaded course of the river, or through the avenues and glades of the forest, already dark from the shadow of the pine-trees, the woodcocks keep up a continual flight, passing and repassing in all directions, as if in search of each other. As the twilight comes on, in the open part of the country, they leave the shade of the woods and fly down to the swamps and pools near the sea-shore and elsewhere, to feed during the night. When watching in the evening for wild ducks or geese near the swamps by the shore, I have constantly seen them pitch close to me, and commence feeding in their peculiar manner. These birds must probably come from the Altyre woods, the nearest point of which is at a distance of two or three miles. In the evening the woodcock's flight is rapid and steady, instead of being uncertain and owl-like, as it often is in the bright sunshine. I consider their vision to be peculiarly adapted to the twilight, and even to the darker hours of night—this being the bird's feeding-time. In very severe and protracted snowstorms and frosts I have seen them feeding at the springs during the daytime; but in moderate weather they pass all the light hours in the solitary recesses of the quietest parts of the woods, although occasionally one will remain all day in the swamp, or near the springs on the hill-side, where he had been feeding during the night. When they first arrive, about the month of November, I have sometimes fallen in with two or three brace far up on the mountain, while grouse-shooting. They then sit very close, and are easily killed. The first frost, however, sends them all to the shelter of the woods. No bird seems less adapted for a long flight across the sea than the woodcock: and it is only by taking advantage of a favourable wind that they can accomplish their passage. An intelligent master of a ship once told me, that in his voyages to and from Norway and Sweden, he has frequently seen them, tired and exhausted, pitch for a moment or two with outspread wings in the smooth water in the ship's wake; and having rested themselves for a few moments, continue their weary journey.

Although those that remain here breed so early in the year, the woodcocks that migrate do not leave England till the end of March or beginning of April. In the wild extensive woods of Sussex, I have often seen them in the evenings, about the beginning of April, flying to and fro in chase of each other, uttering a hoarse croaking, and sometimes engaging each other at a kind of tilting-match with their long bills in the air. I remember an old poaching keeper, whose society I used greatly to covet when a boy, shooting three at a shot, while they were engaged in an aerial tournament of this kind.

There was a sporting turnpike-man (a rare instance of such a combination of professions) on Ashdown forest, in Sussex, who used to kill two or three woodcocks every evening for a week or two in March and April—shooting the birds while he smoked his pipe and drank his smuggled brandy and water at his turnpike-gate, which was situated in a glade in the forest, where the birds were in the habit of flying during the twilight.

I rather astonished an English friend of mine, who was staying with me in Inverness-shire during the month of June, by asking him to come out woodcock-shooting one evening. And his surprise was not diminished by my preparations for our battue, which consisted of ordering out chairs and cigars into the garden at the back of the house, which happened to be just in the line of the birds' flight from the woods to the swamps. After he had killed three or four from his chair, we stopped murdering the poor birds, which were quite unfit to eat, having probably young ones, or eggs, to provide for at home, in the quiet recesses of the woods, along the banks of Loch Ness, which covers afford as good woodcock-shooting as any in Scotland.

The female makes her nest, or rather, lays her eggs—for nest she has none—in a tuft of heather, or at the foot of a small tree. The eggs are four in number, and resemble those of a plover. They are always placed regularly in the nest, the small ends of the eggs meeting in the centre. When disturbed from her nest, she flutters away like a partridge, pretending to be lame, in order to take the attention of the intruder away from her young or eggs. It is a singular but well-ascertained fact, that woodcocks carry their young ones down to the springs and soft ground where they feed. Before I knew this, I was greatly puzzled as to how the newly-hatched young of this bird could go from the nest, which is often built in the rankest heather, far from any place where they could possibly feed, down to the marshes. I have, however, ascertained that the old bird lifts her young in her feet, and carries them one by one to their feeding-ground. Considering the apparent improbability of this curious act of the woodcock, and the unfitness of their feet and claws for carrying or holding any substance whatever, I should be unwilling to relate it on my own unsupported evidence; but it has been lately corroborated by the observations of several intelligent foresters and others, who are in the habit of passing through the woods during March and April.

The woodcock breeds a second time in July and August. I am of opinion that all those which are bred in this country emigrate about the beginning of September, probably about the full moon in that month. At any rate they entirely disappear from woods where any day in June or July I could find several brace. In September and the beginning of October I could never find a single bird, though I have repeatedly tried to do so. A few come in October; but the greatest number which visit this country arrive at the November full moon; these birds invariably taking advantage of the lightest nights for their journey. In many parts of the country near the coast, the day, and almost the hour, of their arrival can be accurately calculated on, as also the particular thickets and coverts where the first birds alight.

The snipe[1] also begins to breed in March, though it is not quite so early a bird as the woodcock. Snipes hatch their young in this country, breeding and rearing them in the swamps, or near the springs on the mountains. During the pairing time the snipes fly about all day, hovering and wheeling in the air above the rushes where the female bird lies concealed, and uttering their peculiar cry, which resembles exactly the bleating

---

[1] Both snipe and jack-snipe lay four eggs (C. St. J.) Owing to the reclaiming of marshland, their numbers are decreasing in many parts of Scotland.

of a goat, and from which they have one of their Gaelic names, which signifies the air-goat.

About the end of July and first week in August the snipes descend from the higher grounds, and collect in great numbers about certain favourite places. They remain in these spots for a week or ten days, and then disperse. The rest of the season we have but few in this part of the country. Particular ditches and streams near my house always afford me two or three snipes; and as fast as I kill these, others appear.

Occasionally flights of jack-snipes come here; generally about the end or middle of October; and last year I find, on referring to my game-book, that on the 19th of October I killed eight brace of jack-snipes in an hour or two, finding them all in a small rushy pool and in the adjoining ditch. Usually, however, I only find three or four during a day's shooting; but in this manner I kill a great many in the course of the season, as there appears to be a constant succession of these birds from October to March, when they leave us. The jack-snipe never remains to breed here. I can scarcely call the solitary snipe a bird of this country; never having seen but one in Scotland, and that was in Sutherlandshire.

DONALD AND THE SEAL.

CHAPTER XXIX

Seals—Destruction to Fish and Nets—Shooting Seals in River and Sea—Habits of Seals—Anecdotes—Seal and Dog—Seal and Keeper—Catching Seals—Anecdotes.

SEALS,[1] which a few years ago abounded along this coast, are now comparatively rare, and before long will be entirely banished to the undisturbed and unfrequented rocks of the more northern islands. The salmon-fishers on the coast wage a constant war against them, in consequence of the great damage they do to their stake-nets, which are constantly torn and injured by these powerful animals. Nor is the loss they occasion to the salmon-fishers confined to the fish which they actually consume or to

---

[1] The colour of seals varies very much. When first born they are cream-coloured. It is soon drowned when entangled in a net, but when undisturbed can remain a considerable time under the water. Does not always devour the fish which it captures under the water.—C. St. J.

The true fur seals of the far North, many thousands of which are killed annually in Davis Straits and round Spitzbergen and Greenland, are *Cystophora cristata*, *Phoca barbata* and *P. grœnlandica*. A few specimens of these (with the exception of *P. barbata*) have been taken on our coasts.

the nets that they destroy, for a seal hunting along the coast in the neighbourhood of the stake-nets keeps the salmon in a constantly disturbed state, and drives the shoals of fish into the deep water, where they are secure from the nets. There is consequently a constant and deadly feud between the fishermen and the seals, which has almost totally expelled the latter from this part of the coast. An old seal has been known to frequent a particular range of stake-nets for many years, escaping all attacks against him, and becoming both so cunning and so impudent that he will actually take the salmon out of the nets (every turn of which he becomes thoroughly intimate with) before the face of the fishermen, and retiring with his ill-gotten booty, adds insult to injury by coolly devouring it on some adjoining point of rock or shoal, taking good care, however, to keep out of reach of rifle-ball or slug. Sometimes, however, he becomes entangled in the nets, and is drowned, but this seldom happens to a full-grown seal, which easily breaks through the strongest twine if he can find no outlet. From the shore opposite Cromarty I one day saw a large seal swim into the stake-nets and take out a salmon, with which he retired to a small rock above the water, and there devoured it entirely in a very short space of time.

Sometimes at high-water and when the river is swollen a seal comes in pursuit of salmon into the Findhorn, notwithstanding the smallness of the stream and its rapidity. I was one day, in November, looking for wild ducks near the river, when I was called to by a man who was at work near the water, and who told me that some " muckle beast " was playing most extraordinary tricks in the river. He could not tell me what beast it was, but only that it was something " no that canny." After waiting a short time, the riddle was solved by the appearance of a good-sized seal, into whose head I instantly sent a cartridge, having no balls with me. The seal immediately plunged and splashed about in the water at a most furious rate, and then began swimming round and round in a circle, upon which I gave him the other barrel, also loaded with one of Eley's cartridges, which quite settled the business, and he floated rapidly away down the stream. I sent my retriever after him, but the dog, being very young and not come to his full strength, was baffled by the weight of the animal and the strength of the current, and could not land him; indeed, he was very near getting drowned himself, in consequence of his attempts to bring in the seal, who was still struggling. I called the dog away, and the seal immediately sank. The next day I found him dead on the shore of the bay, with (as the man who skinned him expressed himself) "twenty-three pellets of large hail in his craig."

Another day, in the month of July, when shooting rabbits on the sand-hills, a messenger came from the fishermen at the stake-nets, asking me to come in that direction, as the "muckle scalgh" was swimming about, waiting for the fish to be caught in the nets, in order to commence his devastation.

I accordingly went to them, and having taken my observations of the locality and the most feasible points of attack, I got the men to row me out to the end of the stake-net, where there was a kind of platform of netting, on which I stretched myself, with a bullet in one barrel and a cartridge in the other. I then directed the men to row the boat away, as if they had left the nets. They had scarcely gone three hundred yards from the place when I saw the seal, which had been floating, apparently unconcerned, at some distance, swim quietly and fearlessly up to the net. I had made a kind of breastwork of old netting before me, which quite concealed me on the side from which he came. He approached the net, and began examining it leisurely and carefully to see if any fish were in it; sometimes he was under and sometimes above the water. I was much struck by his activity while underneath, where I could most plainly see him, particularly as he twice dived almost below my station, and the water was clear and smooth as glass.

I could not get a good shot at him for some time; at last, however, he put up his head at about fifteen or twenty yards' distance from me; and while he was intent on watching the boat, which was hovering about waiting to see the result of my plan of attack, I fired at him, sending the ball through his brain. He instantly sank without a struggle, and a perfect torrent of blood came up, making the water red for some feet round the spot where he lay stretched out at the bottom. The men immediately rowed up, and taking me into the boat, we managed to bring him up with a boathook to the surface of the water, and then, as he was too heavy to lift into the boat (his weight being 378 lbs.), we put a rope round his flippers, and towed him ashore. A seal of this size is worth some money, as, independently of the value of his skin, the blubber (which lies under the skin, like that of a whale) produces a large quantity of excellent oil. This seal had been for several years the dread of the fishermen at the stake-nets, and the head man at the place was profuse in his thanks for the destruction of a beast upon which he had expended a most amazing quantity of lead. He assured me that £100 would not repay the damage the animal had done. Scarcely any two seals are exactly of the same colour or marked quite alike, and seals frequenting a particular part of the coast become easily known and distinguished from each other.

There is a certain part of the coast near the sand-hills where I can generally get a shot at a seal. I have frequently killed them, but seldom get the animal, as the water is deep at the place and the current strong. The spot I allude to is where the sea, at the rise of the tide, flows into a large basin through a narrow channel, the deep part of which is not much more than a hundred yards in width. If there are any seals hunting this part of the coast, they come into this basin at every tide in search of fish, or to rest in the quiet water. My plan is to be at the place before the tide has begun to rise, and then, having made up a breastwork of sand and weed, I wait for the appearance of the seals, which frequently, before the tide has risen much, come floating in, with their heads above the water. If they do not perceive my embankment, I am nearly certain of a shot, but if they do, they generally keep over on the opposite side of the channel, watching it so closely that on the least movement on my part they instantly dive. So quick are their movements in the water, that I find it impossible to strike a seal with ball if he is watching me, for quick and certain as is a detonating gun, they are still quicker, and dive before the ball can reach them. As for a flint gun, it has not a chance with them. Within the memory of some of the people here, seals were very numerous about this part of the coast, and were constantly killed by the farmers for the sake of their oil, and with no weapons except their hoes or spades, with which they attacked them when lying on the sand-banks. It is but seldom that I see them resting on the shore, but occasionally watch them in that situation, as they either lie sleeping on the banks or play about, which, notwithstanding their unwieldy appearance, they sometimes do. At other times they engage in the most determined battles with each other, fighting like bulldogs, and uttering loud mournful cries. In waiting for seals, attention must be paid more to the state of the tide than to the time of day, although certainly, like all wild animals, they appear less on their guard at early dawn than at any other hour. The seal generally takes the same course every day at the same height of tide, and basks on the same rock or sand-bank during low-water. They show themselves much less in cold and stormy weather than when it is warm and fine. Knowing this, and having seen a seal show himself in a particular channel or basin of the sea, you may be nearly sure of seeing him there the next day, about the same height of tide.

The young appear about July. When first born they are nearly white, and the hair is rough and long: they gradually become spotted and of a darker colour, like the old ones. The very young ones that I have seen here were probably born about the rocks and caves of the Ross-shire coast. Some rocks off the coast near Gordonston were till very lately the constant resort of seals, but owing to workmen having been employed there of late years in building a lighthouse and other works, they very seldom rest on them at present. They were also much frightened by a plan for catching them adopted by some of the workmen. Observing that the seals when disturbed tumbled off the rocks in great confusion, two fellows, during low-water, fixed firmly into the rock several strongly-barbed iron hooks, with the points turned upwards. This done, the first time that they saw any great assemblage of seals basking on the rock, near their hooks, they got into a boat and rowed quickly up to the place, firing guns and making all the noise that they could. The poor seals, in their hurry to escape, came tumbling over the side of the rocks where the hooks were placed. Several were much torn and wounded, and one was held till the men got up and despatched him. This cruel proceeding had the effect of keeping them from the place for a considerable time afterwards. Notwithstanding the great timidity, of the seals, they have immense strength in their jaws, and, indeed, great muscular power in every part of their body. A farmer near the coast here, seeing several basking on the sand-banks, and not being possessed of a gun, hit upon what seemed to him the capital plan of setting a strong bulldog at them, hoping that the dog would hold one of them till he could get up and kill it with his spade. The dog reached the seals before they could get into the water, and attacked one of the largest. The seal, however, with a single bite completely smashed the head of the dog, and flinging him to one side, scuffled away into the water, leaving the farmer not much inclined to attempt seal-hunting again.

My man, one day while we were waiting in our ambuscade for the seals, gave me an account of a curious adventure he had with one near the same spot a few years back.

He was lying at daybreak ensconced close to the water's edge, waiting in vain for a shot at some grey geese that frequented the place at the time, when he saw a prodigiously large seal floating quietly along with the tide, not thirty yards from the shore. Donald did not disturb the animal, but went home early in the day, and, having cast some bullets for his gun and made other preparations, retired to rest. The next morning he was again at the shore, well concealed, and expecting to see the seal pass with the flowing tide; nor was he disappointed. About the same period of the rise of the tide, the monster appeared again. Donald cocked his gun, and crouched down behind his ambuscade of seaweed and shingle, ready for the animal's head to appear within shot. This soon happened, but instead of swimming on with the tide, the seal came straight to the shore, not above ten yards from where his mortal enemy was lying concealed. The water was deep to the very edge, and the great unwieldy beast clambered up the steep beach, and was very soon high and dry, a few yards from the muzzle of Donald's gun, which was immediately pointed at him, but from the position in which the seal was lying he could not get a shot at the head, the only part where a wound would prove immediately fatal. Donald waited some time, in hopes that the animal would turn or lift his head, but at last losing patience, he gave a low whistle, which had the immediate effect of making the animal lift its head to listen. The gun was immediately discharged, and the ball passed through the seal's neck, close to the head. Up ran Donald, and flinging down his gun, seized one of the immense fins or flippers of the beast, which he could scarcely span with both hands. The seal was bleeding like a pig at the throat, and quite stunned at the same time, but though it did not struggle, it showed a kind of inclination to move towards the water, which obliged Donald to stick his heels into the ground, and to lean back, holding on with all his strength to prevent the escape of the enormous beast. "'Deed, Sir," said Donald, "if you believe me, he was as big as any Hieland stirk in the parish." Well, there the two remained for above an hour—motionless, but always straining against each other, Donald's object being to keep the seal in the same place till the tide had receded to some distance, and then to despatch him how he best could. Many a wistful glance he cast at his gun, which he had so rashly flung down without reloading; the said gun being, as he said, "but a bit trifling single-barrelled thing, lent him by a shoemaker lad, who whiles took a shot along the shore"—in other words, who poached more hares than he made shoes.

After they had remained in this uncomfortable position for a long time, till Donald's hands had become perfectly cramped and stiff, the seal suddenly seemed to recover himself, and turning round to see what was holding him, looked the man full in the face, with a bewildered air of astonishment; then seeing what kind of enemy he had to deal with, he gave a tremendous shake, casting Donald off like a "bit rag," as he expressed it, and leaving him prostrate in the pool of blood that had come out of the bullet-hole, moved slowly into the water, and quietly went down to the bottom. Donald, in utter disgust and wretchedness at losing his prize, walked straight home, and went to bed to sleep off his disappointment. The next morning, however, on considering over the matter, he came to the conclusion that the seal must be dead, and would probably, as the tide ebbed, be grounded on one of the adjacent sand-banks; so he returned to the bay at low-water, and the first thing he saw was his seal lying dead on a sand-bank, and looking like a coble keel uppermost. And a perfect argosy did it turn out, producing more pints of oil and a larger skin than ever seal produced before or since.

I have seen these animals caught by placing a strong net,

made for the purpose, across a deep and narrow channel through which they escaped when frightened off a sand-bank, where they were in the habit of resting at low-water. We quietly laid the net down, fixing it at each end with an anchor; we then rowed round to the bank, and away went the seals, splattering over the wet sands into the channel; we came after them as hard as we could row. At first, when they struck the net, some turned back, but frightened on by our shouts, they made a rush at the net. We got to one end of it, detached the anchor, and began to haul it round, so as to enclose the seals; then began a noise and clamour which surpassed anything of the kind I ever heard—the seals splashing and snorting like drowning horses, while we were all straining every nerve to row round the boat, with the weight and struggles of seventeen seals, large and small, against us; my crew of six Highlanders shouting, cursing, and swearing, and encouraging each other in Gaelic—presently a more furious shout from the leader of the crew announced that something unexpected had happened, and looking round, we saw that thirteen of the seals had escaped, partly by jumping over the net, and partly by breaking through a weak part of it. One very large seal, which we afterwards found had left her young one within the net, returned in her maternal fondness to rescue it; she swam round, and finding her offspring in the midst of all the confusion, swam away again from the net, leading the way for the little one to escape also. I snatched up my gun and fired, killing her on the spot, so that she fell back into the net, and we managed to land her, and the other four, and despatched them, despite their struggles, to the great joy of the salmon-fishers of the Cromarty Firth. At another time, several years ago, I was put into rather a dilemma by one of these animals: we had shot a three-parts grown seal, as she was asleep on an isolated rock. Having got her into our very frail and crazy boat, we proceeded towards the land in high spirits; but before we were half-way across, our seal, who had only been stunned, the shot having merely grazed her head, came to life, and finding herself in so unwonted a position, commenced an indiscriminate attack on everything in her way; our legs being more so than anything else, we had to throw our feet up on the gunwale of the boat, and despatch her how we could, as she was tearing away, with immense strength, at the woodwork within her reach, and we expected that she would have made a hole in the bottom of the boat. We managed, however, with some difficulty, to stun her again, with the handle of an oar, and got safe to land with our prize, the first of the kind I had ever captured.

LOOKING UP THE FINDHORN VALLEY FROM DULSIE BRIDGE

FOX-HUNTING IN THE HIGHLANDS

CHAPTER XXX

Fox-hunting in the Highlands

I HAVE very little to say on this most momentous of all sporting subjects; and that little will, I fear, be sadly

> "Unmusical to Melton ears,
> And harsh in sound to Quorn."

But what are a set of poor fellows like us to do, living here amongst mountains, and ravines, and torrents, and deep watercourses, and morasses, against none of which the best horse that ever put foot on turf could contend for five minutes? It took me, I must confess, some time before I could get over all the finer tone of my Leicestershire feelings; and I have no doubt that I blushed a perfect scarlet the first time that I doubled up a fox[1] with a rifle-ball; but now, rendered callous by use and necessity, I can do execution upon him without a pang.

[1] The fox is still common in Scotland, but the enmity of farmers and shepherds, together with guns and traps, have reduced its numbers of late years. Mr. J. Colquhoun in *The Moor and the Loch*, vol. ii., has a good chapter on the Highland fox. It lives much on sheep and lambs, whereas an English fox only kills lambs in times of scarcity or when it has cubs. But there is no reason to suppose the two are of different species.

In Scotland the fox holds the first place among "vermin." I do not think that a mountain-fox would live long before a pack of regular fox-hounds, but in his own country he is well able to take care of himself. He is a handsome powerful fellow; and in size and strength more like a wolf than a Lowland fox, and well he may be, since his food consists of mutton and lamb, grouse and venison. His stronghold is under some huge cairn, or among the fragments that strew the bottom of some rocky precipice, perhaps three thousand feet above the sea. In those mountain solitudes he does not confine his depredations to the night; I have often encountered him in broad daylight; and through my deer-glass have watched his manner of hunting the ptarmigan, which is not so neat, but appears quite as successful, as the tactics of the cat. By an unobservant eye, the track of a fox is easily mistaken for that of a dog. The print is somewhat rounder, but the chief difference is the superior neatness of the impression, and the exactness of the steps, the hind-foot just covering the print of the fore-foot. The fox makes free with a great variety of game, and the demands of his nursery require a plentiful supply.[1] In the hills he lives on lambs, sheep, grouse, and ptarmigan; in the low country, the staple of his prey is rabbits, where these are plentiful; but nothing comes amiss to him, from the field-mouse upwards. The most wary birds, the wood-pigeon and the wild duck, do not escape him, and he destroys a considerable number of the young of the roe. The honey of the wild bee is one of his favourite delicacies; and vermin-trappers have found no bait more effective to lure him than a piece of honey-comb. His nose is very fine, and he detects the taint of human footstep or hand for days after it has been communicated. Several ways are tried for evading his suspicions. Some trappers place three or four traps in a circle, and leave them well covered for some days without any bait; and at the end of that time, when all taint must have left the traps, they place a bait in the centre. Another way is to place the traps in shallow water, and a bait on some bank where he cannot reach it without running a good chance of treading on them. Even when the enemy is in the trap, the victory is not won; and if

---

[1] The fox is fond of the sea-shore, where it feeds on dead fish, etc., thrown up by the sea. It manages to catch old wild ducks and other birds. It also kills young roe, lambs, and cats.—C. St. J.

he escapes, whether whole or maimed, after being trapped, he is too well warned ever to be caught again. Altogether, trapping has never been very successfully practised against the fox in the Highlands, and the old native practice of "fox-hunting," as the professional mode of killing them is called here, is still much preferred.

Of all ways of earning a livelihood, perhaps there is none that requires a greater degree of hardihood and acuteness than the trade of a vermin-killer in the Highlands—meaning by "vermin," not magpies, crows, and "such small deer," but the stronger and wilder carnivorous natives of the mountain and forest—the enemies of the sheep and lambs. In the Highlands he is honoured with the title of "The Fox-hunter"; but the Highland fox-hunter leads a very different life, and heads a very different establishment, from him of Leicestershire. When you first come upon him in some wild glen, you are somewhat startled at his appearance and bearing. He is generally a wiry active man, past middle age, slung round with pouches and belts for carrying the implements of his trade; he wears a huge cap of badger-skin, and carries an old-fashioned long-barrelled fowling-piece. At his feet follow two or three couple of strong gaunt slow-hounds, a brace of greyhounds, rough, and with a good dash of the lurcher, and a miscellaneous *tail* of terriers of every degree.

A short time ago the foxes having made too free with the lambs, the sheep-farmer of the glen summoned the fox-hunter to his assistance, and I joined him with my rifle. Before daylight, the fox-hunter and myself, with two shepherds, and the usual following of dogs, were on the ground, and drew some small hanging birch-woods near the scene of the latest depredations. While the whole pack of dogs were amusing themselves with a marten-cat in the wood, we found a fresh fox-track on the river bank below it, and after considering its direction leisurely, the fox-hunter formed his plans. The hounds were coupled up, and left to the charge of the two shepherds, whilst we started with our guns for a steep corrie, where he expected we could command the passes. It was a good hour and half of a jog-trot, which seemed a familiar pace to my companion. We at length turned off the great glen, and proceeded up a small, rapid, rocky burn, tracing it to where it issued through a narrow fissure in the rocks, down which the water ran like a mill-race. Scrambling up to the head of the ravine, we found ourselves in the corrie, a magnificent amphitheatre of precipitous grey rocks. The fox's favourite earth was known to be far up on the cliff, and as only two passes could easily lead to it, we endeavoured to command them both. My station was high up, on a dizzy enough crag, which commanded one of the passes for a considerable way, and sufficiently screened me from all the lower part of the corrie. Having with some difficulty got to my place, and arranged the best vista I could command whilst keeping myself unseen, I had a few minutes to admire the wild scene below me. It was a narrow corrie, with a small clear stream twisting and shining through an endless confusion of rugged grey rocks.

I had not been placed many minutes when a deep bay reached me through the clear morning air. I listened with eagerness; and soon heard the whole pack in full cry, though at a great distance, and apparently not coming quite in our direction. While watching, however, the different entries to the corrie, I saw a fox come leisurely down a steep slope of loose stones, towards where the fox-hunter was concealed. Presently he stopped, and quietly sitting down, appeared to listen for the dogs; and, not hearing their cry come nearer, he came quietly and leisurely along, till he reached the track where we had crossed the corrie; when, cautiously stopping with his nose to the ground, he changed his careless manner of running to a quick canter, halting now and then, and snuffing the air, to find out where the enemy was concealed. Just then, too, the hounds appeared to have turned to our direction, and another fox came in view, entering the corrie to my right hand at a great pace, and making directly towards me, though still at a mile's distance. The first fox had approached within sixty or seventy yards of the fox-hunter, when I saw a small stream of smoke issue from the rocks, and the fox staggered a little, and then I heard the report of the gun. The foxes both rushed down the hill again, away from us, one evidently wounded; when, the echo of the shot sounding in every direction, first on one side of the corrie, then on another, and then apparently on every side at once, fairly puzzled the poor animals. The wounded fox turned back again, and ran straight towards where the fox-hunter was, while the other came towards me. He was within shot, and I was only waiting till he got to an open bit of ground, over which I saw he must pass, when the hounds appeared in full cry at the mouth of the corrie by which he had entered. Reynard stopped to look; and stretching up his head and neck to do so, gave me a fair shot at about sixty yards off. The next moment he was stretched dead, with my ball through him; while the other, quite bewildered, ran almost between the legs of my fellow-chasseur, and then turned back towards the dogs; who, meeting him full in the face, wounded as he was, soon caught and slew him. In a short time the whole of our troops, dogs, shepherds, and all, were collected; and great were the rejoicings over the fallen foe. I must say, that though our game was ignoble, the novelty of the proceedings, and the wildness and magnificence of the scenery, had kept me both amused and interested. I forget the name of the corrie: it was some unpronounceable Gaelic word, signifying the "Corrie of the Echo."

HIGHLAND MOWING.

BADGER AND WASPS' NEST

CHAPTER XXXI

The Badger: Antiquity of; Cleanliness; Abode of; Food; Family of—Trapping Badgers—Anecdotes—Escape of Badger—Anecdotes—Strength of—Cruelty to.

AMONGST the aboriginal inhabitants of our wilder districts, who are likely to be soon extirpated, we may reckon that ancient, peaceable, and respectable quadruped, the badger;[1] of an ancient family he certainly is—the fossil remains which have been found prove his race to have been co-existent with that of the mammoths and megatheriums which once wandered over our islands. Though the elk[2] and beaver have long since ceased

[1] Not uncommon in wooded parts of Morayshire; it destroys the nests of wild ducks, partridges, etc., sometimes catching the old bird on her eggs and eating her. In the winter they turn up the ground in the turnip-fields after the manner of a pig, travelling far from their holes for this purpose.—C. St. J.

[2] *Megaceros Hibernicus*. Remarkable from the fact that it is the sole survivor from the Pleistocene into the Prehistoric Age which has since become extinct, and also from having existed in vast numbers in Ireland, while its bones are rarely found in Britain. It has, however, been discovered in the marl below the peat in the parish of Maybole, Ayrshire.—Dawkins, *Early Man in Britain*, 1880, p. 257, 8.

to exist amongst us, our friend the brock still continues to burrow in the solitary and unfrequented recesses of our larger woods. Persevering and enduring in his every-day life, he appears to have been equally so in clinging to existence during the numerous changes which have passed over the face of the globe since the first introduction of his family into it. Notwithstanding the persecutions and indignities that he is unjustly doomed to suffer, I maintain that he is far more respectable in his habits than we generally consider him to be. "Dirty as a badger," "stinking as a badger," are two sayings often repeated, but quite inapplicable to him. As far as we can learn of the domestic economy of this animal when in a state of nature, he is remarkable for his cleanliness—his extensive burrows are always kept perfectly clean, and free from all offensive smell; no filth is ever found about his abode; everything likely to offend his olfactory nerves is carefully removed. I once, in the north of Scotland, fell in with a perfect colony of badgers; they had taken up their abode in an unfrequented range of wooded rocks, and appeared to have been little interrupted in their possession of them. The footpaths to and from their numerous holes were beaten quite hard; and what is remarkable and worthy of note, they had different small pits dug at a certain distance from their abodes, which were evidently used as receptacles for all offensive filth; every other part of their colony was perfectly clean. A solitary badger's hole, which I once had dug out, during the winter season, presented a curious picture of his domestic and military arrangements—a hard and long job it was for two men to achieve, the passage here and there turned in a sharp angle round some projecting corners of rock, which he evidently made use of when attacked, as points of defence, making a stand at any of these angles, where a dog could not scratch to enlarge the aperture, and fighting from behind his stone buttress. After tracing out a long winding passage, the workmen came to two branches in the hole, each leading to good-sized chambers: in one of these was stored a considerable quantity of dried grass, rolled up into balls as large as a man's fist, and evidently intended for food; in the other chamber there was a bed of soft dry grass and leaves—the sole inhabitant was a peculiarly large old dog-badger. Besides coarse grasses, their food consists of various roots; amongst others, I have frequently found about their hole the bulb of the common wild blue hyacinth. Fruit of all kinds and esculent vegetables form his repast, and I fear that he must plead guilty to devouring any small animal that may come in his way, alive or dead; though, not being adapted for the chase, or even for any very skilful strategy of war, I do not suppose that he can do much in catching an unwounded bird or beast. Eggs are his delight, and a partridge's nest with seventeen or eighteen eggs must afford him a fine meal, particularly if he can surprise and kill the hen-bird also; snails and worms which he finds above ground during his nocturnal rambles are likewise included in his bill of fare. I was one summer evening walking home from fishing in Loch Ness, and having occasion to fasten up some part of my tackle, and also expecting to meet my keeper, I sat down on the shore of the loch. I remained some time, enjoying the lovely prospect: the perfectly clear and unruffled loch lay before me, reflecting the northern shore in its quiet water. The opposite banks consisted, in some parts, of bright green sward, sloping to the water's edge, and studded with some of the most beautiful birch-trees in Scotland; several of the trees spreading out like the oak, and with their ragged and ancient-looking bark resembling the cork-tree of Spain—others drooping and weeping over the edge of the water in the most lady-like and elegant manner. Parts of the loch were edged in by old lichen-covered rocks; while farther on a magnificent scaur of red stone rose perpendicularly from the water's edge to a very great height. So clearly was every object on the opposite shore reflected in the lake below, that it was difficult, nay impossible, to distinguish where the water ended and the land commenced—the shadow from the reality. The sun was already set, but its rays still illuminated the sky. It is said that from the sublime to the ridiculous there is but one step;—and I was just then startled from my reverie by a kind of grunt close to me, and the apparition of a small waddling grey animal, which was busily employed in hunting about the grass and stones at the edge of the loch; presently another, and another, appeared in a little grassy glade which ran down to the water's edge, till at last I saw seven of them busily at work within a few yards of me, all coming from one direction. It at first struck me that they were some farmer's pigs taking a distant ramble, but I shortly saw that they were badgers, come from their fastnesses rather earlier than usual, tempted by the quiet evening, and by a heavy summer shower that was just over, and which had brought out an infinity of large black snails and worms, on which the badgers were feeding with good appetite. As I was dressed in grey and sitting on a grey rock, they did not see me, but waddled about, sometimes close to me; only now and then as they crossed my track they showed a slight uneasiness, smelling the ground, and grunting gently. Presently a very large one, which I took to be the mother of the rest, stood motionless for a moment listening with great attention, and then giving a loud grunt, which seemed perfectly understood by the others, she scuttled away, followed by the whole lot. I was soon joined by my attendant, whose approach they had heard long before my less acute ears gave me warning of his coming. In trapping other vermin in these woods, we constantly caught badgers—sometimes several were found in the traps; I always regretted this, as my keeper was most unwilling to spare their lives, and I fancy seldom did so. His arguments were tolerably cogent, I must confess. When I tried to persuade him that they were quite harmless, he answered me by asking—" Then why, Sir, have they got such teeth, if they don't live, like a dog or fox, on flesh?—and why do they get caught so often in traps baited with rabbits?" I could not but admit that they had most carnivorous-looking teeth, and well adapted to act on the offensive as well as defensive, or to crunch the bones of any young hare, rabbit, or pheasant that came in their way. When caught in traps, they never left part of their foot behind them and so escaped, as foxes and other vermin frequently do; but they display very great strength and dexterity in drawing up the peg of the trap, and this done, they will carry off the heaviest trap to an amazing distance, over rock or heather. They never attempt to enter their hole with a trap dangling to their foot, but generally lie up in some furze-bush or thicket; on these occasions we invariably found them, by tracking them with a dog which generally attended the trapper, and which dog was peculiarly skilful in tracking animals of this kind. Rover (for that was his name), a strong water-spaniel, was very fond of, and took great interest in, trapping; if he accompanied the keeper when placing his traps overnight, he would often start alone in the morning to take a survey of them, and either kill any animal he found captive, or, if he was not very confident of being the strongest, he would return impatiently for the man, and, running before him, point out plainly where every head of vermin was caught. As for getting into a trap himself, he was far too cunning, but always halting a few yards to leeward of them, and sniffing the air, would at once know if anything was caught. If a cat, marten-cat, or any smaller animal was there, he at once rushed in and killed it; but he waited for the assistance of his friend the keeper to despatch any larger animal.

To return to the badger, and his food. One of his most favourite repasts is the contents of the nest of the wasp or wild bee, great numbers of which he must destroy. However far under ground the hive may be, and in however strong and difficult a situation, he digs them up, and, depending on his rough coat and long hair as a protection from their stings, devours comb, larvæ, honey, and insects. Many a wasps' nest I have found dug up in this way, and often far from the badger's usual abode; but the tracks of the animal always made it evident who had been the robber.

The badger is easily tamed, and will (if taken young and well used) become much attached to his master. When first caught, their efforts to escape show a degree of strength and ingenuity which is quite wonderful, digging and tearing at their prison with the strength of a rhinoceros. When first imprisoned, if looked at, he immediately rolls himself up into a ball and remains quite motionless. As soon as the coast is clear again, he continues his attempts to escape; but if unsuccessful, he soon becomes contented in his confinement. I one day found a badger not much hurt in a trap. Tying a rope to his hind leg, I drove him home before me, as a man drives a pig, but with much less trouble, for he made no attempts at escape, but trotted quietly ahead, only occasionally showing a natural inclination to bolt off the main path whenever he passed any diverging road, all of which were probably familiar haunts of the unlucky beast. When at home I put him into a paved court, where I thought he could not possibly escape. The next morning, however, he was gone; having displaced a stone that

I thought him quite incapable of moving, and then digging under the wall, he got away.

The badger always puts me in mind of a miniature bear, and to this family he evidently belongs. His proportions are similar to those of the bear; his manner of placing his feet on the ground is like that of a bear, and is very peculiar. Beyond the marks of his toes, which, five in number, mark the ground in a nearly straight line, are the impressions of his strong, sharp nails, apparently unconnected with, and at the distance of an inch or two from the rest of his track. These long and powerful nails are a formidable weapon, and in engagements with dogs he makes good use of them, inflicting fearful and sometimes fatal wounds. Though a quiet animal, and generally speaking not much given to wandering, I have occasionally fallen in with his unmistakable track miles from any burrow. His habits are wholly nocturnal, and it is only in the summer evenings, when the darkness lasts but a few hours, that he is ever met with whilst it is light. During winter he not only keeps entirely within his hole, but fills up the mouth of it to exclude the cold and any troublesome visitor who might intrude on his slumbers. Frequently, however, tempted by mild weather in the winter, he comes out for some good purpose of his own —either to enjoy the fresh air or to add to his larder; but never does he venture out in frost or snow. Sometimes I have known a badger leave the solitude of the woods and take to some drain in the cultivated country, where he becomes very bold and destructive to the crops, cutting down wheat and ravaging the gardens in a surprising manner. One which I know to be now living in this manner derives great part of his food during the spring from a rookery, under which he nightly hunts, feeding on the young rooks that fall from their nests or on the old ones that are shot. This badger eludes every attempt to trap him. Having more than once run narrow risks of this nature, he has become so cunning that no one can catch him. If a dozen baited traps are set, he manages to carry off the baits and spring every trap, always with total impunity to himself. At one time he was watched out to some distance from his drain, and traps were then put in all directions round it, but, by jumping over some and rolling over others, he escaped all. In fact, though a despised and maltreated animal, when he has once acquired a certain experience in worldly matters, few beasts show more address and cunning in keeping out of scrapes. Though eaten in France, Germany, and other countries, and pronounced to make excellent hams, we in Britain despise him as food, though I see no reason why he should not be quite as good as any pork.

The badger becomes immensely fat. Though not a great eater, his quiet habits and his being a great sleeper prevent his being lean.

The immense muscular power that he has in his chest and legs enables him to dig with great rapidity, while his powerful jaws (powerful, indeed, beyond any other animal of his size) enable him to tear away any obstacle in the shape of roots, etc., that he meets with. He can also stand with perfect impunity a blow on his forehead which would split the frontal bone of an ox. This is owing to its great thickness, and also to the extra protection of a strong ridge or keel which runs down the middle of his head. A comparatively slight blow on the back of his head kills him. In his natural state he is more than a match for any animal that would be inclined to molest him, and can generally keep at bay any dog small enough to enter his hole. Fighting at advantage from behind some stone or root, he gives the most fearful bites and scratches, while the dog has nothing within his reach to attack save the badger's formidable array of teeth and claws.

Though nearly extinct as one of the *feræ naturæ* of England, the extensive woods and tracts of rocks in the north of Scotland will, I hope, prevent the badger's becoming, like the beaver and other animals, wholly a creature of history, and existing only in record. Much should I regret that this respectable representative of so ancient a family, the comrade of mammoths and other wonders of the antediluvian world, should become quite extirpated. Living, too, in remote and uncultivated districts, he very seldom commits any depredations deserving of death or persecution, but subsists on the wild succulent grasses and roots, and the snails and reptiles which he finds in the forest glades, or, on rare occasions, makes capture of young game or wounded rabbits or hares, but I do not believe that he does or can hunt down any game that would not otherwise fall a prey to crow or weasel, or which has the full use of its limbs. It is only wounded and injured animals that he can catch.

It is difficult to understand how any person who is not lost to every sense of humanity and shame can take delight in the cowardly and brutal amusement of badger-baiting—instead of amusement, I should have said, the disgusting exhibition of a peaceable and harmless animal worried by fierce and powerful dogs. The poor badger, too, has probably been kept for a length of time in a confined and close hutch, thereby losing half his energy and strength; while the dogs, trained to the work and in full vigour of wind and limb, attack him in the most tender and vulnerable parts. Truly, I always feel a wish to make the badger and his keeper change places for a few rounds. Not that I would pay the former so bad a compliment as to suppose that he would take delight in tormenting even so great a brute as his gaoler must be.

GROUP OF HIGHLAND DOGS. FROM SIR E. LANDSEER, R.A.

"THE NEXT MOMENT HE WAS PASSING FULL BROADSIDE TO ME"

CHAPTER XXXII

Autumn Day on the Mountain—Stags and Hinds—A Bivouac—Death of the Stag

IN the same ratio that steam-boats, railways, coaches, and every other kind of conveyance were crowded in the months of July and August with men, dogs, and guns, all travelling northwards, every road is in October occupied by travellers to the south; for the cold blasts of the mountain, and the uncertain state of the weather, in the Highlands, drive most of our English sportsmen back again to the more solid comforts of their own homes. Nevertheless, there are, perhaps, more variety of sport and more objects of interest to the hunter and naturalist to be met with during the autumn and winter months in the northern parts of

Scotland than during any other season of the year. And, as for weather, after the first burst of the equinoctial winds and rains, the climate is as good as in any part of Great Britain. The fine clear bracing frosts of the autumn are nowhere to be felt with greater enjoyment than on the mountains. It is not, indeed, quite so desirable to bivouac out, "sub Jove frigido," in the month of October or November, with no covering but a plaid and a heap of heather, as it is in July or August; still I have done so, and been none the worse for it.

Some years back I remember sleeping under a rock in the beginning of October with much satisfaction, and no ill consequences to myself.

The red deer had just commenced what is called by the Highlanders roaring,[1] *i.e.* uttering their loud cries of defiance to rival stags, and of warning to their rival mistresses.

There had been seen, and reported to me, a particularly large and fine-antlered stag, whose branching honours I wished to transfer from the mountain side to the walls of my own hall. Donald and myself accordingly, one fine morning early in October, started before daybreak for a distant part of the mountain, where we expected to find him; and we resolved to pass the night at a shepherd's house far up in the hills, if we found that our chase led us too far from home to return the same evening.

Long was our walk that day before we saw horn or hoof; many a likely burn and corrie did we search in vain. The shepherds had been scouring the hills the day before for their sheep, to divide those which were to winter in the low ground from those which were to remain on the hills. However, the day was fine and frosty, and we were in the midst of some of the most magnificent scenery in Scotland; so that I, at least, was not much distressed at our want of luck. Poor Donald, who had not the same enjoyment in the beauty of the scene, unless it were enlivened by a herd of deer here and there, began to grumble and lament our hard fate; particularly as towards evening wild masses of cloud began to sweep up the glens and along the sides of the mountain, and every now and then a storm of cold rain and sleet added to the discomfort of our

---

[1] The old word for this is "bell" (*i.e.* bellow), see *Marmion*, iv. 15:

"The wild-buck bells from ferny brake."

position. There was, however, something so very desolate and wild in the scene and the day, that, wrapt in my plaid, I stalked slowly on enjoying the whole thing as much as if the elements had been in better temper, and the Goddess of Hunting propitious.

We came in the afternoon to a rocky burn, along the course of which was our line of march. To the left rose an interminable-looking mountain, over the sides of which were scattered a wilderness of grey rock and stone, sometimes forming immense precipices, and in other places degenerating into large tracts of loose and water-worn grey shingle, apparently collected and heaped together by the winter floods. Great masses of rock were scattered about, resting on their angles, and looking as if the wind, which was blowing a perfect gale, would hurl them down on us.

Amongst all this dreary waste of rock and stone, there were large patches of bright green pasture and rushes on the level spots formed by the damming up of the springs and mountain streams.

Stretching away to our right was a great expanse of brown heather and swampy ground, dotted with innumerable pools of black-looking water. The horizon on every side was shut out by the approaching masses of rain and drift. The clouds closed round us, and the rain began to fall in straight hard torrents; at the same time, however, completely allaying the wind.

"Well, well," said Donald, "I just dinna ken what to do." Even I began to think that we might as well have remained at home; but, putting the best face on the matter, we got under a projecting bank of the burn, and took out our provision of oat-cake and cold grouse, and having demolished that, and made a considerable vacuum in the whisky flask, I lit my cigar, and meditated on the vanity of human pursuits in general, and of deer-stalking in particular, while dreamy visions of balls, operas, and the last pair of blue eyes that I had sworn everlasting allegiance to, passed before me.

Donald was engaged in the more useful employment of bobbing for burn trout with a line and hook he had produced out of his bonnet—that wonderful blue bonnet, which, like the bag in the fairy tale, contains anything and everything which is required at a moment's notice. His bait was the worms which in a somewhat sulky mood he kicked out of their damp homes about the edge of the burn. Presently the ring-ousel began to whistle on the hill-side, and the cock grouse to crow in the valley below us. Roused by these omens of better weather, I looked out from our shelter, and saw the face of the sun struggling to show itself through the masses of cloud, while the rain fell in larger but more scattered drops. In a quarter of an hour the clouds were rapidly disappearing, and the face of the hill as quickly opening to our view. We remained under shelter a few minutes longer, when suddenly, as if by magic, or like the lifting of the curtain at a theatre, the whole hill was perfectly clear from clouds, and looked more bright and splendidly beautiful than anything I had ever seen. No symptoms were left of the rain, excepting the drops on the heather, which shone like diamonds in the evening sun. The masses of rock came out in every degree of light and shade, from dazzling white to the darkest purple, streaked here and there with the overpourings of the swollen rills and springs, which danced and leapt from rock to rock, and from crag to crag, looking like streams of silver.

"How beautiful!" was both my inward and outward exclamation. "'Deed it's not just so dour as it was," said Donald; "but, the Lord guide us! look at yon," he continued, fixing his eye on a distant slope, at the same time slowly winding up his line and pouching his trout, of which he had caught a goodly number. "Tak your perspective, Sir, and look there," he added, pointing with his chin. I accordingly took my perspective, as he always called my pocket-telescope, and saw a long line of deer winding from amongst the broken granite in single file down towards us. They kept advancing one after the other, and had a most singular appearance as their line followed the undulations of the ground. They came slowly on, to the number of more than sixty (all hinds, not a horn amongst them), till they arrived at a piece of table-land four or five hundred yards from us, when they spread about to feed, occasionally shaking off the raindrops from their hides, much in the same manner as a dog does on coming out of the water.

"They are no that canny," said Donald. "*Nous verrons,*" said I. "What's your wull?" was his answer; "I'm no understanding Latin, though my wife has a cousin who is a placed minister." "Why, Donald, I meant to say that we shall soon see whether they are canny or not: a rifle-ball is a sure remedy for all witchcraft." Certainly there was something rather startling in the way they all suddenly appeared as it were from the bowels of the mountain, and the deliberate, unconcerned manner in which they set to work feeding like so many tame cattle.

We had but a short distance to stalk. I kept the course of a small stream which led through the middle of the herd; Donald followed me with my gun. We crept up till we reckoned that we must be within an easy shot, and then, looking most cautiously through the crevices and cuts in the bank, I saw that we were in the very centre of the herd: many of the deer were within twenty or thirty yards, and all feeding quickly and unconscious of any danger. Amongst the nearest to me was a remarkably large hind, which we had before observed as being the leader and biggest of the herd. I made a sign to Donald that I would shoot her, and left him to take what he liked of the flock after I fired.

Taking a deliberate and cool aim at her shoulder, I pulled the trigger; but, alas! the wet had got between the cap and nipple-end. All that followed was a harmless snap: the deer heard it, and starting from their food rushed together in a confused heap as if to give Donald a fair chance at the entire flock, a kind of shot he rather rejoiced in. Before I could get a dry cap on my gun, snap, snap, went both his barrels; and when I looked up, it was but to see the whole herd quietly trotting up the hill, out of shot, but apparently not very much frightened, as they had not seen us, or found out exactly where the sound came from. "We are just twa fules, begging your honour's pardon, and only fit to weave hose by the ingle," said Donald. I could not contradict him. The mischief was done; so we had nothing for it but to wipe out our guns as well as we could and proceed on our wandering. We followed the probable line of the deer's march, and before night saw them in a distant valley feeding again quite unconcernedly.

"Hark! what is that?" said I, as a hollow roar like an angry bull was heard not far from us. "Kep down, kep down," said Donald, suiting the action to the word, and pressing me down with his hand; "it's just a big staig." All the hinds looked up, and, following the direction of their heads, we saw an immense hart coming over the brow of the hill three hundred yards from us. He might easily have seen us, but seemed too intent on the hinds to think of anything else. On the height of the hill he halted, and stretching out his neck and lowering his head, bellowed again. He then rushed down the hill like a mad beast: when half-way down he was answered from a distance by another stag. He instantly halted, and looking in

"ON THE HEIGHT OF THE HILL HE HALTED"

that direction roared repeatedly, while we could see in the evening air, which had become cold and frosty, his breath coming out of his nostrils like smoke. Presently he was answered by another and another stag, and the whole distance seemed alive with them. A more unearthly noise I never heard, as it echoed and re-echoed through the rocky glens that surrounded us.

The setting sun threw a strong light on the first comer, casting a kind of yellow glare on his horns and head, while his body was in deep shade, giving him a most singular appearance, particularly when combined with his hoarse and strange bellowing. As the evening closed in, their cries became almost incessant, while here and there we heard the clash of horns as two rival stags met and fought a few rounds together. None, however, seemed inclined to try their strength with the large hart who had first appeared. The last time we saw him, in the gloom of the evening, he was rolling in a small pool of water, with several of the hinds standing quietly round him, while the smaller stags kept passing to and fro near the hinds, but afraid to approach too close to their watchful rival, who was always ready to jump up and dash at any of them who ventured within a certain distance of his seraglio. "Donald," I whispered, "I would not have lost this sight for a hundred pounds." "'Deed, no, it's grand," said he. "In all my travels on the hill I never saw the like." Indeed it is very seldom that chances combine to enable a deer-stalker to look on quietly at such a strange meeting of deer as we had witnessed that evening. But night was coming on, and though the moon was clear and full, we did not like to start off for the shepherd's house, through the swamps and swollen burns among which we should have had to pass, nor did we forget that our road would be through the valley where all this congregation of deer were. So, after consulting, we turned off to leeward to bivouac amongst the rocks at the back of the hill, at a sufficient distance from the deer not to disturb them by our necessary occupation of cooking the trout, which our evening meal was to consist of. Having hunted out some of the driest of the fir-roots which were in abundance near us, we soon made a bright fire out of view of the deer, and after eating some fish and drying our clothes pretty well, we found a snug corner in the rocks, where, wrapped up in our plaids and covered with heather, we arranged ourselves to sleep.

Several times during the night I got up and listened to the wild bellowing of the deer: sometimes it sounded close to us, and at other times far away. To an unaccustomed ear it might easily have passed for the roaring of a host of much more dangerous wild beasts, so loud and hollow did it sound. I awoke in the morning cold and stiff, but soon put my blood into circulation by running two or three times up and down a steep bit of the hill. As for Donald, he shook himself, took a pinch of snuff, and was all right. The sun was not yet above the horizon, though the tops of the mountains to the west were already brightly gilt by its rays, and the grouse cocks were answering each other in every direction.

Having discharged our guns, which we did close to a steep and very noisy cascade in the burn, so that the report could scarcely be heard beyond the place we were in, we dried the locks as well as we could, and after a meagre breakfast on the remains of the trout and some very wretched remnants of oatcake, we proceeded on our journey. The deer had moved from the valley where we had left them the previous evening; but Donald, who knew every mountain and glen in the country, having ascertained exactly the way the wind came from, led me off in an easterly direction. The sun was well up when we came towards the summit of a hill from which he expected to see the herd, and his anticipations proved to be correct; on looking carefully down into the extended valley below us, we saw the whole of them. They had apparently finished feeding, and were retiring to rest on a hill-side which faced the morning sun; the hinds were in a compact body, while the largest hart kept a little to their rear, and constantly employed himself in keeping off a number of smaller stags which were moving about; occasionally one of these would make an impatient rush into the centre of the herd of hinds, but was as quickly driven out by the large stag, who then returned to his post in the rear. When they had ascended to near the summit, the hinds began to drop one by one into the long heather, until they were all lying down, with the exception of five or six who kept constantly fidgeting about, turning their long ears and snuffing the air in all directions. The old stag walked quietly about, going round and round the herd; now and then lying down for a few moments, and then rising again, to see that no other stag intruded too near. The smaller stags kept continually circling round the whole herd; occasionally two of these youngsters would meet, but after a few tilts at each other, separated again and continued their watchful march. I saw no chance of getting near the big-antlered leader, though one of the smaller stags could easily have been shot. After consulting with Donald, I sent him to make a large circuit, and when he got quite round them he was to show himself in the distance to the deer. We reckoned on their leaving the glen by a particular pass, close to which I stationed myself. I kept both gun and rifle with me. From my position, though I could not see Donald, I had a good view of the deer. After waiting for nearly an hour, I saw one of the smaller stags suddenly stop in his rounds, and having gazed for a moment or two in the direction in which I knew Donald was, he trotted nearer to the hinds, still, however, halting occasionally, and turning an anxious glance down the valley. I saw by his manner that he had not quite made up his mind as to whether there was an enemy at hand; not having got the wind of Donald, but probably having caught a glimpse of some part of his cap or dress.

The stag then stood motionless on a small hillock, with his head turned towards the suspected quarter, though none of his rivals took any notice of him. The hinds, one and all, kept a most anxious watch on his movements, evidently aware that he suspected some danger. In the meantime Donald seemed to have got a little more to windward of the deer. Presently one old hind got up and snuffed the air, then another and another, till all were on their legs; still they were not decided as to the danger. At last a general panic seemed to seize the hinds, and they all trotted together a short way up the hill; the large stag had got up also, but seemed not at all disposed to make off. The hinds came to a halt near the top of the first slope of the hill, and were joined immediately by about a dozen stags, which, collecting together, galloped up the hill to join them; this seemed to arouse the old fellow, and he trotted up after them. The hinds only waited for his joining them, and then the whole herd set off towards my pass. They had to cross a trifling hollow, during which time I lost sight of them. When they emerged their order had quite changed; first of all came eight stags in a body, jostling each other as they hurried up through the narrow passes of the rocks; then came the whole lot of hinds, mostly in single file, but breaking into confused flocks as they passed over pieces of heather and open ground; next to them came the object of our manœuvres, and at a small distance behind him the rest of the stags, four or five in number. On they came, sometimes in full view and sometimes half concealed from me. Donald, too, now showed himself, waving his plaid. The hindmost deer halted on seeing him, and then rushed on to the main herd, who now all got into rare confusion as they hurried on to the pass through which they left the glen. The foremost stags were now passing one by one within forty yards of me ; just at that point they had to make a spring over a kind of chasm in their road. I kept quite motionless, and they did not observe me, half concealed as I was amongst the grey rocks. Now came the hinds, with a noise like a rushing stream ; amongst them were four or five stags ; they were trotting quickly past me, when an unlucky hind caught sight of my rifle-barrel as a ray of the sun fell upon it ; the rest of the herd took the alarm from her manner, and they all rushed through the pass in the most mad confusion. The difficult part was only a few yards in length, and once through this, they got into regular order again. But where is their lord and leader ? I was afraid to look over my ambuscade for fear of turning him. Just as I was about to do so, however, I heard his step on the stones, and in the next moment he was in full view passing broadside to me, but going slowly and undecided whether to proceed or turn back, having perceived the panic of the rest of the flock. When he came to the difficult point where the rest had leaped, he halted for a moment, looking round. The next moment my rifle-ball passed through the top of his shoulder, just too high ; the blow, however, knocked him down, and before he was up I had my gun in my hand ; the poor brute rose, and looked wildly round ; not knowing where the enemy was, nor which way to go, he stood still, looking with anxious glance at his companions, who were galloping off up an opposite slope. Expecting him to drop dead every moment, I did not pull the trigger, but kept my aim on him. The way the rest had gone seemed too rough for him, and after standing for a minute gazing after them, he turned round with the intention, probably, of going down the hill to some well-known burn where he had been in the habit of bathing, and cooling his limbs. He twice fell to his knees before he had gone five yards, and then walked slowly away. I thought he might recover strength, and taking a deliberate aim, I fired. This time he fell without a struggle, perfectly dead. Donald joined me by the time I had bled him, and examined the shot-marks. One had broken the very top of his shoulder, but just missed the large arteries ; the other ball seemed to have passed through his heart. The Highlander was vastly delighted at our getting the stag we had determined on, but his enjoyment was somewhat damped by my not having sent both barrels into the middle of the hinds. "Aiblins your honour would have tuk down twa or three at each shot, and the brutes will all be off our march in an hour's time. Lord, Sir, if I had only been where your honour was, with the dooble-barrel loaded with swan-post, I'd hae rattled it about their lugs; I fairly suspect I'd have put down half-a-dizen." I consoled Donald with a dram, and we set to work to prepare our stag for taking home, which, with the help of a shepherd's pony, we succeeded in doing before night.

Donald, though, professedly, he cared for neither wind nor weather, was in bed all the next day, from what he called rheumatiz, but what I called whisky toddy, taken to counteract any bad effects of his cold bivouac; for my own part, I did not feel at all the worse for our cool couch, and was quite ready to renew the campaign.

THE RAVEN

CHAPTER XXXIII

Peculiarities and Instinct of Different Animals—Feeding Habits—The Beaks of Birds—Wings of Owl—Instinct in finding Food—Ravens—Knowledge of Change of Weather—Fish.

I CANNOT conclude these hasty sketches without remarking that few people are aware of the numberless subjects of interest and observation to be found in the habits and structure of the commonest birds and animals which pass before our eyes every day of our lives. How perfectly are all these adapted to their respective modes of living and feeding. In every garden and shrubbery the naturalist finds amusement in watching its living tenants. Look at the chaffinch, how it adapts the colour and even the shape of its nest to the spot in which it is placed, covering the outside with materials of the same colour as the bark of the tree in which it is. So do also all the other small birds. Again, they line their nests with materials of the same colour as their eggs. The chaffinch lines it with wool and feathers mixed together, giving it a background of nearly the same hue as the shell of the eggs. The greenfinch lines it with light-coloured feathers, collected from the poultry-yard, as her eggs are nearly white. The yellow-hammer has a greyish egg with stripy marks; she lines her nest with horsehair. The robin's eggs being of a reddish-brown, she makes use of dried grass and similar substances. The prevailing colour of the hedge-sparrow's nest is green, and her eggs are of a greenish-blue; and in the same manner all our common and unregarded birds adapt both the outside and the lining of their nests to the colour of the surrounding substances and that of their own eggs respectively. In the same manner they all have bills adapted to the food on which they live—the grain-feeding birds have short, strong mandibles, while those of the insectivorous birds are longer and more slender, and as perfectly adapted for searching in crannies and corners for the insects and eggs that may be hidden there, as the former are for cutting and shelling the seeds and grain on which they feed.

Look, too, at the eggs of lapwings and of all those birds that hatch on the bare ground. Those that lay on fields have their eggs of a brownish-green, while those that lay on the stones and pebbles have them of a sandy and brown mottled colour, so like the substances which surround them, that it is most difficult for the passer-by to distinguish the egg from the stone. In the same manner the young of all birds which live on the ground resemble the ground itself in colour, thereby eluding many of their enemies. Look also at the birds whose residence and food are placed in the marshes and swamps—the woodcocks and snipes, for example, which feed by thrusting their bills into the soft mud for the purpose of picking out the minute red worms and animalcules which abound in it, have the bill peculiarly adapted for this purpose. The upper mandible has a kind of knob at the end, which overlaps the under mandible, and not only prevents its being injured, but makes it quite easy for the bird to pass its bill both into and out of the ground without obstruction. How peculiarly well the bill of these birds is adapted for this purpose is perceived at once by drawing it through the fingers. The end of the mandible, too, is full of nerves, which enables the bird to distinguish the soft and minute substances on which it feeds without seeing them. The oyster-catcher, which feeds on shell-fish and similar food, has a bill with hard, sharp points, with which it can dig into and break the strong coverings of its prey; no tool could be made to answer the purpose better. The curlew's long curved bill is also a perfect implement for worming out the sea-slugs, which it extracts from the wet sands. The birds that live chiefly on the insects and water-plants which are found in swamps and muddy places have their feet of great size and length, which enables them to walk and run over muddy and soft places without sinking. The water-hen and water-rail, indeed, often run along the floating leaves of the water-plants without bearing them down by their weight. The bald coot, too, a bird that lives almost wholly in muddy places, has its feet and toes formed purposely for running on a soft surface. How different from the strongly retractile talons of the hawk and owl, made purposely to seize and hold their struggling prey.

Thus also the beak of these carnivorous birds is formed for tearing and rending, while the strong wedge-shaped mandibles of the raven and carrion-crow are the best possible implements for the half-digging, half-cutting work which they are called upon to perform in devouring the dead carcasses of large animals. The goosander and merganser, which feed principally on small eels and fish, have a row of teeth-like projections inside their bill, which, slanting inwards, admits of the easy entrance of their slippery prey, but effectually prevents its escape; while the cormorant, whose food consists of larger fish, instead of these numerous teeth has a strong curved beak, well fitted for holding the strongest sea-trout or haddock. Put your finger into the bill of a common duck, and you will see how easily it goes in, but how difficult it is to draw it out again, in consequence of the sloping projections, by means of which the bird is enabled to hold worms and snails. No bill but that of a crossbill could cut and divide the strong fir-cones from which it extracts its food. The common woodpecker bores holes with its strongly-tipped wedge-shaped bill in the hard beech-trees, with a precision and regularity not to be excelled by the best carpenter; while with its long worm-like tongue it darts upon and catches the small insects which take refuge in the chinks and crevices of the bark. The swallows, which catch their insect prey while flying at speed in the air, are provided with large wide-opening mouths, which enables them to capture the swiftest-flying moth or midge. In fact, if we take the trouble to examine the manner of feeding and the structure of the commonest birds, which we pass over without observation in consequence of their want of rarity, we see that the Providence that has made them has also adapted each in the most perfect manner for acquiring with facility the food on which it is designed to live. The owl, that preys mostly on the quick-eared mouse, has its wings edged with a kind of downy fringe, which makes its flight silent and inaudible in the still evening air. Were its wings formed of the same kind of plumage as those of most other birds, it is so slow a flier that the mouse, warned by the rustling of its approach, would escape long before it could pounce upon it. The heron has also a quantity of downy plumage about its wings, which are also of a very concave form, and the bird alights in the calm pool without making a ripple, and whilst standing motionless, knee-deep in the water, it is almost invisible in the gloom of evening, owing to its grey shadowy colour. So also is the colour of the wild duck, partridge, and other birds which hatch on the ground, exactly similar in its shade to the dry foliage among which they sit—insomuch so, that even when they are pointed out to one by another person it is very difficult to distinguish these birds.

How curiously quick is the instinct of birds in finding out their food. Where peas or other favourite grain is sown, wood-pigeons and tame pigeons immediately congregate. It is not easy to ascertain from whence the former come, but the house-pigeons have often been known to arrive in numbers on a new-sown field the very morning after the grain is laid down; although no pigeon-house from which they could come exists within several miles of the place.

Put down a handful or two of unthrashed oat straw, in almost any situation near the sea-coast where there are wild ducks, and they are sure to find it out the first or second night after it has been left there.

There are many almost incredible stories of the acuteness of the raven's instinct in guiding it to the dead carcass of any large animal, or even in leading it to the neighbourhood on the near approach of death. I myself have known several instances of the raven finding out dead bodies of animals in a very short space of time. One instance struck me very much. I had wounded a stag on a Wednesday. The following Friday I was crossing the hills at some distance from the place, but in the direction towards which the deer had gone. Two ravens passed me, flying in a steady straight course. Soon again two more flew by, and two others followed, all coming from different directions, but making direct for the same point. "'Deed, Sir," said the Highlander with me, "the corbies have just found the staig; he will be lying dead about the head of the muckle burn." By tracing the course of the birds, we found that the man's conjecture was correct, as the deer was lying within a mile of us, and the ravens were making for its carcass. The animal had evidently only died the day before, but the birds had already made their breakfast upon him, and were now on their way to their evening meal. Though occasionally we had seen a pair of ravens soaring high overhead in that district, we never saw more than that number; but now there were some six or seven pairs already collected—where from, we knew not. When a whale, or other large fish, is driven ashore on the coast of any of the northern islands, the ravens collect in amazing numbers, almost immediately coming from all directions, and from all distances, led by the unerring instinct which tells them that a feast is to be found in a particular spot.

Ducks go out to the grass-fields to search for the snails which they know will be found before the coming shower; the field-mouse covers up her hole in due time before the setting in of cold weather. Fish have the strongest instinct with regard to changes of the weather, refusing obstinately to rise at the most tempting baits or flies when clouds charged with thunder or rain are passing through the air. Indeed most birds and animals have a singular foreknowledge of changes in the weather; shifting their quarters according as the coming rain or the dryness of the atmosphere warns them.

The grouse foretell the approaching rains before the most weather-wise shepherd can do so, by betaking themselves to the dry heights, where they sit or walk about with erect heads and necks, in quite a different manner from their usual gait. So do the mountain sheep change their feeding-ground to the lee side of the hills before severe blasts of wind and rain. I have often been warned of an approaching change in the weather by the proceedings of the wild fowl in the bay; and before changes of wind these birds betake themselves to those places which will afford them the best shelter during the coming storm.

There are few animals which do not afford timely and sure prognostications of changes in the weather. It is proverbial that pigs see the wind; and they undoubtedly become restless, and prepare their straw beds prior to a severe storm, some hours before human organs are aware of its approach.

In fine, there is matter not only for amusement but for admiration in the actions and habits of every animal that we see, even down to the most common small birds and quadrupeds: and the unoccupied man may always find wherewithal to amuse himself profitably in watching the instinct which prompts the everyday proceedings of the animals which are always around us.

HIGHLAND BAROMETERS

THE STAG AT BAY

CHAPTER XXXIV

Coursing Deer

THOUGH I am by no means of opinion that running red deer with the rough deer-hound is so exciting or so satisfactory a sport as stalking the noble animal, and attacking him in his fastnesses with the aid only of a rifle, I have sometimes seen runs with the deer-hounds which fully answered all my expectations. It much oftener happens, however, that after the first start nothing more is seen of dogs or deer until they are found at bay in some rocky burn or stream, the whole run having taken place out of sight of the sportsman. Moreover, the dogs run a great risk of being disabled and injured either by the stag or by the sharp and rugged rocks and stones over which they take their headlong course. The deer-hound is so noble and handsome an animal, that, independently of his actual and marketable value, he is invariably a pet and favourite of his master, so that any accident which happens to him is the more regretted. With good management the experienced stalker can generally secure his dogs from running at young deer or hinds unfit to be killed. Indeed, many deer-hounds have a wonderful instinct in singling out the biggest head of horns in a herd of deer, and in sticking to this one, regardless of the rest of the herd. It will often happen, however, that the dogs set off after some hind or young stag, which leads both them and you away a long chase, unsatisfactory both in its commencement and termination, disturbing the ground and taking up twice as much time as would be required to kill the fine old ten-antlered stag, whose head you covet for your lobby, and whose haunches you wish to send to your English friend, to show him what size a mountain-fed stag will grow to. A large heavy hart is also much sooner blown and brought to bay than a younger and lighter deer.

The breed of deer-hounds, which had nearly become extinct, or at any rate was very rare a few years ago, has now become comparatively plentiful in all the Highland districts, owing to the increased extent of the preserved forests and the trouble taken by different proprietors and renters of mountain shootings, who have collected and bred this noble race of dogs, regardless of expense and difficulties. The prices given for a well-bred and tried dog of this kind are so large, that it repays the cost and trouble of rearing him. Fifty guineas is not an unusual price for a first-rate dog, while from twenty to thirty are frequently given for a tolerable one.

My object, however, in commencing this Chapter was not to enter into a disquisition concerning greyhounds, but to describe some of their performances which have fallen under my own observation, and which I noted down at the time.

September 22, 18—.—Started this morning at daybreak with Donald and Malcolm Mohr, as he is called (Anglicè, Malcolm the Great, or big Malcolm), who had brought his two deer-hounds, Bran and Oscar, to show me how they could kill a stag. Malcolm himself is as fine a looking "lad" (of thirty-five years old, however) as ever stepped on the heather; a head and shoulders taller than Donald, who, for this reason, and I believe for no other, affects to treat his capabilities as a deer-stalker with considerable contempt, always ending any description of a sporting feat of Malcolm's with the qualification, "'Twas no that bad for so long-legged a chiel as yon."

The dogs were perfect. Bran, an immense but beautifully-made dog, of a light colour, with black eyes and muzzle; his ears of a dark brown, soft and silky as a lady's hand, the rest of his coat being wiry and harsh, though not exactly rough and shaggy like his comrade Oscar, who was long-haired and of a darker brindle colour, with sharp long muzzle, but the same soft ears as Bran, which, by the bye, is a distinctive mark of high breeding in these dogs. Malcolm Mohr and I took no guns with us; but Donald, as usual, had his old "*dooble*-barrel," as he calls it, an ancient flint-and-steel affair; the barrels by Manton, and therefore excellent when you could get them off, which the stock and locks, apparently the workmanship of a Highland carpenter and blacksmith, generally prevented me from doing, the triggers being inaccessible to any ordinary forefinger, and the stock about half the length of any other gunstock that ever came in my way. Donald, however, was in the habit of relating great feats which he had performed amongst red deer with this gun, and he always coddled it up with great care from wet or damp, either when laid up in ordinary at home or when carried by himself over mountain and glen. On the present occasion he had a very snuffy and dirty-looking cotton handkerchief tied over the muzzle, and a footless stocking knotted over the locks, to keep out the morning mists.

Our path for some time was along the course of the river, where the great yellow trout were plainly to be seen in the perfectly clear water, waiting for the insects as they fell off the weeping branches of the birch-trees which overhung the still pools, as if admiring their own elegance in the water, where every leaf was as plainly reflected as it would have been in the costliest mirror; and as we made our way up the hill-side the autumnal air felt fine, fresh, and exhilarating.

On coming out of the scattered wood which clothed the

glen on each side of the stream, we saw a fine roebuck feeding in a grassy spot a few hundred yards out of the wood. I and Donald also were much tempted to run the dogs at him, as he was so far from cover; but as Malcolm voted against it, I yielded, though Donald was obliged to take sundry pinches of snuff before he quietly acquiesced in my determination to leave the buck unmolested. As we edged off from him in order that the dogs might not see him and be tempted by his starting off to break away from us, the buck lifted his head, and Bran's quick eye immediately caught sight of him; and the dog stood immovable, with his ears erect, and one fore-foot raised from the ground. The sensible creature, however, instead of straining at his leash, looked up inquiringly at his master, asking him plainly, "Am I to chase that beauty?" Oscar, who was trotting quietly behind Donald, who held him, seeing that Bran had game in view by his manner of gazing, and following the direction of his eyes, also saw the buck. Not being so well broken as Bran, he no sooner saw the buck than he sprang forward, pulling the old keeper down on the flat of his back. Luckily, Donald had the strap twisted round his arm, or the dog would have escaped after the deer. As it was, Donald managed to hold him, and having got up, rubbed his back, and vented his ill-humour in numberless Gaelic imprecations against the dog for upsetting him, and against Malcolm, "the muckle fule," as he called him, for laughing at his mishap, he got under way again. In the meantime the roe had disappeared down some hollow of the ground, and we proceeded on our way.

After leaving the woods, we traversed a long range of broken ground, where we had but small chance of seeing the deer, though their tracks were tolerably fresh here and there; our object was to find the animals in certain places more adapted for the running of the dogs than the ground we were then passing. We therefore did not examine two favourite but rugged and steep corries, where deer were generally found.

Our forbearance was rewarded, for on coming to a point overlooking a long and wide stretch of hill-side, through the centre of which ran a winding but not very rapid burn, we immediately distinguished nine deer still feeding, though the morning was somewhat advanced; they were scattered about a green spot at the head of the burn, and feeding on the coarse grass and rushes which grew about the springs and marsh that fed the main stream. They could not have been better placed, and after a short consultation—which, however, lasted longer than it need have done, owing to Donald's determined and customary opposition to every proposal made by his tall rival —we turned back behind the shoulder of the hill, in order to get into a hollow of the ground which would enable us to reach the course of the burn: for, this done, our task was comparatively easy.

As the water, owing to the dry weather, was but shallow, and the little wind which there was, was blowing right down the stream, by keeping its course we hoped to reach the deer unobserved. Before starting, I took a good look at them through my glass, and saw that the herd consisted wholly of hinds, except one tolerably handsome stag. The dogs instinctively perceived that we had found game, and changed their careless and slouching trot for an eager and quick walk; every now and then they looked with pricked-up ears and an inquiring glance at Malcolm's face, as if to ask him where the deer were, and how soon they would be seen.

Malcolm proposed to me that Donald should get up to a height of the hill, from whence he could see for a long distance on the other side, in case the deer crossed the top, and went to bay in any of the burns that were within his view, and after a slight demur, rather at the proposer than at the proposal, Donald started off, with his "*dooble*-barrel" still carefully swaddled up under his arm.

Malcolm and I proceeded carefully, though with great ease, till we got into the burn; I led Oscar, while Bran was under his guidance—we waded and scrambled with no great difficulty, excepting that now and then Oscar was a little annoyed at not being close to his master, as both dogs seemed perfectly aware of what was going on, and in momentary expectation of seeing the deer. Never was ground more favourable: till we were within four hundred yards of the deer, we had scarcely occasion to stoop our heads. Having come at length to rather a difficult pass, Malcolm asked me to look up carefully, that we might know exactly where the deer were, while he held the dogs. Raising my head gradually, I looked through a tuft of rushes, and saw first the horns of the stag, and then the heads of five of the hinds; they had lain down in the long heather, near the spot they had been feeding on. But where were the remainder of the herd? I looked for two or three minutes in vain, keeping my head perfectly motionless. Presently, however, the rest of the deer appeared from amongst some broken ground, a hundred yards higher up the hill than the others. Having looked anxiously round them, they all dropped quietly down to rest, with the exception of one lanky-looking hind, who stood motionless on a small hillock, with her eyes and ears turned with great attention in the direction of Donald's place of ambuscade: she evidently had some kind of suspicion of danger from that quarter, though she had not yet quite made up her mind as to the reality of it. I lowered myself as gradually as possible, and looked back at Malcolm. He was kneeling on one knee with a dog held in each hand; the dogs themselves were a perfect picture, as they stood, with the most intense expression of anxiety, watching my movements, and snuffing the air in the direction in which I had been looking; the wind was too light, however, for them as yet to scent the deer. As they stood motionless, and scarcely drawing their breath, I could plainly see their hearts beating with anxiety and eagerness; I explained the position of the deer to Malcolm, and we immediately agreed that no time was to be lost, lest they should take alarm at Donald, whose whereabouts the hind seemed strongly to suspect.

We had a difficult task in advancing the next fifty yards with the dogs. The sensible animals, however, crouched when we did, and were wonderfully little in the way, considering the nature of the ground which we had to pass. The old hind's ears were visible, but no more of her, as we crept along; she appeared to be still intently watching in the same direction as before. Having crawled over a small height, we got into a hollow place, and then proceeded to put the dogs' collars and straps in a state to enable us to slip them at a moment's warning. Both Bran and Oscar stood motionless, and almost seemed to turn their necks in order to assist us in the operation.

We then advanced with great care and silence, on our hands and knees, for a couple of hundred yards along a cut in the ground that took us away from the burn. Everything had favoured us, the deer's attention had been taken off by

Donald, and the ground had been the easiest I ever stalked a deer in. We were now within about a hundred yards of them, and could get no nearer unobserved; so, patting the dogs and whispering a word of encouragement to them, we led them in front of us, and rising up in full view of the deer, pointed towards them. We had no need, however, to show their game to the noble hounds, for the deer starting up as soon as they saw us, were at once caught sight of by both Bran and Oscar. Away went the deer; those which were the farthest off waited for their comrades to join them, and then all took the hill in a compact body, and the dogs with an impatient whine darted off the instant they were released from their collars.

The deer ran in a sloping direction up the hill, apparently not exerting themselves very much, but in reality getting over the ground at a very quick pace; the two dogs ran neck and neck, not exactly straight at the deer, but almost parallel, sloping a little, however, towards them, and gaining slowly, but still perceptibly, on their game. This lasted for half a mile or so, when the dogs had gained so much, that they were within forty yards of the deer. Nearer and nearer they approached, the hinds running in a close body, the stag now and then lagging behind a few yards, and then with a great effort joining them again, his greater weight and fat beginning to tell on his wind. Malcolm danced and shouted with eagerness: for my own part I went along at a quiet trot, in order not to lose sight of the run in case they turned up the hill and got over the height.

Presently the dogs seemed to be in the midst of the deer; and the next moment we saw the stag coming straight down the hill with tremendous strides, and the dogs ten yards behind him—Bran rather the first; his thinner coat telling in his favour. As for the hinds, they dispersed for a moment, then collected again, and went off up the hill; being intent on the stag, I saw nothing more of them; they probably did not halt till they had crossed the hill and the river too.

Down came the stag at a pace and with bounds that seemed likely to smash his legs every moment. Luckily for the dogs the ground was (as it had been all along) most favourable. I lost view of all three as they got into the course of a burn, which joined the one we had come up. The dogs were then at his haunches, but unable to get hold. Bran's point of attack was always at the shoulder, or fore-leg, while Oscar had a habit of biting at the hind-leg above the hock, frequently cutting through the flesh and tendons in a most extraordinary manner, and tumbling the deer over very quickly. He had, however, not yet got a fair chance at his present chase. Once in the burn, I knew that neither dog could do much, excepting to bring the stag to bay. I ran as hard as I could towards them, and soon saw the deer rattling down the stream, with stones and water flying about him in all directions. The dogs were still keeping up as well as they could in the narrow and rough path the stag had chosen, and sometimes springing at him, but unable to get a hold. Malcolm and myself were in great dread that they would be injured or killed. When within fifty yards of us, both dogs were thrown down, after making an ineffectual attempt at holding the deer, who broke away, and, getting a little ahead of his pursuers, came to bay under a rock in a pool of the burn which reached to his knees. The dogs had recovered themselves almost immediately, and, crouching in the water, bayed furiously at the stag, who, with his back to the rock, presented only his armed front to them. Knowing their business well, from having gained experience in many hard-fought battles, they did not risk their lives by rushing at his horns, but contented themselves by keeping him there, while they now and then looked round at Malcolm, as if to ask for his assistance. "Down, good dogs, down," he said, when, seeing us approach, they seemed inclined to rush in.

The deer now and then appeared anxious to break off, but whenever he attempted to move, the hound nearest the direction towards which he turned sprang in front of him, baying and preventing his leaving the spot.

Not seeing Donald and his gun, we consulted together as to what was to be done, and at last Malcolm determined, by cautiously attacking the deer from above with his stick, to make him turn from the dogs, and give them a chance of fixing on him without risk from his horns; if they succeeded, I was to run in, and act as circumstances permitted, and, if possible, to help the dogs by stabbing the deer in the throat. As soon as Malcolm had commenced his part of the business, by going round the deer, I called off the dogs in order that they should not be trampled down by the first rush of the poor beast.

They came quite willingly, evidently placing entire confidence in our manner of attack. Malcolm got just above the stag, and then flinging his heavy stick at his legs, and shouting loudly, frightened him so that he rushed out of the pool, passing close to me.

"Now, then, good dogs, at him"; and the next moment the stag was tumbled over, with both hounds fixed on him—Bran at his shoulder and Oscar at his throat. I easily managed my part of the affair, and put an end to the poor animal's pain with my hunting-knife. "Well done, Sir, well done," said Malcolm; "that was quickly finished."—"Deed, ay," said Donald, who just then came up, panting like a walrus. "No that bad either"; this being the utmost praise that he ever bestowed on any one. The hounds, as soon as they saw that the stag was quite dead, left him, and, lying quietly down, began to lick the bruises and cuts they had received in the run; luckily there were none of any consequence. Every now and then one of the dogs would get up, and, going up to the deer, examine him all over, as if to satisfy himself that there was no life remaining. We examined the dogs' limbs to see that there was no serious strain or cut, and then, after rubbing the dirt and blood off their skins, set to work to open the deer, and dispose of the body, ready to be carried off the next day. This done, we sat down, talked over the run, and consulted as to our proceedings for the rest of the day; and as it was still early, we agreed to try some more ground, in the contrary direction to that in which the hinds had gone, and, if kept out late, to sleep at a shepherd's house some distance up in the hills.

We searched many a corrie and glen in vain, till towards evening, Donald, who had been examining the rushy ground that fringed the sides of a considerable mountain stream, in hopes of seeing some deer at feed, suddenly shut up the telescope, and as he deliberately wiped the glasses, and placed it in its case, said, without looking up, "I'm seeing a fine stag down yonder, Sir." Then having taken a long pinch of snuff, he added, "He is just the beast that the shepherd up there was telling me of last Sabbath"—Sunday being the day on which Donald invariably heard all the hill news.

The evening was coming on, so having no time to lose, and a considerable retrograde movement to make before we could approach the stag with any hope of success, off we set at once, and we had a quick and difficult march of it for nearly half an hour before we got into the burn, up the course of which we proposed to keep, as it led straight to the deer. The banks, however, were not so high as those of the former stream, and the water ran over loose round stones, which made our task much more difficult.

We were within five hundred yards, and had got over the worst of our ground, when, on looking up, we saw the deer trotting deliberately but steadily up the hill away from us, evidently having been moved by some suspicion of danger, though we were positive he had not seen or scented us. "See to that; the brute is clean gone," said Donald; and, indeed, clean gone he was for that evening, as just then we lost sight of his antlers as he got over the crest of the hill. On taking the glass, and examining the whole country round, I soon saw the object of his alarm in the person of the very shepherd whose house we were making for. The man was passing at some distance on his way homewards, quite unconscious of our presence or the mischief he had done, as he trudged along towards us with his plaid over his shoulder, and his two colley dogs trotting slowly at his heels. "Oh, but we'll give him a bonny fleg for spoiling our sport the night," said Malcolm. Accordingly Donald and he concealed themselves in the burn, one above and the other below the point at which the shepherd appeared likely to cross it, while I remained hid in a hollow of the moss, a quiet spectator of their attack on the poor fellow's nerves.

The shepherd had just put his foot in the burn, when Malcolm shouted at the top of his voice, "Willie Young, Willie Young," this being the man's name. He stopped short, and with a frightened look at seeing no one, was going on his way again, when Donald took up the chorus, "Willie Young, Willie Young." "Wha's you?" said the shepherd, turning towards Donald. "Willie Young, Willie Young," then shouted Malcolm, and at his voice the unhappy proprietor of the name wheeled round as on a pivot. I could not refrain from joining in the persecution, and Willie Young was kept for ten minutes, turning from side to side, on hearing his name called by his unseen tormentors, till he got so terribly frightened that I thought it as well to show myself, or I firmly believe the man would have gone mad. I never saw a poor fellow more relieved in my life than he was on seeing that his persecutors were mere flesh and blood like himself, and not spirits of the air or flood as he had imagined. Having laughed at him for his fright, and appeased his somewhat reasonable anger, we found out from him that this stag was constantly about the same place, and had got so accustomed to seeing the shepherd pass to and fro, that he invariably returned to the same glen within a few hours.

It was getting late, so we postponed attacking him till the next morning. The shepherd also told us that, although the stag had not particularly fine antlers, he was one of the heaviest and largest deer that had been in that part of the country for some years. He knew him by his large track, and also by his colour, which was peculiarly light. We accompanied Willie Young home to his domicile; and having taken our frugal supper of porridge and milk, followed, however, by some whisky-and-water of no mean flavour and strength, which Mr. Young informed us in confidence had been made by some "lads down the glen yonder," we retired to our sleeping-places. For my own part, I took up my quarters in the building dignified by the name of barn, where, rolled in my plaid, and burrowed in the straw, I slept free from the ten thousand nightly visitants called fleas, which would have eaten me up in Willie Young's house, where, on a former occasion, I had discovered that they rivalled the celebrated plague of Egypt in number and power of tormenting. My two attendants, Donald and Malcolm, slept somewhere near me, as I heard them talking till a very late hour, probably consulting about their plans of attack for the next day.

Before the sun was above the heathery brae which was to the east of us, I looked out and saw the opposite mountain tops already lighted up, and illuminated in the most beautiful and fanciful manner—the glare catching the projecting peaks and angles, and throwing the other parts of the rocks and heights into the deepest shade. Donald was sitting on a stone, rubbing his eyes and his gunlocks alternately with his ancient "pocket napkin," as he called it. Malcolm and the shepherd were leaning against the corner of the house chattering Gaelic, while the rather pretty wife of the latter, bare-headed and bare-legged, was coming over from the cow-byre with a tin pail of fresh and frothing milk. " I hope your honour slept weel ; I'll be taking your breakfast ben the house directly," said pretty Mrs. Young. The two hounds were yawning and stretching themselves in front of the door, and received me with a joyful though rough welcome, Bran putting his front paws on my shoulders, and Oscar almost knocking me down by running and rubbing against my legs. The shepherd's two colley-dogs were standing down at the burn side with their tails between their legs, barking and howling at their unusual four-legged visitors, who occasionally looked, first at the colleys and then at me, as much as to say, " Shall we punish their impertinence, or not ? " One word of encouragement would have sent the two hounds full chase after the yelping curs.

Breakfast done, we started to look for the stag. The shepherd went with us, anxious to see the sport, and we were glad of his assistance in finding the deer, as he was so well acquainted with the animal's haunts. On our way he told us that he had no doubt we should at once find him, but that the dogs would have hard work to kill him, as he was an old cunning fellow, and was supposed to be the same stag who had killed the greyhound of Rory Beg, the fox-hunter, last year, in a corrie at some distance off. The dog having got after the deer (as Rory said, *by accident !*), and being close alongside of him, was killed dead on the spot by a single blow of his antler ; the stag having struck him without stopping, simply turning his head and striking him as he ran alongside. We examined the glen where we had seen the deer, but without success ; no mark of him was to be seen. The shepherd, however, told us to wait till about nine o'clock ; it was nearly that hour now, and he would probably be seen coming in to lie down for the day, on the slope of the hill above the burn. We accordingly lay down quietly in a concealed place, and, as he had predicted, we presently saw the magnificent fellow appear on the top of the hill, where he halted for full ten minutes, looking carefully over the glen in order to see that it was free from any enemy. The morning sun shining on his bright hide made him look of even a lighter and brighter colour than he really was. His horns, though not exactly of first-rate size, loomed large and wide, as seen in clear relief between us and the sky. After standing some time, looking like the solitary spirit of the mountain, he seemed to have made up his mind that all was right and safe, and he walked slowly and deliberately half-way down the hill, and after stopping again to reconnoitre for a short time, he dropped at once down into the heather. I watched him for a few minutes through the glass, as he lay motionless, excepting that now and then he turned his horn down to scratch a fly off his side, or shook his ears when the gnats were particularly troublesome about his head.

We saw that he had taken up too wary and commanding a position to admit of our approaching him with the dogs; so after some consultation, and, as usual, much opposition from Donald, we adopted my plan of driving him, taking the chance of his leaving the glen at his usual pass, where Malcolm and I were to hold the dogs. The shepherd was to move him; and Donald was to be placed with his gun in a burn over the hill, to which we judged he would probably run, and go to bay, when pressed by the hounds. Donald, having loaded his gun with an immense charge of slugs in one barrel and a ball in the other, started off. The shepherd took a long circuit to get below the deer, while Malcolm and I took up our post in a capital hiding-place near the line by which the game had entered the glen. There was not a breath of wind blowing from any direction, everything was as calm as it could possibly be, so that although we had no fear of being scented by the stag, we had to take the extremest care not to make the least noise in going to our place of ambuscade. We held the dogs in our handkerchiefs as the quickest way of slipping them. The stag was easily seen without much risk of his observing us, as we looked through a crevice in the rocks.

After waiting an anxious half-hour or more, we saw the deer suddenly spring up, and, after standing at gaze for a moment, trot up the hill, but not exactly in our direction. He came to a flat spot, and then halted again, and looked earnestly down into the glen. The shepherd was now in full view, and the deer having looked at him fixedly for a minute, seemed to recognise an old and harmless acquaintance; and then turning, trotted deliberately, at no great pace, straight towards us. We heard every step he took as he trotted up the hard hill-side; now and then he crossed a sloping piece of loose gravel which rattled as his hard hoofs struck the stones, and at one time he had to pick his way through a wet splashy piece of marsh, which he did deliberately and slowly, occasionally looking round at the shepherd below him. At this time we could not move or lift our heads for fear of being seen, but had to wait till the deer had passed the rocks amongst which we were concealed, that we might let slip the hounds at a distance of about thirty or forty yards. The deer was now close to us, not more than ten yards off, but we did not want to let the dogs go for fear of turning him back again into the valley from which he had come, where the ground was not nearly so favourable for the dogs as the slope on the other side of us. We heard him tramp past us as he trotted slowly along on the other side of the rocks behind which we were concealed. The next moment he had cleared the rocky ground, and was in full view about thirty yards from us, on a wide expanse of good heather-ground. The dogs saw him too, and getting to our feet, we slipped them.

With one affrighted glance behind him, away went the stag, at first along the top of the slope, as if anxious to keep above the dogs; but finding himself hard pressed, he turned his head down the hill, and the race began. Down they went, the dogs close on the stag. Now and then they tried to spring on him, but his strength and quickness always enabled him either to shake them off or to elude them; indeed after running for some distance he seemed rather to gain on the dogs than to lose ground. Finding this, they seemed more intent upon trying to tire him out than to seize him, and galloped along, keeping somewhat above him, as if to drive him into the burn, where he would come to bay. The stag tried again to ascend the slope, but could not manage it; his wind began to fail, and he turned straight down, gaining a little on the dogs. Crossing some rather wet ground, they were again up to him, and he only escaped being pulled down by his great strength, which enabled him to shake off the hounds more than once. It was clear that his object was now to gain the burn. All three were evidently beginning to fail, as the chase had already lasted some time.

Malcolm and I had now reached the burn also, having made for it in a straight line as soon as the dogs were slipped. As luck would have it, deer and hounds all passed us down the stream, the dogs panting, and the deer with his tongue hanging out and blowing like a porpoise. He soon came to bay, and the dogs were glad to get a rest, and lying down in the water, opposite his head, they alternately bayed at him, and rolled in the stream to cool themselves. We came up, and the deer immediately broke his bay, and rushing over the dogs, trampled them under foot, and striking Oscar a sharp blow (which luckily only grazed him) with his antler, took down the stream again. We looked round for Donald, and presently saw him crouched on a rock immediately above the stream, and about two hundred yards below us. The dogs recovered quickly, and were again close on the stag. He stopped two or three times for a few moments, turning fiercely on the hounds, and at last came to bay in a determined style, under the very rock where Donald was concealed. The next moment we saw the deer stagger and fall in the water, and immediately heard the report of Donald's gun. Before the stag could recover, both hounds were on him, worrying at his throat like bulldogs, and after one or two efforts to rise, the poor animal's head sank into the pool, which was soon red with the blood that bubbled up from his mouth and nostrils. Donald had shot him just behind the heart with his single ball, which had cut the large blood-vessels.

"Puir brute, puir brute, it's just a sorrow to see him," said Malcolm : and, now that the excitement of the chase was over, I also would have given much to have been able to bring the gallant animal to life again. We got him out of the water, and were soon joined by Willie Young, who sighed more than once, and took a vast pinch of snuff out of Donald's box, half sorry to see his old acquaintance, the white stag, as he called him, lying dead and bloody on the heather.

As Oscar had got a rather awkward, though not very deep cut, and Bran seemed rather the worse for his bruises, I left Donald and the shepherd to attend to the removal of the deer, and walked straight for home with Malcolm and the two dogs, which had both of them done their duty so well.

Of the different runs which I have seen with deer, these two were certainly the best, both as regards our having the game almost constantly in view, and as to our being well up at the conclusion of each chase.

I certainly have not had much experience in running with greyhounds ; but those who have, speak with raptures of this way of killing deer. For my own part, I prefer my rifle, with a good dog. A high-bred English smooth greyhound sometimes kills red deer well and cleverly, having the advantage in wind and speed over the rough dogs, and also possessing the most dashing courage when in pursuit of game. It wants weight, however, to enable it to pull down so large an animal as a stag; though I have seen a small greyhound tumble over a deer, and kill it very quickly, by catching the animal under the shoulder, when in full speed, which at once upset him, and then flying at the throat, he soon finished the business.

MALCOLM HOLDING THE DOGS

YOUNG DUCKS CATCHING MOTHS

CHAPTER XXXV

Tameness of Birds when Sitting

July 1*st*.—In walking over a field, the grass of which had been cut the day before, but was not yet carried, I disturbed a landrail, who was still sitting on her eggs, notwithstanding the great change that must have come over her abode, which, from being covered with a most luxuriant crop of rye-grass and clover, was now perfectly bare. How the eggs had escaped being broken, either by the scythe or by the tramping of the mowers' feet, it is difficult to understand; but there was the poor bird sitting closely on her eggs, as if nothing had happened, and on my near approach she moved quietly away, looking more like a weasel than a bird as she ran crouching with her head nearly touching the ground.

In another part of the same field I passed a nest of landrails in which the young ones were on the point of, or rather, in the very act of being hatched, some of the young having just quitted the shell, while others were only half out of their fragile prison. Both old birds were running around the nest while I stooped to look at their little black progeny, and were uttering a low kind of hissing noise, quite unlike their usual harsh croak. The mowers told me that they had seen several nests in the same field, but had avoided breaking the eggs whenever they perceived them in time. Though innumerable landrails arrive here during the first week in May, always coming regularly to their time, the period and manner of their departure are quite a mystery to me. Although in general their young are not hatched till the first or second week in July, they seem to have entirely vanished by the time that the corn is cut: it is very rare indeed to find one when you are beating the fields in September.

The partridges here are chiefly hatched about the last week in June. Like the landrail, the hen bird sits very close, and during that time will almost allow herself to be taken up in the hand, especially when near her time of hatching. They seem to be quite confident in the forbearance of my boys, who have an intimate acquaintance with almost every nest in the neighbourhood of the house, the old bird allowing them to peer closely into her nest, and even to move aside the grass and herbage which conceal it, when they want to see if she is on her eggs. A retriever one day caught an old hen partridge on her nest, but let her go again on my rating him, without doing more damage to her than pulling out some feathers. Notwithstanding this she returned to the nest, and hatched the whole of the eggs the next day. Had she not been so near her time of hatching, I do not suppose that she would have returned again. All birds have the same instinctive foreknowledge of the time of hatching being near at hand, and do not, when this is the case, leave their nest so easily as when disturbed at an earlier period of incubation. Some small birds are much tamer in this respect than others. A bullfinch will often allow herself to be taken off her nest, and replaced again, without showing the least symptom of fear. Indeed, this bird if put into a cage with her nest of young ones will continue to feed them as readily as if her habitation was still in its original situation. Blackbirds also are very unwilling to fly off from their eggs.

The common wren, on the contrary, immediately forsakes her nest if it is at all handled and examined before she has laid her eggs. She will abandon it if she merely observes people looking too closely at it; but when she has commenced to sit I have known her to be caught on her nest, and replaced, and still not forsake it. A small blue-headed tomtit formed her nest this year in a chink in my garden wall, and allowed the children to take out an egg to examine it from underneath her, without leaving the nest. In fact, instead of being frightened at the intrusion of their hands into her little warm, well-feathered domicile, she pecked courageously at their fingers, hissing and spluttering at them, and never seeming inclined to fly off. When the young ones were hatched, the activity and perseverance of the old birds in providing them with caterpillars and blue-bottle flies were perfectly wonderful. They appeared to fly backwards and forwards to their young family every minute of the day, always bringing some insect in their bills. The good done by these little birds in destroying grubs and flies ought to earn them an immunity from all danger from trap or gun. Gardeners are always too much inclined to wage war against all small birds, forgetting that they invariably feed their young, not with seeds, but with different kinds of grubs and caterpillars, in this way amply repaying any little mischief they may do to the early-sown seeds. For my own part, I never trust a gun in my gardener's hands, but let the blackbirds and thrushes take as many cherries as they like, in return for which they destroy thousands of grey snails, etc., besides giving me many a moment of pleasure by their song. I admit that I do occasionally shoot the crows and jackdaws when they destroy too many of the cherries, particularly as these active marauders come from some distance in large flocks as soon as the fruit becomes red on the trees. I invariably observe that at this season one or two jackdaws arrive first, flying round and round at a great height above the garden. After some chattering between themselves, they fly away, returning some hours afterwards with the rest of their family, four or five in number; and if not checked by a few charges of shot, these first intruders soon invite every jackdaw in the country to the feast, their numbers increasing every day, till I am obliged to take active steps against them.

About the second week in July the young wild ducks begin to fly. Those hatched high up in the country usually make their way down to the sea-side in that month. They follow the course of some stream or river till they arrive at their destination. Like the fable of the ostrich hiding her head when pursued, the young wild ducks when chased on the river will frequently dip their heads under the water, and keeping them there till they are nearly drowned, fancy themselves secure, although their whole body is exposed. If taken up, and put into some enclosed yard or garden, they will soon become tolerably tame, and get very fat if well fed. The whole of my poultry-yard (as far as ducks are concerned) is supplied by a breed of half-wild and half-tame ducks, originating in some young drakes caught, and turned out with the tame ducks—the tame drakes being all sent away, in order to ensure the proper cross in the breed. The birds are very much improved for the table by this cross, and are quite as tame as the common domestic duck, only showing their wild parentage in an inclination to hide their nests, and to build at a distance from home—always, however, if allowed so to do, bringing home their broods as soon as they are hatched. At other seasons they never seem inclined to wander, though they are always to be seen at the very earliest dawn of the morning, before it is quite light, spread out over the grass-field adjoining the house, hunting it in a regular line of advance for worms and snails. As the evening comes on, too, it is amusing to see them bent on the same pursuit, and displaying the greatest activity and skill in catching the large evening moths, as these insects rise from the grass or fly low over it.

CURLEW AND GOLDEN PLOVER

CHAPTER XXXVI

Variety of Game

THE list of game killed by my own gun on the 21st of October appears in my game-book to have been as follows:—

Grouse .	.	6	Teal . .	1
Partridge	.	13	Curlew . .	3
Woodcock	.	1	Plover . .	4
Pheasant	.	1	Jacksnipe .	2
Wild duck	.	1	Hare . .	5
Snipe .	.	4	Rabbit . .	2

Though the number of animals in this list may not seem great to many of my sporting friends in England and Scotland, a prettier variety of game could scarcely be killed by one gun in any single locality, and the whole of them were shot during a few hours' walk, and on a most stormy and windy day. I had promised to send a hamper of game to a friend in Edinburgh, and knowing that he would prize it more if I could make up a variety than if I sent him double the quantity of any one kind, I determined to hunt a wild part of my shooting-ground, where I should have a chance of finding ducks, snipes, etc.

I started after breakfast with a single pointer, and my everlasting companion, an old retriever. As the steam-boat for Edinburgh started the next day, I was obliged, though the wind blew nearly a hurricane, to make the best of it, and face the wind in the dreary and upland ground, which I had determined to beat, and where I had sent an attendant to meet me.

Passing over a long tract of furze and broom, I killed a couple of hares, and drove some partridges off down to windward; but as they flew quite out of the direction in which I meant to shoot, I did not follow them. My pointer stood immediately on getting into an extensive piece of grazing-ground; his head high up showed me that the birds were at some distance. He drew on for some two or three hundred yards, when two large coveys of partridges rose, and, unable to face the wind, drifted back over my head like leaves. Bang, bang—and a brace of them fell dead sixty yards behind me, though shot when nearly over my head, and killed at once. I marked down the rest, and got a brace more, when they went straight away, as if determined to make their next resting-place somewhere about Norway. But my line was to windward still, in order to hunt some ground where there was a chance (though a bad one) of a brace or so of grouse.

Picking up a snipe or two, and a hare, I worked up hill against the wind along a tract of wild heather and pasture-ground. In the midst of this was a small peat-bog, and, when passing it, I flushed a brace of mallards, which, after drifting about and trying to make their way to the sea, turned and alighted in a swampy piece of ground, where there were some small pools. By their manner I was sure that they had some companions where they alighted, so, desiring the man who accompanied me to hold the pointer, I tried to stalk unperceived to the spot where they were, allowing my old retriever (who was well accustomed to duck-shooting) to accompany me. I had got to within a hundred yards, when an old mallard, whom I had not seen, rose at my feet out of a pool, and quacked an alarm that made six more rise out of shot of me. I avenged myself, however, on him, bringing him down quite dead at a considerable distance. Several pairs of ducks rose at the report, and all went off to the sea.

I had scarcely commenced hunting again with the pointer, when he stood at something close to his nose, stopping dead short in the midst of his gallop. I walked up, expecting a jacksnipe; when, out of a small hollow, or rather hole in the heather, rose eight grouse. They flew wild, but I killed one with my first barrel, and two with the second—the wind blowing them up into a heap just as I pulled the trigger: the rest flew over a height not far up, right in the eye of the wind. I knew the violence of the gale must stop them; and accordingly I found them again, immediately over the ridge, and killed a brace more, marking down the rest close to a cottage. My next two barrels killed one only. The rest went off a long distance. The star of my friend's larder was still in the ascendant, for before I turned to beat homewards I killed two jack-snipes; thus making up four partridges, six grouse, four snipes, three hares, and a wild duck. Not a bad bag already. I beat on towards the coast, killing some partridges, a brace of rabbits, a woodcock, and a hare or two.

Near the shore I saw an immense flock of curlews and other birds in a tolerably good situation for getting near them. Of all shore-birds there is none, not even the wild duck, so difficult of approach as a curlew. With the most acute sense of hearing, their organs of smelling are so sensitive, that the moment you get "betwixt the wind and their nobility" they take wing, giving the alarm by their loud shrill whistle to every other bird within hearing. I got, however, unperceived to within forty yards of them, and having loaded one barrel with a cartridge, I fired right and left at the flock.

There was a rare confusion and scuffling amongst them, and my retriever brought me, one by one, three curlews and four golden plovers. Some other birds dropped here and there out at sea, but I could only get the above number. A brace of teal rose at the shot and alighted in a ditch in the adjoining field; so, loading quickly, I walked to the place: as they rose rather wild, I only bagged one, the other bird going away hard struck. I then followed the course of the rushy ditch, or rather rivulet, which led towards my house, having already a fair quantity of game. My dog pointed, and I killed a snipe; I did not reload the barrel, as I was near home, but hunted on along the rushes, expecting another snipe to present my remaining charge to. The dog presently stood, and then drew slowly on till he came very near to the end of the rushes, when he pointed dead at something close to him. I walked about the rushes, but could find nothing, till, just as I was giving it up, a magnificent old cock pheasant, which had wandered away from the woods, rose in a furrow of the field adjoining the rushes. He was rather far off, but I killed him dead, making as pretty a climax or tail-piece to a day's wild shooting as I could have wished; and though I have very often far exceeded the number which I killed that day, I do not ever remember bagging a handsomer collection of animals in so short a time. Every bird, too, was in beautiful plumage and condition, and when laid out, ready to be packed up, made quite a picture.

An account of a day's shooting is rather a dry affair, but I have given it as showing the great variety of game which is to be found in this part of the country. I had, indeed, as good a chance of killing a roebuck as anything else, as I passed through a piece of ground where I have repeatedly killed roe. I saw an old blackcock too, but he was in a bare place, and rose out of shot.

Golden plovers and curlews collect on the low grounds in immense flocks at this time of the year, previous to settling down in their winter quarters. Both these birds breed generally in very high situations, and though wary in the winter, and difficult to approach, yet during the summer, when crossing the mountains, I have been absolutely annoyed by the continued clamour of curlews flying and screaming within a few yards of my head, and following up their persecutions for a considerable distance, when it would probably be taken up by another pair with fresh lungs, whose breeding-place I might be approaching.

The golden plover has a plaintive and rather sweet note as he flits rapidly round the traveller who intrudes on his domain. Indeed in the spring the note of the golden plover, as he ascends with rapid wheelings high above your head, is quite musical, and approaches nearly to the note of a thrush or blackbird. Not only the whistle of the plover, but even the harsh cry of the landrail, and the monotonous call of the cuckoo, are always grateful to my ear, because, being heard only in the spring-time, they are associated in my mind with the idea of the departure of winter and the return of fine weather. It is often a matter of astonishment to me how the throat of a bird so tender and delicately formed as the landrail can emit such hard and grating cries, which sound more as if they were produced by some iron or brazen instrument than from the windpipe of a bird. The raven or crow look as if they ought to be the owners of a harsh and croaking voice, and a shrill note comes appropriately from the throat of a barn-door cock; but a landrail appears to be a bird quite unfitted to produce a sound like that of a piece of iron drawn along the teeth of a rusty saw. There is a way of imitating their cry so exactly as to bring the bird to your feet, but I never could succeed in doing so, or indeed in making it answer me at all, though I have tried the plan which I was told was infallible, of drawing the edges of two horse's ribs against each other, one of them being smooth and the other notched like a saw. Although the fields were swarming with the birds at the time, I never succeeded in persuading even a single one to answer me.

www.ingramcontent.com/pod-product-compliance
Lightning Source LLC
Chambersburg PA
CBHW030320240426
43673CB00040B/1221